access to history

America: Civil War and Westward Expansion 1803–90

ALAN FARMER

FIFTH EDITION

HODDER
EDUCATION
AN HACHETTE UK COMPANY

The Publishers would like to thank Nicholas Fellows and David Ferriby for their contribution to the Study Guide.

The Publishers would like to thank the following for permission to reproduce copyright material:

Photo credits: p15 Library of Congress, LC-DIG-cwpbh-05089; **p60** Library of Congress, LC-DIG-cwpbh-00880; **p71** Bettmann/Corbis; **p79** Library of Congress, LC-USZ62-15984; **p97** Library of Congress, LC-DIG-cwpbh-00879; **p104t** Library of Congress, LC-DIG-ppmsca-22982; *b* Library of Congress, LC-DIG-ppmsca-32284; **p128t** Library of Congress, LC-USZ62-12380, *b* Library of Congress, LC-DIG-pga-02502; **p133** Library of Congress, LC-USZ62-132749; **p137** Library of Congress, LC-DIG-ppmsca-35499; **p149** Corbis; **p157** Library of Congress, LC-DIG-ggbain-34127; **p159** Library of Congress, LC-DIG-ds-05168; **p167** Library of Congress, LC-USZ62-1770; **p169** Electoral campaign poster for the Union nomination with Abraham Lincoln running for President and Andrew Johnson for Vice-President (colour litho), American School, (19th century)/Private Collection/Bridgeman Images; **p185** Corbis; **p198** Library of Congress, LC-USZ62-13017; **p210** Library of Congress, LC-USZ62-128619; **p218** Library of Congress, LC-USZ62-16181; **p241** LegendsOfAmerica.com; **p245** Library of Congress, Printed Ephemera Collection; Portfolio 134, Folder 13; **p249** Library of Congress, LC-DIG-ppmsca-08372.

The Publishers thank OCR for permission to use specimen exam questions on pages 258 and 262, from OCR's A Level History A specification H505 © OCR 2014. OCR have neither seen nor commented upon any model answers or exam guidance related to these questions.

Acknowledgements: Harper & Row, *Slavery: History and Historians* by Peter J. Parish, 1989. HarperCollins, *The Lincoln–Douglas Debates* by Harold Holzer, editor, 1993. Harvard University Press, *The Last Best Hope of Earth* by Mark E. Neely, Jr, 1993. Krieger Publishing, *Fifty Basic Civil War Documents* by L.L. Snyder, editor, 1982. Penguin Books, *Battle Cry of Freedom* by James McPherson, 1990. Time Life Books, *The Old West: The Indians* by Ezra Brown, editor, 1973. Touchstone, *The Causes of the Civil War* by Kenneth M. Stampp, editor, 1991. University of Missouri Press, *Shades of Blue and Grey: An Introductory Military History of the Civil War* by Herman Hattaway, 1997.

Every effort has been made to trace all copyright holders, but if any have been inadvertently overlooked the Publishers will be pleased to make the necessary arrangements at the first opportunity.

Although every effort has been made to ensure that website addresses are correct at time of going to press, Hodder Education cannot be held responsible for the content of any website mentioned in this book. It is sometimes possible to find a relocated web page by typing in the address of the home page for a website in the URL window of your browser.

Hachette UK's policy is to use papers that are natural, renewable and recyclable products and made from wood grown in sustainable forests. The logging and manufacturing processes are expected to conform to the environmental regulations of the country of origin.

Orders: please contact Bookpoint Ltd, 130 Milton Park, Abingdon, Oxon OX14 4SB. Telephone: +44 (0)1235 827720. Fax: +44 (0)1235 400454. Lines are open 9.00a.m.–5.00p.m., Monday to Saturday, with a 24-hour message answering service. Visit our website at www.hoddereducation.com

© Alan Farmer 2015

First published in 2015 by
Hodder Education
An Hachette UK Company
Carmelite House, 50 Victoria Embankment
London EC4Y 0DZ

Impression number	10	9	8	7	6	5	4	3	
Year		2019	2018	2017	2016	2015			

Cover photo: © Francis G. Mayer/Corbis
Produced, illustrated and typeset in Palatino LT Std by Gray Publishing, Tunbridge Wells
Printed and bound by CPI Group (UK) Ltd, Croydon CR0 4YY

A catalogue record for this title is available from the British Library

ISBN 978 1471839061

Contents

Dedication

Keith Randell (1943–2002)

The *Access to History* series was conceived and developed by Keith, who created a series to 'cater for students as they are, not as we might wish them to be'. He leaves a living legacy of a series that for over 20 years has provided a trusted, stimulating and well-loved accompaniment to post-16 study. Our aim with these new editions is to continue to offer students the best possible support for their studies.

CHAPTER 1

Mid-nineteenth-century USA

In the mid-nineteenth century most Americans were proud of the achievements of their country and optimistic about its future. There seemed good cause for this optimism. The USA had the most democratic system of government in the world; it was also one of the world's most prosperous and enterprising nations. However, there was a threatening cloud on the horizon: northern and southern states were growing apart, economically, socially, culturally and politically. This chapter considers the differences between the states through four main themes:

★ The US political system

★ Social and economic development

★ The growth of sectionalism

★ The nature of American slavery

The key debate on *page 20* of this chapter asks the question: How benign was the system of slavery in the USA?

Key dates

1787	Founding Fathers drew up the US Constitution	1831	**Jan.**	Publication of *The Liberator*
1793	Invention of the cotton 'gin'		**Aug.**	Nat Turner's revolt
1808	USA declared African slave trade illegal	1833		Formation of National Anti-Slavery Society

1 Introduction

▶ *Why was the USA so successful during the mid-nineteenth century?*

Before 1861 the history of the USA had been in many ways a remarkable success story. The small, predominantly English settlements of the early seventeenth century had expanded rapidly, so much so that by the end of the eighteenth century they had been able to win independence from Britain. The USA, which in 1776 had controlled only a narrow strip of land along the Atlantic seaboard, expanded westwards. In 1803 the USA doubled in size when it purchased the

Louisiana territory from France (see Figure 2.1, page 40). By 1860 the original thirteen states had increased to 33 and the nation extended from the Atlantic to the Pacific.

By 1860 white Americans enjoyed a better standard of living than any other people on earth. Prosperity and the rapidly expanding economy attracted large-scale immigration. In 1860 the USA had a population of 31 million people (slightly more than Britain): four million were foreign born.

The USA's political system – **republican**, **federal** and **democratic** – was the pride of most Americans and the envy of most British and European radicals. By the mid-nineteenth century, many Americans considered themselves to be the world's most civilised and fortunate people. However, not everyone benefited from the 'great experiment'.

- During the 250 years that had elapsed since the coming of the first English settlers, Native Americans had lost a huge amount of land.
- The other major ethnic group that might have questioned the notion of a 'great experiment' were African Americans, whose ancestors had been transported to America as slaves. The fact that slavery continued in the American South was a great anomaly in a country based on the Declaration of Independence's assertion 'that all men are created equal'. In the opinion of many northerners, the fact that slavery still existed was the major failing of the 'great experiment'.

If slavery was the USA's main failing pre-1861, the Civil War (1861–5) remains the greatest failure in US history. Some 620,000 Americans were to die in the conflict, as many as in almost all America's subsequent wars put together. In the century of its greatest growth, the USA came very close to splitting apart.

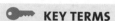

KEY TERMS

Republican A form of government without a monarch (or someone who supports such a government).

Federal A government in which several states, while largely independent in home affairs, combine for national purposes.

Democratic A form of government in which ultimate power is vested in the people and their elected representatives.

Constitution A set of rules by which an organisation or a country is governed.

Founding Fathers The American politicians who drew up the American Constitution.

Federal government The national government.

Sovereignty Supreme power.

2 The US political system

▶ *How did the US system of government operate?*

The 1787 **Constitution**, drawn up by the **Founding Fathers**, had created a system whereby power would be divided between the **federal government** in Washington and the individual states. The Founding Fathers, accepting that **sovereignty** should be founded on the people, set out to create a system of checks and balances that would prevent any branch of government being in a position to tyrannise the people or any group of people being able to ride roughshod over the rights of others. The federal government had well-defined executive, legislative and judicial branches, each of which was able to check the actions of the others (see Figure 1.1, page 3). And the people, in theory, were able to check the actions of each branch.

State governments tended to replicate the federal government: each state had its governor, its own legislative body and its own Supreme Court. In the late eighteenth century the USA had devised a system for admitting new states. New areas first assumed **territorial status**, electing a territorial government. Once the population of a territory had reached 60,000 it could submit its proposed constitution (invariably cribbed from other states) to Congress and apply to become a state. By 1850 the USA comprised 30 states.

KEY TERM

Territorial status Areas in the USA that had not yet become states and which were still under federal government control.

THE AMERICAN PEOPLE
ELECT

CONGRESS (The Legislative)

Congress makes laws, has the power of the purse, declares war and checks the work of the President.

Senate	House of Representatives
• Two Senators represent each state (no matter how large or small the state). • Senators sit for six years – one third come up for re-election every two years.	• Members of the House represent constituencies based on population. • The House is elected *en masse* every two years.

- Both houses of Congress need to agree before a law can be carried out.
- Congress may override a presidential veto.
- Congress may impeach and remove the President from office.

THE PRESIDENT
(The Executive)
- Elected every four years by the Electoral College (Electoral College representatives are selected by the party with the most votes in each state).
- If the President resigns or dies, the Vice-President takes over.
- The President is head of state but also has some real powers. He may call special sessions of Congress, may recommend legislation and may veto bills.
- Presidents appoint their own ministers, or secretaries, who sit in the cabinet but who are forbidden to sit in Congress.
- The President is the Commander-in-Chief of the armed forces.

THE SUPREME COURT (The Judiciary)
- This is the highest court. It approves the laws and decides whether they are Constitutional.
- The (usually nine) Supreme Court Judges are appointed by the President.
- The Senate ratifies the President's appointments.

Figure 1.1 The US Constitution.

American democracy

By the 1820s almost all white males had the right to vote. The rise of democracy is often associated with President **Andrew Jackson** (1829–37), who claimed to represent the common man against the interests of privilege. In truth, Jackson benefited from, rather than created, the democratic tide. While there were limits

KEY FIGURE

Andrew Jackson (1767–1845)

A self-made man from Tennessee, Jackson was a successful soldier. A slave-holding landowner, he was American president from 1829 to 1837.

to that tide – women and most blacks, for example, could not vote – the USA was far more democratic than Britain.

Democrats and Whigs

By the mid-nineteenth century the USA had two main political parties: the Democrats and the Whigs. President Jackson was very much the catalyst generating the development of the **second party system**. Many Americans loved him. Others hated him. His supporters called themselves Democrats. His opponents eventually were known as Whigs. The two parties, although operating nationally, were not as internally united as modern political parties. They were really an assortment of state parties that only came together every four years to nominate a presidential candidate and devise a national **platform**.

The Democrats believed that the best form of government was the least form of government, arguing that most issues (not least slavery) should be decided at state, not federal, level. Democrats opposed government intervention in economic matters and held the view that the USA would prosper if **tariffs** were lowered and the USA expanded westwards. The party was strongest in the south and west but could also count on the support of many voters in northern cities, not least from Irish Catholics.

The Whigs favoured government intervention in economic and social matters. They supported higher tariffs and government-sponsored internal improvements (for example, railway building). Northern Whigs often supported causes such as the abolition of slavery.

Political involvement

In presidential elections, when efforts were made to win as much support as possible, both parties put forward platforms that evaded most controversial issues. However, in general, the two parties did articulate contrasting platforms, especially with regard to economic matters, which were of major concern to most Americans in the 1840s.

Political campaigns generated real excitement and high voter turnouts. Both parties held barbecues and torchlight processions, and distributed a massive amount of campaign literature. Party-subsidised newspapers helped to shape political sentiment and raised tensions by indulging in scurrilous attacks on the enemy.

Throughout the 1840s most Americans committed themselves to one of the two parties. In many respects political allegiances were similar to present-day football allegiances. Indeed politics was the most popular spectator and participant 'sport' of the day: party activities offered excitement, entertainment and camaraderie. The political game was highly competitive: Whigs and Democrats looked forward to defeating the enemy. Political rallies drew large attendances and 'fans' often dressed for the occasion wearing the regalia of their party. Oddly, the main 'stars' – the presidential candidates – rarely participated much in the campaigns. Instead, they retreated to their homes and let their supporters do the dirty work for them.

Presidential campaigns were by no means the only political 'events'. Elections were far more frequent at state and local level. Different states held elections in different months and in different years. In virtually every month of every year, Congressmen or state legislatures were elected somewhere in the USA.

Limited government

Despite the fierce inter-party rivalry, government had a limited impact on the lives of most Americans. It was unusual for one party to control the presidency, both houses of Congress and the Supreme Court at the same time. It was thus difficult for the federal government to do very much. The fact that many matters were seen as state and not federal concerns was another limiting factor. So too was the notion, strongly held by the Democrats, that it was not government's responsibility to interfere in social and economic matters.

The federal government was made up of only a handful of departments: State, Treasury, Interior, Navy, War and the Post Office. In 1860 there were 36,672 people on the federal government payroll (excluding the armed forces). Over 30,000 of these were employed by the Post Office.

The vast majority of those who worked in the departments were political appointments: so, too were the **postmasters**. Whig presidents appointed Whig civil servants (and postmasters); Democrats did the same. This **patronage** or 'spoils system' was an essential way of preserving and promoting party unity. The 'spoils' of office – jobs and government contracts – were what the game of politics was all about for some of those involved in it.

Presidents were more figureheads and distributors of patronage than active policy-makers. Congress, essentially a talking shop, rarely passed major legislation. Indeed it was rarely in session: it met in December and only sat until March. Apart from the postmaster, Americans rarely came across a federal official. The actions of state legislatures had more influence on most Americans' day-to-day lives than the actions of the federal government. Even so, although states were responsible for matters such as education and public health, state governments did not impinge greatly on people's lives.

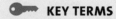

KEY TERMS

Postmaster The person in charge of a local post office.

Patronage The giving of jobs or privileges to supporters.

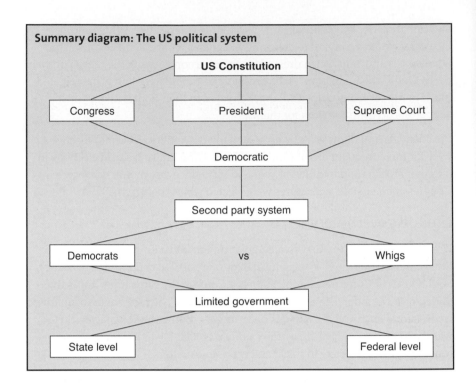

Summary diagram: The US political system

3 Social and economic development

▶ *To what extent were Americans a 'society of equals' and a 'people of plenty'?*

In the 1830s a perceptive Frenchman, Alexis de Tocqueville, visited the USA and wrote a book recounting his experiences. What struck him was the fact that the country was far more equal than societies in Europe. He noted that there was no 'feudal' hierarchy: no sovereign, no royal court, no established aristocracy or church leaders. Instead, there were opportunities for men of talent and ambition to rise to the top.

Historians today are suspicious of this early notion of the **American Dream**. Black slaves, Native Americans and women were far from equal. Moreover, there were great inequalities of wealth among white males. In 1860 the top five per cent of free adult males owned 53 per cent of the wealth. The bottom 50 per cent owned only one per cent. Family standing and inherited wealth were vital assets in terms of individual advancement in America as in most European societies.

Nevertheless, de Tocqueville's claim did have some basis. People were more likely to rise from 'rags to riches' in the USA than in Europe.

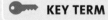 **KEY TERM**

American Dream The idea that the American way of life offers the prospect of economic and social success to every individual.

From Alexis de Tocqueville, *Democracy in America*, 1835.

The great advantage of the Americans is … that they are born equal instead of becoming so … . Never before has a people found for itself such a happy and fruitful basis of life. Here freedom is unrestrained, and subsists by being useful to every one without injuring anybody. There is undeniably something feverish in the activity it imparts to industry and to the human spirit.

> To what extent is Source A useful for understanding the concept of equality in early nineteenth-century USA?

Women's status

Mid-nineteenth-century America assigned distinctly unequal roles to men and women. Women were seen, and saw themselves, as homemakers. Only 25 per cent of white women worked outside the home before marriage and fewer than five per cent did so while they were married. The notion that women's place was in the home was disseminated by both the Church and the press.

Today, historians debate the extent to which the **cult of domesticity** was a setback for women. Many would claim it was. Women were denied the same social and political rights as men. They could not vote. In many states wives could not even own property.

Some historians have argued that the cult of domesticity actually gave women some power. They had responsibility for their children. (By 1850 the average white woman had five children.) Often seen as the guardians of morality, women tended to set family values and were more frequent churchgoers than men. Middle-class women also participated in many of the reform movements that were a feature of mid-nineteenth-century American life, especially **abolitionism** and **temperance**.

A 'people of plenty'

Historian David Potter (1976) described mid-nineteenth-century Americans as a 'people of plenty'. Prosperity and growth seem to be the two words that best describe America's economic development in the early nineteenth century. The country had enormous reserves of almost every commodity – fertile land, timber, minerals – and an excellent network of navigable rivers. In the period 1800–50 the USA's **gross national product** increased seven-fold and the income of ordinary American families more than doubled.

Population growth

The USA's population grew rapidly, doubling every 25 years or so. In 1840 it stood at 17 million; by 1860 it had reached 31 million. Most of the growth came from natural increase: plenty of children were born and Americans lived longer than most people in the world. Population growth was also the result of huge immigration, especially from Ireland and Germany.

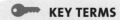 **KEY TERMS**

Cult of domesticity The notion that women's place was in the home.

Abolitionism The desire to end slavery.

Temperance Opposition to the drinking of alcohol.

Gross national product The total value of all goods and services produced within a country.

Western expansion

In the early nineteenth century, Americans populated the area between the Appalachian Mountains and the Mississippi River. Between 1815 and 1850 the population west of the Appalachians grew three times as quickly as the population of the original thirteen states (see pages 27–46).

Agriculture

Most Americans were farmers. Small family farms still characterised agriculture, north and south, east and west. Between 1840 and 1860 food production increased four-fold. This was largely due to the opening up of new tracts of land in the West. The development of more scientific techniques – fertilisation, crop rotation and the use of new machinery – also helped.

Industrialisation

America's industrial revolution mirrored that of Britain. There were important technological developments in textiles, coal, iron and steel, and in the use of steam power. New machines were introduced and constantly improved. The USA, fortunate in its enormous mineral wealth, could also count on British investment.

Transport

Massive changes in transport help to explain the agricultural and industrial changes that were underway. The development of steamboats revolutionised travel on the great rivers. By 1850 there were over 700 steamships operating on the Mississippi and its tributaries. The country also developed an impressive canal system. However, by 1850 canals were facing competition from railways. In 1840 the USA had over 3000 miles (5000 km) of track. By 1860 this had increased to over 30,000 miles (50,000 km) – more track than the rest of the world combined.

Urbanisation

Fewer than one in ten Americans lived in towns (defined as settlements with more than 2500 people) in 1820; one in five did so by 1860. Some cities experienced spectacular growth. Chicago had only 40 people in 1830; by 1860 it had 109,000. New York had over 800,000 inhabitants by 1860.

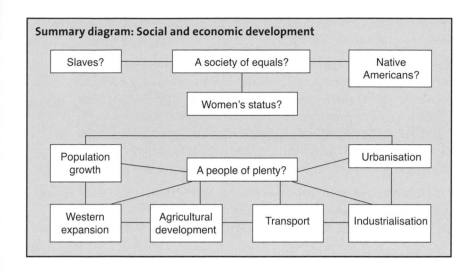

Summary diagram: Social and economic development

Slaves? — A society of equals? — Native Americans?

Women's status?

Population growth — A people of plenty? — Urbanisation

Western expansion — Agricultural development — Transport — Industrialisation

 # The growth of sectionalism

▶ *What were the main differences between North and South?*

For much of the early nineteenth century there were rivalries between the newer western states and the older established eastern states. Far more important, however, were the differences between North and South. Some historians have underplayed the differences, stressing instead the similarities between the two regions:

- a common language
- a shared religion
- the same legal, political and racial assumptions
- a celebration of the same history.

Other historians, however, believe that there were deep divisions between North and South: divisions that helped to bring about war.

Economic differences

Historians once claimed that the Civil War was a conflict between a backward, **agrarian**, planter-dominated South and a modern, industrialised and **egalitarian** North. This view is far too sweeping. In reality, there was not one but many 'Souths' encompassing several distinct geographical regions. Eastern states such as Virginia were very different from western states such as Texas. The lower (or Deep) South was different from the upper South. Accordingly, it is difficult to generalise about the 'Old' South.

There were also many 'Norths'. Moreover, in many respects, those 'Norths' were not dissimilar economically to the 'Souths'. The North was industrialising, not

 **KEY TERMS**

Agrarian Relating to land and farming.

Egalitarian A society in which people are equal.

industrialised. Only four northern manufacturing industries employed over 50,000 people in 1860. The northwest was still overwhelmingly rural.

Nor was the South economically backward. Many southerners grew tobacco, sugar and particularly cotton. By the mid-nineteenth century, cotton sales made up at least half of the USA's total exports. Trade in cotton ensured that white southern society was prosperous and enterprising and that most southerners had an economic interest in a good railway and telegraph network. Nor was the South totally lacking in industry. The Tredegar Iron Works in Richmond, Virginia, ranked fourth among the nation's producers of iron products by 1840.

The North was not more egalitarian than the South. In 1860 the wealthiest ten per cent of northerners owned 68 per cent of the wealth; these figures were almost identical in the South. The typical northerner was a self-sufficient farmer, owning 20–200 hectares of land. The same was true of the South. In 1860, 75 per cent of southern families did not own slaves.

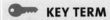 **KEY TERM**

Planters Men who owned plantations with twenty or more slaves.

Southern planters

Planters, who comprised less than five per cent of the white population, owned the South's best farmland and the major portion of its wealth, including most of its slaves. Historian Eugene Genovese believed that the planters led southern politics and set the tone of social life, especially in states such as Virginia and South Carolina. However, in the North a minority of wealthy men wielded similar power. Rich Americans, North and South, found it easier to involve themselves in politics than ordinary Americans, as they could find the time and money to pursue their 'hobby' or 'conviction'.

There was fluidity in southern society. Sons of planters did not automatically become planters themselves. There were opportunities for self-made men to become planters, and then, perhaps, to involve themselves in politics. Of the eight governors of Virginia in the two decades before the Civil War, only one had been born a planter. Three had risen from relative obscurity. If planters involved themselves in politics (and by no means all did), they had to appeal to large electorates. Nor did they speak with one voice. Some were Whigs and some were Democrats.

North–South differences

Nevertheless, there were economic and social differences between North and South.

Table 1.1 Percentage of labour force in agriculture

Year	North	South
1800	68%	82%
1860	40%	81%

Industry

The North was more industrial (see Table 1.1). The southern states, with about 35 per cent of the USA's population, produced only ten per cent of the nation's manufactured output in the 1850s. The North had twice as much railway track as the South.

Urbanisation

The North was far more urban (see Table 1.2). In 1860 the southern states had only twenty towns over 5000 people. Even cities like Charleston and Richmond had populations of under 40,000. Only New Orleans with 175,000 inhabitants was comparable to northern cities in size and diversity. Only one southerner in fourteen was a town dweller compared with one in four northerners.

Immigrants

Unlike the South, the North had a growing number of immigrants. Between 1830 and 1860 most of the five million immigrants to the USA settled in the North. Thus, one in six northerners in 1860 was foreign born compared with one in 30 southerners.

Southern economic grievances

The two regions had different economic interests. The tariff (see page 4) was a source of constant grievance to most southerners, who argued that it benefited northern industrialists at the expense of southern farmers. The South felt exploited in other ways. Southerners depended on northern credit to finance the growing of cotton, tobacco, sugar and rice; they relied on northerners to market these goods; and they were reliant on northern vessels to transport them. Inevitably much of the profits from **King Cotton** ended up in Yankee (northern) pockets.

SOURCE B

From an Alabama newspaper report, 1851.

We purchase all our luxuries and necessities from the North. Our slaves are clothed with northern manufactured goods, have northern hats and shoes, work with northern hoes, ploughs and other implements. The slaveholder dresses in northern goods, rides in a northern saddle, sports his northern carriage, reads northern books. In northern vessels his products are carried to market, his cotton is ginned with northern gins, his sugar is crushed and preserved with northern machinery, his rivers are navigated by northern steamboats.

Southern honour

Historian Wyatt Brown (1985) claimed that southerners were more concerned about their personal, family and sectional honour than northerners. In Brown's view, southern males were highly sensitive to personal insult, reacting violently to even trivial incidents, which included resorting to duelling.

Values

Many southerners, disliking what they saw in the North, had no wish to industrialise and urbanise. There was a general southern belief that old agrarian ways and values were better than Yankee materialism. Southerners remained

Table 1.2 Percentage of population living in towns of 2500 or more

Year	North	South
1820	10%	5%
1840	14%	6%
1850	26%	10%

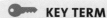 **KEY TERM**

King Cotton Cotton was so important to the US economy that many Americans claimed that 'cotton was king'.

Why was the situation, as described in Source B, a problem for southerners?

proudly and defiantly rooted in the past. Many held a 'romantic' view of the southern way of life, seeing themselves as gracious and hospitable. Yankees, in contrast, were seen as ill-mannered, aggressive and hypocritical.

There were other differences. Northerners were generally better educated than southerners and more responsive to new ideas. While northerners espoused movements for reform, southerners tended to condemn all radical '-isms', associating them with abolitionism and viewing them as a threat to old values and institutions (not least slavery). Not unnaturally, northerners saw southerners as backward and out of touch with 'modern' ideas and ideals. The main difference between the regions, and the main reason for the growth of sectionalism, was slavery.

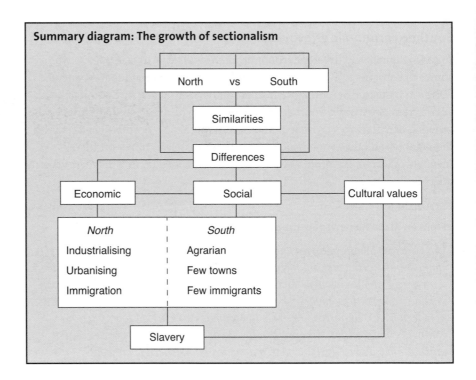

Summary diagram: The growth of sectionalism

5) The nature of American slavery

▶ *Why were southerners so committed to slavery and some*
northerners so strongly opposed to it?

The settlement of North America was an African as well as a European
enterprise. Virtually all the Africans who 'settled' in the seventeenth and
eighteenth centuries came as enslaved people. By 1808, when the African slave
trade was declared illegal, there were over a million slaves in the USA. Slavery
divided Americans. It continues to divide historians.

Slavery pre-1830

In 1776 slavery existed in all the thirteen colonies. However, it was of major
importance only in the South, largely because the northern climate was not
suited to **plantation agriculture**. In the final decades of the eighteenth century
some Protestants, especially **Quakers**, condemned slavery as a moral evil.
Others thought it inconsistent with enlightened ideas that stressed liberty,
equality and free enterprise. Northern states abolished slavery, some at a stroke,
others gradually. In 1787, Congress passed an ordinance that kept slavery out of
the North West Territory. In 1808, the USA banned the slave trade with Africa.
Even some southerners regarded slavery as an evil (albeit a necessary one) and a
few freed their slaves.

King Cotton ensured that slavery survived and throve. In 1790 only 9000 bales
of cotton were produced in the USA. Eli Whitney's invention of a cotton engine
(or 'gin') in 1793 revolutionised southern agriculture. It enabled short-fibre
cotton (the only cotton which easily grew in the South) to be quickly separated
from its seed. Suddenly it became highly profitable to grow cotton and southern
farmers cashed in. By the 1830s the South was producing 2 million bales per
year. King Cotton soon outstripped all other plantation crops in economic
importance. Such was the demand (mainly from Britain), and such were
the profits, that the cotton belt spread westwards – to Kentucky, Tennessee,
Alabama, Mississippi, Arkansas and Texas. Cotton production needed a
large amount of unskilled labour. Slave labour was ideal. Cotton and slavery,
therefore, were interlinked.

Most southerners were committed to their **peculiar institution**. The Founding
Fathers in 1787 had realised that they could not tamper with slavery in the
South. While they had avoided using the word 'slave', they acknowledged
slavery's existence. Slaves were accepted, for representation and taxation
purposes, as three-fifths of a free person. Events in Haiti in the 1790s, where
slaves had won their freedom, massacring most of the white population in the
process, convinced most whites that slavery must be maintained as a means of
social control.

 KEY TERMS

Plantation agriculture
Sugar, rice, tobacco and
cotton were grown on
southern plantations.

Quakers Members of the
Religious Society of Friends,
founded in England by
George Fox in the 1640s.
Quakers were (and remain)
committed to pacifism.

Peculiar institution
Southerners referred to
slavery as their 'peculiar
institution'.

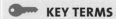
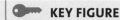
Abolitionists

Most abolitionists in the first three decades of the nineteenth century supported gradual **emancipation**, with financial compensation for slave owners. They also believed that freed slaves should be encouraged to return to Africa. In 1822 the USA purchased Liberia, on the west coast of Africa, as a base for returning ex-slaves. However, this policy had little success. Only 10,000 African Americans had gone to Africa by 1860; in the same period the USA's slave population increased by 2 million. There were never enough funds to free and then transport more than a fraction of the slaves. Moreover, most ex-slaves had no wish to move to Liberia, which would have been as alien to them as it would have been to white Americans.

William Lloyd Garrison

In the early 1830s a new and far more strident abolitionist movement developed. This was associated with **William Lloyd Garrison** who, in 1831, launched a new abolitionist journal, *The Liberator*. Convinced that slavery was a sin, Garrison demanded (without any notion of how it could be done) immediate abolition. For the next four decades he was to be one of the leading abolitionists.

The growth of the abolitionist movement

In 1833 a militant National Anti-Slavery Society was established. This organisation soon mushroomed and by 1838 it had 250,000 members. Most of its leaders were well educated and fairly wealthy. Women played a crucial role. So too did African Americans, some of whom, like Frederick Douglass (see page 15), were ex-slaves. Helped by the new steam-driven printing press, abolitionists churned out a mass of anti-slavery literature. They also organised frequent and massive petitions to Congress. To prevent North–South division, Congress introduced the 'gag rule' in 1836, which ensured that abolitionist petitions were not discussed.

Historians have tried to explain why the abolitionist movement suddenly became so strong in the North in the 1830s. Some stress that it was part of a worldwide phenomenon, in which Britain in particular played an important role. British anti-slavery writings certainly had a receptive audience in the USA. (Britain abolished slavery throughout its colonies in 1833.)

Other historians stress American roots. Mid-nineteenth-century America was a religious society and the Church had a powerful effect on most people's lives. Although Catholic Church membership was growing as a result of immigration, most Americans were Protestants: Baptists, Methodists, Unitarians, Presbyterians and Episcopalians. In the early nineteenth century, there was an upsurge in **evangelical** Protestantism known as the Second Great Awakening. Evangelical preachers fired up Americans to do battle against the sins of the world, including slavery.

Frederick Douglass

1818	Born into slavery
1835	Escaped to the North
1839	Joined the abolitionist movement
1845	Published a best-selling *Narrative* of his life
1847	Founded the *North Star*
1859	Refused to join Brown's raid on Harper's Ferry (see page 80)
1889–91	US Consul General to Haiti
1895	Died

Douglass became the most famous and influential African American of his time. His mother was a slave; his white father was his mother's owner. He learned to read and write while working as a household slave in Baltimore. After becoming a plantation field-hand, he escaped (posing as a sailor) to the North, first working in New York but then moving to Massachusetts. In 1841 he gave his first speech to the Massachusetts Anti-Slavery Society. He was so successful that he was hired to conduct a regional speaking tour and quickly became a leading campaigner for abolition. In 1847 he founded his own paper, *North Star*. He was a great writer and also an inspiring speaker. 'I appear this evening as a thief and robber', Douglass told northern audiences. 'I stole this head, these limbs, this body from my master and ran off with them.'

Abolitionist problems in the North

The extent of the abolitionists' success must not be exaggerated. The movement had only limited appeal in the North. De Tocqueville commented: 'The prejudice of race appears to be stronger in the states that have abolished slavery than in those where it still exists.' Many northerners, fearing a northern exodus of liberated slaves and fearful of the effect that the new crusade would have in the South, hated the abolitionists. Anti-slavery meetings (and abolitionist printing presses) were sometimes broken up by angry northerners. In 1837 Elijah Lovejoy, a Presbyterian minister and newspaper editor, became the first abolitionist martyr when he was murdered by a mob in Illinois.

The abolitionists also had limited political success. Failing to win the support of either the Whig or Democrat parties, abolitionists set up their own Liberty Party. In 1840 its presidential candidate won only 7000 votes. Not all abolitionists supported the Liberty Party's creation. Many preferred to work through the existing parties. Garrison tried to ignore what he regarded as the sordid business of politics altogether, refusing to vote under the US Constitution, which he regarded as a pro-slavery document.

Abolitionists were unable to agree about other strategies. Some wanted to initiate a slave revolt. Most, realising that a revolt would be suicidal for the slaves, favoured 'moral' force and hoped to win white support in the South. A plethora of different opinions, coupled with individual feuds, resulted in a major schism in the Anti-Slavery Society in 1840.

Abolitionist problems in the South

The abolitionists had no success in winning southern white support. They were not helped by the fact that in 1831, **Nat Turner** led a slave revolt in which 55

 KEY FIGURE

Nat Turner (1800–31)

A Virginian slave who had literacy and carpentry skills which gained him the respect of fellow slaves. This enabled him to organise and lead the bloodiest slave rebellion in US history.

whites (mainly women and children) were killed before the insurrection was crushed. The revolt appalled southerners, who blamed abolitionists for inciting trouble among the slaves.

Abolitionist attacks goaded southerners to extol the virtues of their peculiar institution. A clutch of southern writers now argued that slavery was a positive good rather than a necessary evil. History, religion, anthropology and economics were all used to defend slavery.

- All the great civilisations in the past, it was claimed, had been based on slavery.
- The Bible seemed to sanction bondage. At no point did Christ actually condemn slavery.
- Black people were depicted as an inferior species, incapable of taking responsibility for themselves.
- Protected by paternalistic slaveholders, they were better off than most working men in northern factories or freed people in Haiti or Africa.

As well as vigorously defending slavery in print and vocally, southerners took action against abolitionists. Abolitionist literature was excluded from most southern states. In some states, the penalty for circulating 'incendiary' literature among black people was death. Those suspected of having abolitionist sympathies were driven out, often after being physically assaulted. The white South, slaveholders and non-slaveholders alike, was united in its resistance to abolitionism.

The abolitionist crusade, therefore, had little impact on the slaves; indeed it may have made their position worse as many states now placed new restrictions on slaves. Nevertheless, if the abolitionists did little in the short term to help the slaves, they did a great deal to heighten sectional animosity. They stirred the consciences of a growing number of northerners and kept slavery in the forefront of public attention. Southerners, while exaggerating the extent of support for abolitionism, correctly sensed that more and more northerners were opposed to slavery.

The nature of slavery

Historians continue to debate the nature of the peculiar institution. They have a considerable number of sources with which to work: plantation records, census returns, newspapers, diaries, travellers' accounts and political speeches. Unfortunately, there is limited evidence from the slaves themselves, few of whom were literate. The best accounts of what it was like to experience slavery were written by fugitive slaves, some of whom became leading abolitionists. Such men and women were probably not typical slaves. While there are large numbers of reminiscences resulting from interviews with ex-slaves, conducted in the 1930s, these accounts are flawed by the fact that those who provided their recollections had only experienced slavery as children.

Statistical evidence

The census returns of 1850 and 1860 provide a starting point for trying to understand the nature of slavery.

- In 1860 there were nearly 4 million slaves (compared to some 8 million white people) in the fifteen southern states. They were concentrated mainly in the lower South. Slaves outnumbered whites in South Carolina.
- In 1850, one in three white southern families owned slaves. By 1860, as a result of the rising cost of slaves, one family in four were slave owners. The decline in the number of slave owners worried some southern politicians, who believed that the South would be more united if every white family owned a slave and thus had a vested interest in slavery.
- In 1860, 50 per cent of slave owners owned no more than five slaves. Over 50 per cent of slaves lived on plantations with over twenty slaves. Thus the 'typical' slaveholder did not own the 'typical' slave.
- Most slaves were held by about 10,000 families.
- Fifty-five per cent of slaves worked in cotton production, ten per cent in tobacco and ten per cent in sugar, rice and hemp, while fifteen per cent were domestic servants.
- About ten per cent of slaves lived in towns or worked in a variety of industries.

Free black people

By 1860 there were about 250,000 free black people in the South. Many of these were of mixed race and had been given their freedom by their white fathers. Southern free blacks had to carry documentation proving their freedom at all times or risk the danger of being enslaved. They had no political rights and their legal status was precarious. Job opportunities were also limited.

Some 200,000 blacks lived in the North. Northern blacks usually had the worst jobs and **segregation** was the norm in most aspects of life. Only three states allowed blacks to vote on terms of parity with whites in 1860. Some northern states tried to exclude blacks altogether. However, a number of politicians in the decades before the Civil War worked to expand black rights. By 1861 northern blacks had more rights than at any time in the previous 30 years.

The impact of slavery on the southern economy

Economists and politicians in the mid-nineteenth century debated whether slavery was economically profitable. Historians have continued the debate. Much depends on defining just who slavery was profitable for. Few historians claim that slavery was profitable for the slave. Slave owners obviously believed that it was profitable to buy slaves or they would not have done so. Slaveholding enabled planters to increase their cotton acreage and hence their profits.

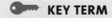 **KEY TERM**

Segregation The system whereby blacks and whites are separated from each other (for example, in schools and housing) on grounds of race.

SOURCE C

How useful is Source C for historians studying the nature of slavery?

Sale of Slaves and Stock.

The Negroes and Stock listed below, are a Prime Lot, and belong to the ESTATE OF THE LATE LUTHER McGOWAN, and will be sold on Monday, Sept. 22nd, 1852, at the Fair Grounds, in Savannah, Georgia, at 1:00 P. M. The Negroes will be taken to the grounds two days previous to the Sale, so that they may be inspected by prospective buyers.

On account of the low prices listed below, they will be sold for cash only, and must be taken into custody within two hours after sale.

No.	Name.	Age	Remarks.	Price.
1	Lunesta	27	Prime Rice Planter,	$1,275.00
2	Violet	16	Housework and Nursemaid,	900.00
3	Lizzie	30	Rice, Unsound,	300.00
4	Minda	27	Cotton, Prime Woman,	1,200.00
5	Adam	28	Cotton, Prime Young Man,	1,100.00
6	Abel	41	Rice Hand, Eyesight Poor,	675.00
7	Tanney	22	Prime Cotton Hand,	950.00
8	Flementina	39	Good Cook, Stiff Knee,	400.00
9	Lanney	34	Prime Cottom Man,	1,000.00
10	Sally	10	Handy in Kitchen,	675.00
11	Maccabey	35	Prime Man, Fair Carpenter,	980.00
12	Dorcas Judy	25	Seamstress, Handy in House,	800.00
13	Happy	60	Blacksmith,	575.00
14	Mowden	15	Prime Cotton Boy,	700.00
15	Bills	21	Handy with Mules,	900.00
16	Theopolis	39	Rice Hand, Gets Fits,	575.00
17	Coolidge	29	Rice Hand and Blacksmith,	1,275.00
18	Bessie	69	Infirm, Sews,	250.00
19	Infant	1	Strong Likely Boy	400.00
20	Samson	41	Prime Man, Good with Stock,	975.00
21	Callie May	27	Prime Woman, Rice,	1,000.00
22	Honey	14	Prime Girl, Hearing Poor,	850.00
23	Angelina	16	Prime Girl, House or Field,	1,000.00
24	Virgil	21	Prime Field Hand,	1,100.00
25	Tom	40	Rice Hand, Lame Leg,	750.00
26	Noble	11	Handy Boy,	900.00
27	Judge Lesh	55	Prime Blacksmith,	800.00
28	Booster	43	Fair Mason, Unsound,	600.00
29	Big Kate	37	Housekeeper and Nurse,	950.00
30	Melie Ann	19	Housework, Smart Yellow Girl,	1,250.00
31	Deacon	26	Prime Rice Hand,	1,000.00
32	Coming	19	Prime Cotton Hand,	1,000.00
33	Mabel	47	Prime Cotton Hand,	800.00
34	Uncle Tim	60	Fair Hand with Mules,	600.00
35	Abe	27	Prime Cotton Hand,	1,000.00
36	Tennes	29	Prime Rice Hand and Coachman,	1,250.00

There will also be offered at this sale, twenty head of Horses and Mules with harness, along with thirty head of Prime Cattle. Slaves will be sold separate, or in lots, as best suits the purchaser. Sale will be held rain or shine.

A notice of a slave sale from 1852.

A more interesting debate is the extent to which the economy of the South gained or lost by slavery. In 1857 a southerner, Hilton Rowan Helper, published an influential book, *The Impending Crisis of the South,* in which he argued that slavery was responsible for the South's economic decline. Since the Civil War a number of historians (for example, Ulrich Phillips) have followed Helper's line. Arguably, slavery did not fully utilise the potential skills of the labour force. It helped to bring manual labour into disrepute among whites, thus helping to undermine the work ethic. It is also possible to claim that slaves were a poor investment and that southern capital would have been better spent on manufacturing and transport. Slavery may have imposed a certain rigidity on the southern mind, ensuring that the South opposed industrialisation and remained dependent on cotton.

A clutch of historians, including Kenneth Stampp, Robert Fogel and Stanley Engerman, have argued (persuasively) that slavery was an efficient form of economic organisation which did not deter the growth of the southern economy. Given that slave prices doubled in the 1850s, investors in slaves received returns similar to those who invested in industry. The fact that the South lagged behind the North in industrial development can be seen as a sign of its economic health. The South was making so much money that it had no incentive to industrialise. From 1840 to 1860, the increase in per capita income in the South exceeded the rate of increase in the rest of the USA. This was largely due to cotton. Given that southern plantations grew cotton more efficiently than any other area in the world, the South faced no immediate threat to its world dominance. Arguably, the planters were entrepreneurial businessmen, obsessed with economic advancement. Fogel and Engerman have claimed that southern slave agriculture, as a result of specialisation, careful management and economies of scale, was 35 per cent more efficient than small-scale family farming.

The future of slavery

Some historians have argued that once cotton prices fell, as surely they must have, then slavery would have withered away and died of its own accord. If this is correct, the bloodletting of the Civil War was unnecessary. However, in 1860 there was still a worldwide demand for cotton and thus no valid economic reason for believing slavery was about to die out. Moreover, slavery was not simply an economic institution. It was also a system of social control. It kept blacks in their place and ensured white supremacy. Even the poorest, non-slaveholding whites felt they had a vested interest in preserving slavery: it kept them off the bottom of the social heap. Southerners feared that an end to slavery would result in economic collapse, social disintegration and race war. Thus, slaveholders and non-slaveholders alike were committed to the peculiar institution, so committed that (ultimately) they were prepared to **secede** from the Union and wage a terrible war in an effort to maintain it. Given this commitment, it is difficult to see how slavery would have withered away without the Civil War.

 KEY TERM

Secede To leave or quit.

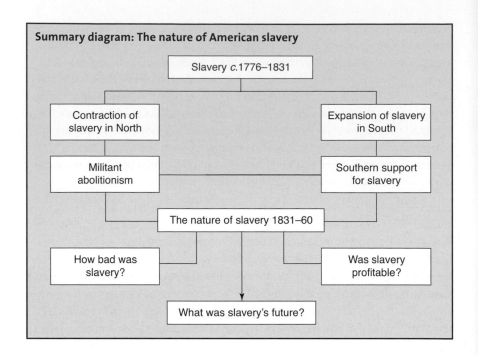

Summary diagram: The nature of American slavery

6 Key debate

▶ *How benign was the system of slavery in the USA?*

Over the past two centuries there have been major debates about whether US-style slavery was a system of ruthless exploitation or whether it was more a kind of welfare state arrangement, offering protection for the slaves from cradle to grave.

In the early twentieth century, white, southern historian Ulrich Phillips wrote two influential books on slavery: *American Negro Slavery* (1918) and *Life and Labour in the Old South* (1929). Philips argued that slavery was as benign and benevolent an institution as slaveholders had always claimed it to be. Most slaves, thought Phillips, were content with their lot. Relationships between the slaves and their owners were marked by 'gentleness, kind-hearted friendship and mutual loyalty'.

In 1956 Stampp, a white northerner, published *The Peculiar Institution*. While accepting that there were massive variations, Stampp held that slavery was harsh rather than benign. He saw little in the way of good relationships between owner and owned. In his view, the typical plantation was an area of persistent conflict between the master and the slaves who were, quite naturally, 'a troublesome property'.

Stampp's thesis, which has been supported by a host of other historians, remains the prevailing view. However, in 1974 Fogel and Engerman produced *Time on the Cross*. After feeding a vast amount of source material into computers, they came up with a host of statistics which, they claimed, displayed precisely what slavery was like. Their conclusions, at least with regard to slave conditions, were similar to those of Phillips. In Fogel and Engerman's view, planters were a 'rational' and humane capitalist class and slavery was a mild and efficient system of labour. Slaves, said Fogel and Engerman, were controlled with minimal force and enjoyed a standard of living comparable to that of northern industrial workers.

The response to *Time on the Cross* was overwhelmingly critical. Many historians attacked Fogel and Engerman's techniques and insisted that their conclusions did not possess the objective scientific status that the authors claimed. Their findings, according to two critics, Richard Sutch and Herbert Gutman, were 'confused, circular and so unsubtle as to be naive. Some of their conclusions can be disproved, while others remain unsupported conjectures, in some cases fanciful speculations.'

Slavery: the benign view

EXTRACT I

From Ulrich B. Phillips, *American Negro Slavery*, written in 1918, available at Project Gutenberg. www.gutenberg.org/ebooks/11490

There were injustice, oppression, brutality and heartburning in the regime – but where in the struggling world are these absent? There was also gentleness, kind-hearted friendship and mutual loyalty to a degree hard for him to believe who regards the system with a theorist's eye and a partisan squint. For him on the other hand who has known the considerate and cordial, courteous and charming men and women, white and black, which that picturesque life in its best phases produced, it is impossible to agree that its basis and its operation were wholly evil.

Those, like Phillips, who have argued that slavery was benign, have made the following points:

- Slaves did not necessarily work much harder or longer than most mid-nineteenth-century Americans. Most did not work on Sundays and received a fair number of holidays; many had half a day's holiday on Saturdays.
- Floggings were rare, if only because slave owners had a vested interest in the maintenance of their property. Just as most owners of expensive cars today take good care of their vehicles, so slave owners looked after their 'property'. (A slave was worth much the same as a modern-day top-of-the-range car.) Most whites were restrained in their treatment of slaves by Christian morality and by their own standards of decency.
- Most owners preferred the carrot as a source of motivation to the stick. Slaves who worked hard were given extra holidays, better clothing and more food.

- Given the standards of the day, slaves were reasonably well fed, clothed and housed.
- There was variety in the nature and organisation of slaves' work. By no means all toiled for long hours on cotton plantations. Within slavery there was a hierarchy, tantamount to a career structure. Hard-working – or lucky – slaves had a good chance of promotion. They could pick up a skill or become a domestic slave, slave driver or plantation overseer.
- By using strategies such as feigning illness or working slowly, slaves were able to modify and subvert the system.
- The slave population increased at much the same rate as white population growth. By 1860 slaves lived almost as long as white southerners.
- The slave family, far from being undermined by the slave system, was the basic unit of social organisation. Slaves usually chose their own partners. Slaves were often traded so that couples who were fond of each other could live together. Slaveholders refrained from selling small children separately from their mothers.
- Slave suicides were rare.
- The fact that there was no major slave revolt – Nat Turner's apart – suggests that slave conditions were not so bad.
- Only a few hundred slaves a year made any serious attempt to escape to freedom.
- Some slaves were granted, or made enough money to purchase, their freedom.
- Historian Eugene Genovese, while not defending slave conditions, has argued that most plantation owners had an aristocratic code of honour. Depicting them as more **paternalistic** than **capitalistic**, he also claimed that they were not particularly racist.
- Although slaves, in strict legal terms, were regarded as 'chattels' (similar to tables and chairs), they were also viewed as human beings. In most states, they had some legal protection, especially if mistreatment was committed by someone other than their owner.

Slavery: the harsh view

EXTRACT 2

From Peter J. Parish, *Slavery: History and Historians*, Harper & Row, 1989, pp. 40–1.

The extraordinarily high labour participation rate [claimed by historians Fogel and Engerman] is in fact another neutral-sounding phrase which is a euphemism for something extremely unpleasant. It means, in fact, that women and children, the aged and the handicapped, even expectant and nursing mothers, were all required to work. This was the consequence of compulsion, not of incentives. Moreover, they were made to work intensively, under constant supervision. Comparisons are hazardous even when they are not odious, but many recent authorities support the conventional view that slaves worked longer hours and had fewer days off even than nineteenth-century industrial workers, and certainly longer hours and fewer days off than free blacks after the Civil War. As a general rule, slave labour was both intensive and extensive.

Most historians remain convinced that slave conditions were harsh.

- Slave owners had unlimited power. Slaves could be sold, separated from their families, punished, sexually exploited and even killed without redress.
- Firm discipline seems to have been the norm. This was an age that believed that to spare the rod was to spoil the child – and slave. On plantations, slaves worked in gangs supervised by a black driver and a white overseer, both of whom used the whip if workers fell behind the pace. 'Uppity' slaves were flogged, branded, mutilated or sold.
- Slaves usually worked longer hours than free Americans. Most slaveholders aimed to make a profit. They thus sought to extract the maximum amount of work for the minimum cost.
- Slaves' normal diet was monotonous (corn and pork were the main components) and resulted in many slaves having vitamin deficiencies.
- Most slaves lived in overcrowded log cabins.
- Slaves had few prospects of promotion: in most states it was illegal for them to be taught to read and write.
- The slave family unit was far from sacrosanct. Possibly a quarter of slave marriages were broken by forced separation. Like other forms of property, slaves were inherited, given as wedding presents, wagered in games of chance and sold to speculators.
- Planters and their sons took advantage of female slaves. Diarist Mary Chesnut, a South Carolina plantation mistress, wrote: 'Like the patriarchs of old, our men live all in one house with their wives and concubines.'
- **Manumission** was rare. By 1860 virtually all the southern states had laws restricting the right of owners to free their slaves.
- It is difficult to establish that most planters were sincerely paternalistic. Most accepted that ultimately they ruled by fear and discipline. Virtually all held racist views.
- The fact that there was no major revolt is not proof that slaves were content. A major revolt was impossible to organise. Slaves were a minority in most states. They were not allowed to own firearms or to congregate in large groups. A slave uprising would have been tantamount to mass suicide.
- It was virtually impossible for a family group to escape. Most individual fugitives were caught within days and severely punished. The '**underground railroad**', despite abolitionist propaganda and southern fears, was far from extensive or well organised. Even those slaves who did make it to the North risked the possibility of being returned to their owners.
- The evidence suggests that most slaves hated slavery. Whenever they had the opportunity of freedom during the Civil War, most took it.

> **?** Which of the two extracts provides the more convincing interpretation of the nature of southern slavery?

 **KEY TERMS**

Manumission Freeing of slaves.

Underground railroad A network of anti-slavery houses that helped runaway slaves to escape to the North and to Canada.

Conclusion

In Stampp's view, 'The only generalization that can be made with relative confidence is that some masters were harsh and frugal; others were mild and generous and the rest ran the whole gamut in between.' Slaves who laboured in the rice- and sugar-growing areas of the Deep South probably endured the worst conditions. Household servants generally had an easier life than field-hands. Historian Paul Escott suggests that slaves on small farms had a worse lot than those on big plantations, if only because they spent much more time under the supervision of their owner and had no sense of belonging to a sizeable slave community.

Chapter summary

By the mid-nineteenth century, the USA had considerably expanded, in terms of both territory and population. The country had the world's most democratic system of government. It was also prosperous. The main problem was sectionalism. There were significant differences between northerners and southerners – differences that were growing as the North's industrial development outstripped that of the South. The North was changing; the South resisted change. By 1850 southerners were conscious of their distinct 'southern-ness'. Northerners and southerners may have spoken the same language but by the mid-nineteenth century (as historian James McPherson has pointed out) they were increasingly using this language to revile each other. Slavery was the key divisive issue. Southerners defended their 'peculiar institution'. A growing number of northern abolitionists condemned it. Historians remain as divided as contemporaries over the exact nature of slavery.

Refresher questions

Use these questions to remind yourself of the key material covered in this chapter.

1 How did the US system of government operate?

2 How democratic was the USA by the mid-nineteenth century?

3 Was the USA 'a society of equals'?

4 Why did the USA's economy prosper in the early nineteenth century?

5 What were the main differences between North and South?

6 Why were southerners so committed to slavery?

7 How important was the abolitionist movement?

8 Was slavery profitable?

9 Was slavery on the point of collapse by the mid-nineteenth century?

10 How benign was southern slavery?

Question practice

ESSAY QUESTIONS

1 'The deep divisions between North and South threatened the unity of the USA by 1850.' Assess the validity of this view.

2 'There was more uniting than dividing North and South in the mid-nineteenth century.' Explain why you agree or disagree with this view.

3 How successful was the abolitionist movement in the USA by 1850?

4 To what extent was southern slavery 'a system of ruthless exploitation'?

SOURCE ANALYSIS QUESTIONS

1 With reference to Sources 1 and 2, and your understanding of the historical context, which of these two sources is more valuable in explaining why there was sectional tension in the mid-nineteenth century?

2 With reference to Sources 1, 2 and 3, and your understanding of the historical context, assess the value of these sources to a historian studying the economic and social impact of slavery.

SOURCE I

From G. Fitzhugh, *Sociology for the South*, 1854. The view of a southerner who tries to defend slavery in a more intellectual way than most southerners.

There is no rivalry, no competition to get employment among slaves, as among free labourers. Nor is there a war between master and slave. The master's interest prevents his reducing the slave's allowance or wages in infancy or sickness, for he might lose the slave by so doing. His feeling for his slave never permits him to stint him in old age. The slaves are all well fed, well clad, have plenty of fuel, and are happy. They have no dread of the future – no fear of want. A state of dependence is the only condition in which reciprocal affection can exist among human beings – the only situation in which the war of competition ceases, and peace, amity and goodwill arise.

SOURCE 2

From H.R. Helper, *The Impending Crisis of the South*, 1857. The view of a southerner who claims that slavery was responsible for the economic decline of the South.

In writing this book, it has been no part of my purpose to cast unmerited opprobrium upon slaveholders, or to display any special friendliness or sympathy for the blacks. I have considered my subject more particularly with reference to its economic aspects as regards the whites – not with reference, except in a very slight degree, to its humanitarian or religious aspects … .

Slavery, and nothing but slavery, has retarded the progress and prosperity of our portion of the Union; depopulated and impoverished our cities by forcing the more industrious and enterprising natives of the soil to emigrate to the free states; brought our domain under a sparse and inert population by preventing foreign immigration; made us a tributary to the North, and reduced us to the humiliating condition of mere provincial subjects in fact, though not in name.

SOURCE 3

From F.L. Olmstead, *The Cotton Kingdom: A Traveller's Observations on Cotton and Slavery in the American Slave States*, 1861. The view of a northerner who travelled widely in the South in 1859.

Slavery withholds all encouragement from the labourer to improve his faculties and his skill; destroys his self-respect; misdirects and debases his ambition, and withholds all the natural motives that lead men to endeavour to increase their capacity of usefulness to their country and the world … .The citizens of the cotton States, as a whole, are poor. They work little, and that little badly; they earn little, they sell little; they buy little and they have little – very little – of the common comforts and consolations of civilized life. Their destitution is not material only; it is intellectual and it is moral … They were neither generous nor hospitable and their talk was not that of evenly courageous men.

CHAPTER 2

The problems of western expansion 1803–54

In the early nineteenth century the USA expanded westwards. Westward expansion benefited millions of white Americans. However, it was a disaster for Native Americans. Westward expansion also led to divisions: divisions between easterners and westerners, but more importantly divisions between northerners and southerners. Indeed, western expansion became the catalyst which threatened to tear the Union apart. This chapter will focus on:

★ Westward expansion 1800–40

★ The Native American experience 1800–40

★ Missouri, Texas and Mexico

★ The impact of the Mexican War 1846–50

★ The 1850 Compromise

★ North–South problems 1850–3

★ The problem of Kansas–Nebraska

Key dates

1803	Louisiana Purchase	1845		Texas joined the USA
1820	Missouri Compromise	1846	May	Start of Mexican War
1825	Erie Canal opened		Aug.	Wilmot Proviso
1830	Indian Removal Act	1848		Treaty of Guadalupe Hidalgo
1836	Texas won independence from Mexico	1850		The 1850 Compromise
1838	Trail of Tears	1854		Kansas–Nebraska Act

Westward expansion 1800–40

▶ *Why did the USA expand westwards so quickly in the early nineteenth century?*

(see Figure 2.1, page 40)

KEY TERM

Native Americans The people, often known as Indians, who first inhabited North America.

In 1800 the USA's western frontier had barely advanced beyond the Appalachian mountains (see Figure 2.1, page 40). Spain claimed much of what is the present USA. **Native Americans** still controlled most of North America. By 1840, the situation had dramatically changed. The Spanish and Native Americans had lost much of their land to US settlers. In 1810 only one American in seven lived west of the Appalachians. By 1840 nearly one in two did. Western expansion was encouraged by federal government action. But economic factors were more important, especially the lure of fertile western land.

Federal government action

American politicians had long envisaged the USA as a bastion of freedom that would extend from the Atlantic to the Pacific Ocean. Federal government action with regard to land policy and the acquisition of territory encouraged western expansion.

Land policy

The 1785 Land Ordinance established the rules by which western lands were to be surveyed and sold. New northwest land was to be surveyed into townships six miles (10 km) square. Each township was then to be divided into 36 sections, each one a mile (1.6 km) square (or 640 acres) (one acre = about 0.40 hectares). Initially, Congress favoured the sale of large parcels of land to wealthy speculators who then sold it in smaller pieces, making a profit in the process, to farmers.

In 1796 the minimum individual purchase was 640 acres, at a price of $2 per acre – too expensive for most would-be settlers. Thereafter, Congress, as a result of popular pressure, reduced the minimum amount – first to 320 acres (in 1800) and then to 160 acres (in 1804). By 1820 it was possible to buy 80 acres and, by 1832, 40 acres. The minimum price per acre steadily fell to about a dollar an acre.

KEY FIGURE

Napoleon Bonaparte (1769–1821)

Napoleon was a brilliant French general. By 1799, he effectively ruled France and in 1804 became French Emperor. For a time, he controlled most of Europe. He was finally defeated by Britain and Prussia at the battle of Waterloo (1815).

The Louisiana Purchase

President Thomas Jefferson (1801–9), believing more land was necessary if the nation was to remain one essentially made up of independent, property-owning farmers, was anxious to expand the 'empire of liberty' – at the expense of Native Americans, the British in Canada and the Spanish. His greatest – and luckiest – triumph as president was the Louisiana Purchase.

In 1800 **Napoleon Bonaparte** had concluded a treaty with Spain providing for the return to France of Louisiana, the vast territory extending westwards from the Mississippi River to the Rockies, and including New Orleans near the

Mississippi's mouth (see the map on page 45). Jefferson was concerned at the prospect of having powerful France as a neighbour rather than enfeebled Spain, particularly as New Orleans was the outlet for the products of nearly half the territory of the USA.

In 1802 Jefferson sent James Monroe to France with instructions to offer $10 million for New Orleans and West Florida (see the map on page 40). By the time Monroe reached Paris, Napoleon had abandoned his designs on America. He offered the USA not only New Orleans but the whole of Louisiana. Monroe, realising the value of what was on offer, determined to exceed his authority. In April 1803 he signed a treaty whereby the USA acquired the whole of Louisiana for $15 million. The Louisiana Purchase gave the USA a tract of some 828,000 square miles (over 2 million km²) at a cost of less than three cents an acre.

The treaty embarrassed Jefferson. To spend $15 million, a sum nearly twice as great as the federal government's annual expenditure, was hardly compatible with his general concern for economy. There was also an issue as to whether he had the constitutional power to acquire additional territory. Swallowing his scruples, Jefferson submitted the treaty to the Senate, which overwhelmingly approved it. In December 1803 the Louisiana territory became part of the USA, more than doubling the national territory (see the map on page 40).

Relations with Britain

In 1812 the USA declared war on Britain. The apparent cause of the war was the problem of American rights at sea, arising from Britain's naval blockade of Continental Europe during the **Revolutionary and Napoleonic Wars**. However, many Congressmen were eager to drive the British from Canada, opening up new land for American settlers. The war did not go as well as Americans hoped. US attempts to seize Canada failed and Napoleon's defeat in 1814 ensured that Britain could focus more attention on the American War. The Treaty of Ghent (December 1814) brought the war to an end. The last battle, a US victory at New Orleans, was fought in January 1815, before news of the peace reached America.

After 1815, US relations with Britain improved. The Convention of 1818 settled most outstanding border issues between the USA and Canada, the 49th parallel becoming the boundary between the two in the west. Given that Britain and the USA could not agree to the borders in Oregon, that region was left open to joint occupancy by citizens of both nations.

Florida

The USA was anxious to **annex** Florida from Spain.

- As long as Spain or any other foreign power controlled Florida it might be used as a base for attacks into US territory.

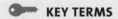 **KEY TERMS**

Revolutionary and Napoleonic Wars The wars, waged by France, lasting from 1792 to 1815. France's main opponents were Britain, Austria, Russia and Prussia.

Annex To take possession of an area.

- Southerners were concerned about Florida becoming a refuge for runaway slaves.
- US politicians claimed that west Florida had been part of the Louisiana Purchase. Spain disagreed.

In September 1810, American settlers seized Baton Rouge and proclaimed a republic of west Florida. In October, President Madison instructed US officials to occupy most of the region. In 1812 it became part of the new state of Louisiana. In 1813 US forces took over the rest of west Florida. Spain, at war with Napoleon and preoccupied with independence movements in several of its Latin American colonies, could do little about it.

President Monroe (1817–25) hoped to acquire the rest of Florida. The thinly populated province had been a thorn in the side of the USA during the war of 1812 as a haven for hostile **Seminole Indians**. In 1817 **Secretary of State** John Quincy Adams began negotiations with Spanish minister Don Luis de Onís to settle border disputes and define the boundary between American and Spanish territory.

In 1817 Monroe authorised a campaign against the Seminoles. General Andrew Jackson, victor of the battle of New Orleans, was given command. His orders allowed him to pursue Seminoles into Spanish territory but not to attack any Spanish fort. Jackson, who had little sympathy for Spaniards or Native Americans, was disinclined to bother with technicalities. In four months he effectively seized much of northern Florida.

While Spain demanded the return of its territory and Jackson's punishment, there was little it could do. Adams supported Jackson, whose actions had strengthened his hand in the negotiations already underway with Luis de Onís. It was now apparent that the USA could seize the whole of Florida whenever it wished.

In 1819 the USA and Spain agreed to the Adams–Onís (or Transcontinental) treaty.

- Spain ceded Florida to the USA.
- The western boundary of the Louisiana Purchase was agreed. The USA gave up its claims to Texas but acquired Spain's claim to the Oregon Territory north of the 42nd parallel.

Economic factors

After 1803 Americans (and European immigrants, mainly from Britain and Germany) poured west in enormous numbers. The main economic pull was the huge swathe of fertile land, much of which was covered with forest, which extended from the Appalachians to the Mississippi River. Western farmers were soon producing enormous quantities of surplus crops: wheat in the northwest, cotton in the southwest.

KEY TERMS

Seminole Indians Native American people of Creek ancestry who migrated from Georgia to Florida in the late eighteenth century. They were regarded by the USA as one of the Five Civilised Tribes.

Secretary of State The US government official responsible for foreign policy.

To a degree, farmers from other parts of the USA were pushed westwards.

- Given western agricultural competition, it was increasingly difficult for farmers to wrest a living from New England's rocky soil.
- While western competition had less dramatic results in the middle Atlantic states, here, too, there was agricultural distress which led to farmers moving west.
- Further south, wasteful methods of cultivation had left a legacy of declining crops and exhausted fields, first in the tobacco states of Virginia, Maryland and North Carolina, then throughout the cotton-producing regions of the Carolinas and Georgia. This encouraged farmers to move westwards.

Land purchase

Some western settlers purchased land from the federal government. Soldiers, who had volunteered to fight in the war of 1812 (see page 29), were given western lands as a military bounty. More frequently, settlers purchased land from speculators. Some settlers just squatted on empty land, clearing the forest, farming the land and then moving on. Squatters' rights proved a difficult issue. The Preemption Act (1841) gave squatters a prior right to purchase lands on which they had settled.

Boom and depression

Economic forces aided and sometimes discouraged expansion. Between 1815 and 1819, for example, wheat and cotton prices climbed sharply. This encouraged western settlement, which, in turn, drove up land prices. But farmers had no control of distant markets. As a result of the overextension of credit and dependence on agricultural exports to repay loans, western farmers – and speculators – were vulnerable to a crash like the **Panic of 1819**. As agricultural and land prices plummeted, speculators lost huge sums of money. Many farmers, unable to meet their debts, moved westwards to squat on new land. As the economic situation improved in the mid-1820s, western expansion continued but at a slower rate than in the 1815–19 boom.

By the 1820s the output of western farmers was immense.

- In the southwest, Mississippi and Alabama produced half of America's cotton.
- The northwest displaced the Atlantic seaboard as the main source of corn, wheat, cattle, sheep and pigs.

The huge increase that occurred in western agricultural production was due not only to the richness of the soil but also to improvements in agricultural technology. Westerners were quick to adopt new labour-saving devices. Jethro Wood's iron plough (developed in 1819), followed in 1837 by John Deere's steel plough, helped to cut and turn the prairie soil. The mechanical reaper, invented in 1831 by Cyrus McCormick, was crucial for enabling large-scale grain production.

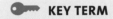 **KEY TERM**

Panic of 1819 A major economic crisis 1819–23. While the entire country was affected, westerners were hit especially hard. It was mainly caused by a decline in demand for US products in Britain and Europe.

Western settlers

Essentially, the West was settled by families who tilled their own soil. But the pattern of ownership was not quite as democratic as many politicians would have wished.

- Given there was no limit on purchases, some westerners accumulated large tracts of land.
- Settlers usually found land too expensive for outright purchase. They were thus forced to borrow at high rates. Hard times forced many into renting their lands.

Most settlers did not stay put for long. Many headed further west. The family of future President Abraham Lincoln was not untypical. Thomas Lincoln, Abraham's father, was born in Virginia in 1778. In 1782 he was taken to Kentucky, where Abraham was born in 1809. In 1816 the Lincolns moved to Indiana. In 1831 Abraham headed further west to Illinois.

Southerners moved into the rich cotton-growing lands of the Mississippi Basin, often taking their slaves with them. Further north, the majority of settlers set up small, family farms. Typical westerners lived in a forest clearing, a clearing usually made by their own axes. Timber was vital. Their houses were made of it, their fields were fenced with it; it provided them with fuel and furniture. Their staple crop was corn, which ensured a sure supply of food.

Transport developments

The movement westwards stimulated improvements in communications. Westerners wanted to be able to send their produce to market in the eastern cities and to receive manufactured goods in return. Transport development, as well as facilitating the movement of goods, encouraged the westward movement of people.

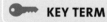 **KEY TERM**

Pioneer settlers Those who were among the first people to explore and occupy a region.

Early movement

Pioneer settlers, of all ages and both genders, moved west by wagon, on foot, on horseback and by boat over lakes and navigable rivers whenever possible. They moved in ones or twos, more usually as families, and sometimes in large groups. Travel was hard: early roads were little more than tracks. Most pioneers settled along major rivers in order to facilitate trade and contact with the outside world.

Road-building

In 1808 work began on the 'National Road' or 'Cumberland Pike'. The road, funded by the federal government, was to run from the Atlantic to Ohio and beyond as the western advance continued. By 1838 it extended some 800 miles (1250 km) to Vandalia, Illinois. The National Road apart, most road-building was the responsibility of state governments and private enterprise.

Steamboats

In 1807 Robert Fulton and Robert Livingstone launched *Clermont*, the world's first commercially successful steamboat, on the Hudson River. Steamboats, however, were to have the greatest impact on the Mississippi and its tributaries. Before the steamboat, western farmers floated their produce downstream in flat boats, essentially rafts. Given the difficulty of hauling craft upstream, most boats were broken up at New Orleans and sold as timber. Steamboats meant that trade could now go both ways on the Mississippi. They quickly cut both the cost and time of transport. In 1817 there were seventeen steamboats on western rivers; by 1836 there were 361. The paddle steamer was never the safest form of transport. Nearly a third of all western steamboats built before 1849 were lost in accidents, usually caused by fire, boiler explosions or collisions with river debris.

Canals

In 1816 the USA had only 100 miles (160 km) of canals. In 1817 work began on the construction of the Erie Canal from Albany to Buffalo on Lake Erie. This was largely the creation of Governor De Witt Clinton of New York. Clinton's 'Big Ditch', running for 363 miles (580 km) with 83 locks and 18 aqueducts, was completed by 1825. It was an economic success. The average freight charges between Buffalo and New York City dropped from 19 cents a ton/mile in 1817 to little more than 2 cents a ton/mile in 1830. Travel time fell from twenty days to eight. Within nine years, the Erie Canal had paid for itself. Its success sparked a nationwide canal building boom. By 1840 there were 3326 miles (5322 km) of canals, mainly financed by state governments.

Railroads

In 1830 the Baltimore and Ohio railroad company opened up a thirteen-mile (21 km) stretch of 'road'. Wagons, initially hauled by horses, were soon pulled by steam locomotives. By the late 1830s, investment in railroads exceeded that in canals. Railroads were built and operated by private companies but these companies were usually offered financial aid by state and city governments. By 1840 the USA had 3328 miles (5325 km) of track – two miles more than its canal system. While canals remained a cheaper way of transporting bulky freight, railroads were faster and had a greater range.

Western cities

Improvements in transport ensured that major cities soon developed in the West. Initially most, like Cincinnati and St Louis, had grown up on the major rivers. The canal system heightened the importance of lake cities such as Buffalo and Chicago, which expanded spectacularly after 1830. The growth of western cities, offering a variety of work, provided another pull for easterners. Overall, however, the West remained essentially agricultural in 1840.

The Far West

Before 1840, Americans referred to the region between the Appalachians and the Mississippi as the 'West'. The Far West – beyond the Mississippi – was largely devoid of white settlers. Nevertheless, Americans had some knowledge of the region.

The Lewis and Clark expedition

In 1803 President Jefferson persuaded Congress to provide money for a transcontinental expedition to explore the western half of North America. In May 1804, a 48-strong team, led by the president's secretary, Captain Meriwether Lewis, and another experienced **frontiersman**, William Clark, set out from St Louis. After following the Missouri to its headwaters, the expedition crossed the Rocky Mountains before descending the Snake and Columbia rivers to reach the Pacific coast. After an epic journey of nearly 4000 miles (6400 km), the explorers returned to St Louis in 1806 with a large collection of maps, drawings, botanical and geological specimens, and a mass of information on Native American customs.

Lieutenant Pike

In 1806–7 Lieutenant Zebulon Pike explored the headwaters of the Arkansas River as far as Colorado and returning by way of Santa Fe. Pike's account, which appeared before that of Lewis and Clark, gave Americans their first detailed information on the Great Plains and Rocky Mountains.

Major Long

In 1819–20 an expedition led by Major Stephen Long travelled across present-day Nebraska and Colorado to the Rockies. Long declared the Plains the Great American Desert, totally unsuitable for white settlers.

Fur traders and trappers

A few white people made serious forays into the Far West in the 1820s. Until the late 1830s furs, especially those of the beaver, were the region's most valuable produce. Trappers and hunters, who generally sold their furs to either Astor's American Fur Company or the Rocky Mountain Fur Company, brought back geographical knowledge of the areas through which they roamed. The (often fictional) printed accounts of the adventures of some of these 'mountain men' (like Kit Carson and Jim Bridger) served to publicise (and romanticise) the Far West.

The situation in 1840

By 1840 the USA was little more than half its present size.

- Mexico, which had won independence from Spain in 1821, controlled a vast swathe of territory in the southwest.

- Although Texas had broken from Mexico in 1835–6, the USA had still not incorporated the new republic into the Union (see pages 41–2).
- Oregon remained a source of dispute with Britain.

Nevertheless, westward expansion in the early nineteenth century had been extraordinary. In 1800 there had been 387,000 settlers west of the Appalachians; by 1840 there were over 7 million (including slaves). By 1840, the US line of settlement had reached the Mississippi and Missouri rivers.

While the federal government had encouraged expansion, the advance was never a planned and organised movement. Instead, it was the work of individual settlers, emigrants from Europe and easterners wanting new land. After a period of territorial government (see page 3), new western states were able to join the Union (see the map on page 40).

There was a measure of rivalry between east and west. Easterners tended to view westerners as uncouth. Westerners chided easterners for their soft lifestyles. Western identity was based on the ideals of self-reliance, simplicity and honesty. Westerners were often intolerant of easterners and other westerners who demonstrated pretensions to gentility.

The frontier possibly brought a new democratic element into US politics. The chief statesmen of the USA in its early years had been wealthy men like Thomas Jefferson. With the growth of western states, new politicians appeared on the scene – men like Andrew Jackson of Tennessee, who were more ready to appeal to popular opinion than previous statesmen.

The western spirit of democracy was not the only effect that the frontier had on US politics. Another – more serious – one soon showed itself. This was the issue of whether the new western states were to be open to slavery. This issue divided westerners. It also divided northerners and southerners (see pages 46–61).

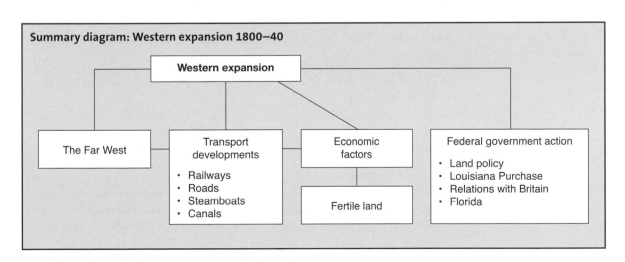

Summary diagram: Western expansion 1800–40

Western expansion

- The Far West
- Transport developments
  - Railways
  - Roads
  - Steamboats
  - Canals
- Economic factors
  - Fertile land
- Federal government action
  - Land policy
  - Louisiana Purchase
  - Relations with Britain
  - Florida

The Native American experience 1800–40

▶ *Why were Native Americans unable to hold on to their ancestral lands?*

US expansion westwards had a shattering effect on Native Americans, who lost their ancestral lands. This did not trouble most white Americans, who regarded Native Americans as savages. 'Is one of the fairest portions of the globe to remain in a state of nature, the haunt of a few wretched savages, when it seems destined by the Creator to give support to a large population and to be the seat of civilization?' asked future President **William Henry Harrison**.

President Jefferson and Native Americans

US administrations in the late eighteenth and early nineteenth centuries made countless treaties with Native Americans, guaranteeing them control of their tribal lands. These treaties proved valueless, for no government could, or wished to, stay the advance of white settlers.

While having a humanitarian interest in their welfare, President Thomas Jefferson was determined to extinguish the title of Native Americans to their lands. He believed they should give up their nomadic hunting lifestyle, settle down to agriculture and merge indistinguishably into American society. Through a series of treaties during Jefferson's administrations, Native Americans were forced or persuaded to hand over their lands.

Native American resistance

Some Native Americans tribes fought desperately to resist the white intruders, engaging in a series of savage skirmishes. Before 1815, the tribes secured some support from Britain and Spain. However, Native American resistance was limited.

- There were relatively few Native Americans – probably fewer than 100,000 – in the mid-west.
- Factionalism and fragmentation among the tribes meant that Native Americans found it difficult to unite against the common threat.
- Superior technology gave white Americans a huge advantage.

Tecumseh, a Shawnee leader, realising the consequences of disunity, attempted to form a confederation of tribes to defend Native American lands. Achieving some success in the northwest, he tried to win over the southern tribes. In his absence, William Henry Harrison, governor of the Indiana Territory, marched to attack Tecumseh's main settlement. On 7 November 1811 the Shawnees attacked Harrison's encampment on the Tippecanoe River. The Shawnees

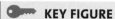

KEY FIGURE

William Henry Harrison (1773–1841)

Harrison was a soldier and politician. Elected as president in 1840, he died in office after one month.

were defeated and Harrison burned their main town. Tecumseh fled to British protection in Canada.

Several northwest tribes fought on Britain's side in the war of 1812 (see page 29). In October 1813, General Harrison defeated a force of British, Canadians and Native Americans at the battle of the Thames in Upper Canada. Tecumseh died in the battle; his dream of Native American unity died with him.

The war of 1812 also brought the USA into conflict with the Creeks in the south. Andrew Jackson waged a successful campaign. After their defeat by Jackson at Horseshoe Bend (March 1814), the Creeks ceded two-thirds of their lands, including most of Alabama, to the USA.

The war of 1812 weakened Native American ability to resist US expansion. After 1815, Native Americans no longer received assistance from Britain or Spain. In the following two decades, by a mixture of bribery and threats, mid-western tribes were prevailed on to sign treaties ceding their lands.

The Indian Removal Act

The notion of relocating Native Americans from the eastern part of the USA into lands west of the Mississippi had long been envisioned. President Andrew Jackson (1829–37) put a relocation policy into effect. Jackson's attitude to Native Americans was the typically western one: they were better off out of the way. With Jackson's backing, Congress passed the Indian Removal Act (May 1830).

- The president was given funds and the power to move Native American tribes from their eastern lands to western lands.
- The western lands (thought unsuitable for white settlement) were to be guaranteed to the tribes 'forever'.
- The government would provide some financial compensation and assistance in moving the Native Americans westwards.
- The act declared that no existing treaties would be violated. This meant that new treaties would have to be negotiated in which tribes agreed to removal.

Some Americans, mainly northerners, opposed the injustice of the removal policy. Most, particularly southerners and westerners, regarding Native Americans as an obstacle to progress, supported it. Some, like Jackson himself, believed that removal was in Native Americans' best interests: they would no longer be cheated by white liquor sellers, dishonest traders and rapacious land dealers. The Indian Territory in the West – a large area in what is now Kansas and Oklahoma – was envisaged as a kind of haven where Native Americans could adapt and assimilate the manners of white civilisation. Some noted the irony: in order to become 'civilised' the Indians were to be moved away from whites.

The removal policy was put into effect with remarkable speed. Some 94 removal treaties were negotiated with Native Americans and by 1835 Jackson announced that the policy had been carried out or was in the process of completion.

The removal policy particularly affected the **Five Civilised Tribes** which occupied large tracts of land in the south. Some tribal groups agreed to move westwards. By the mid-1830s all those who were prepared to move 'voluntarily' – albeit under considerable pressure – had done so. The move often came at a severe cost. The Choctaws lost 1600 people (nearly a tenth of the entire tribe) when they trekked west over the winter of 1831–2.

The main issue came with the Native Americans who refused to move.

The plight of the Cherokee

The Cherokee lived in Georgia and parts of the Carolinas. Many were highly assimilated: the tribal government had a written constitution and a newspaper was published in the Cherokee language. But the tribe faced relentless pressure from white settlers and the Georgian state government.

In an attempt to resist removal, the Cherokees appealed to the Supreme Court. Lawyers representing the tribe argued that Georgia's laws did not apply to them because they were an independent nation within Georgia. While denying this claim, Chief Justice John Marshall ruled that the Cherokees were a 'domestic dependent nation' and thereby entitled to federal protection in Georgia. This had little effect. President Jackson reputedly declared: 'John Marshal has made his decision; now let him enforce it.' Jackson had no intention of doing so. Consequently, Georgian leaders proceeded to pile even more pressure on the Cherokee.

- Cherokee land titles were declared invalid.
- Cherokees were barred from testifying in court against whites.
- Cherokees were forbidden to dig for gold on their lands.

In 1835 one Cherokee faction, regarding removal as the lesser of two evils, agreed to the Treaty of New Echota, ceding 8 million acres (3.2 million hectares) in return for $5 million and a new western homeland. Although it was clear that most Cherokee opposed the treaty, the federal government considered its terms binding on all tribal members.

SOURCE A

From a speech by Major Ridge, a Cherokee leader who favoured making a treaty with the American government.

The Georgians have shown a grasping spirit lately … I know the Indians have an older title than theirs … Yet they are strong and we are weak. We are few, they are many. We cannot remain here in safety and comfort. I know we love the graves of our fathers … We can never forget these homes, I know, but an unbending, iron necessity tells us we must leave them … There is but one path of safety, one road to future existence as a Nation. That path is open before you. Make a treaty of cession. Give up these lands and go over beyond the great Father of Waters [the Mississippi].

? How might an opponent of a move to Indian Territory have responded to Ridge's argument in Source A?

Only about 2000 Cherokee voluntarily emigrated under the terms of the treaty, but over 15,000 remained in the east. These were forcefully evacuated by troops in late 1838. Some 4000 Cherokee died either in the camps where they were assembled for deportation or on the 1200-mile (1900 km) journey westward. They were treated appallingly by the accompanying soldiers, private contractors and whites along the 'Trail of Tears'. The survivors joined some 50,000 other southern Indians in the Indian Territory.

The Seminole War

The Seminoles, led by their chief Osceola, resisted removal from Florida. US troops were sent to deal with them. The Seminole War raged in the Everglade swamps from 1835 until 1842 when the government declared the war over. Some 3000 Seminoles were finally moved to the West. The war cost the USA 1500 men and $50 million. Only a few hundred Seminoles remained in Florida.

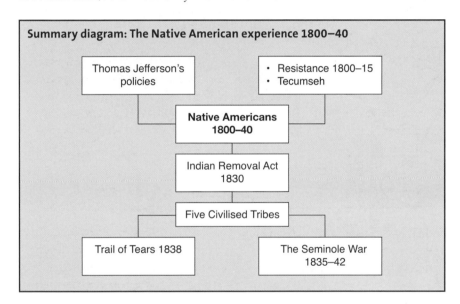

Summary diagram: The Native American experience 1800–40

- Thomas Jefferson's policies
- Resistance 1800–15
- Tecumseh

Native Americans 1800–40

Indian Removal Act 1830

Five Civilised Tribes

Trail of Tears 1838

The Seminole War 1835–42

③ Missouri, Texas and Mexico

▶ *Why was western expansion a problem for the USA in the early nineteenth century?*

Western expansion proved to be major political problem for the USA. As new states applied to join the Union, there was one crucial question in the minds of most Americans: would the new state be free or slave? Southerners regarded the issue as particularly important. They were concerned about the widening disparity in numbers between North and South. In 1790 the population of the northern and southern states had been about equal. By 1850 northerners

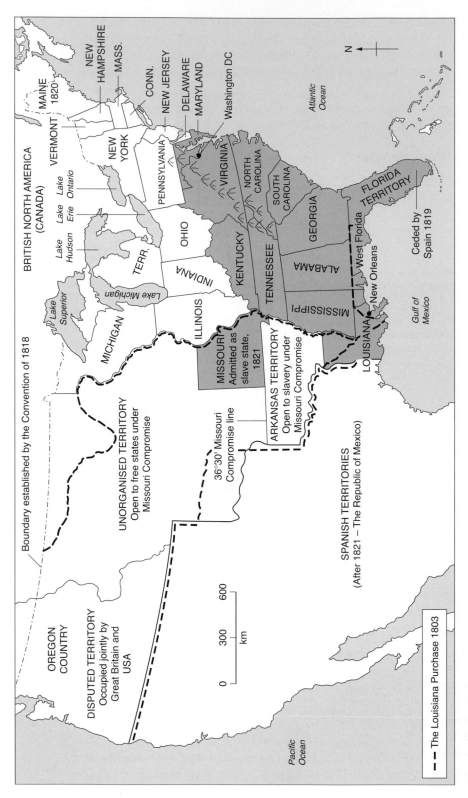

Figure 2.1 The Missouri Compromise.

outnumbered southerners by a ratio of more than three to two. Given that northern states had more seats in the House of Representatives, southerners were determined to maintain a position of equality in the Senate. If this did not happen, they feared that slavery might eventually be abolished.

In the early nineteenth century there were three main crises between northerners and southerners with regard to western expansion. They concerned Missouri, Texas and Mexico.

The Missouri Compromise

By 1819 the original thirteen states had grown to 22. Eleven states were free; eleven were slave. In 1819 Missouri applied to join the Union as a slave state. Given that this would tilt the balance against them, the free states opposed Missouri's admittance. The result was a series of furious debates, with southern and northern Congressmen lined up against each other. In 1820 a compromise was worked out.

- To balance the admittance of Missouri, a new free state of Maine was created.
- Henceforward there should be no slavery in the Louisiana Purchase Territory, north of latitude 36°30′ (see Figure 2.1, page 40). South of that line, slavery could exist.

This 'Missouri Compromise' eased tension. Nevertheless, the issues raised in 1819–20 alarmed many elder statesmen. 'This momentous question, like a fire bell in the night, awakened and filled me with terror', said former President Thomas Jefferson.

Texan independence

Americans had settled in Texas, then part of Mexico, from the 1820s. Most were southerners and many had taken their slaves with them. In 1829 Mexico passed a law to free its slaves and in the following year prohibited further American immigration into Texas. American Texans defied both laws and for some years the Mexican government was too weak to enforce its authority. By 1835 there were about 30,000 American immigrants in Texas (plus 5000 slaves) and only about 5000 Mexicans.

The efforts of the Mexican president, General Santa Anna, to enforce Mexican authority were resented by the American Texans and over the winter of 1835–6 they declared independence. Santa Anna marched north with a large army. A force of 187 Texans put up a spirited defence at the Alamo (a fortified **mission**) but this fell in March 1836. All the Texan defenders were killed. Although US President Jackson sympathised with the Texans, he sent no official help. However, hundreds of Americans from the south and west rushed to the Texans' aid. In April 1836 an American–Texan army, led by Sam Houston, defeated the Mexicans at the battle of San Jacinto. Santa Anna was captured and forced to recognise Texan independence.

 **KEY TERM**

Mission A religious settlement, set up by the Spanish to try to convert Native Americans to Christianity.

Texas and the USA

Although the Mexican government did not ratify Santa Anna's action, Texas was now effectively independent. Most Texans, with southern support, hoped to join the USA. However, many northerners opposed the move, fearing that it would lead to the spread of slavery. So large was Texas that it could be divided into five new slave states, which would tilt the balance between free and slave states heavily in the South's favour. Given that Texas was politically controversial, Jackson shelved the issue. So too did his successor **Martin Van Buren**. The result was that for a few years Texas was an independent republic, unrecognised by Mexico and rejected by the USA.

Texas became a major issue in the 1844 presidential election, fought between the Whig Henry Clay and the Democrat James Polk. Polk, a slaveholder from Tennessee, was elected president on a platform that promised the annexation of both Texas and Oregon – an area claimed by Britain. Outgoing Whig President Tyler, anxious to leave his mark on events, now secured a joint resolution of Congress in favour of the annexation of Texas. Thus, Texas was admitted into the Union, as a single state, in 1845.

Manifest destiny

Polk, committed to western expansion, wished to annex California and New Mexico, provinces over which Mexico exerted little control. Americans were starting to settle in both areas and the Mexican population was small. Many Americans supported expansion. In 1845 Democrat journalist John O'Sullivan declared that it was the USA's **manifest destiny** to control the North American continent (see Source B below). Advocates of manifest destiny invoked God and the glory of democratic institutions to sanction expansion. However, many northern Whigs saw this rhetoric as a smokescreen aimed at concealing the evil intent of expanding slavery.

SOURCE B

From John O'Sullivan, editor of the *New York Morning News*, 1845.

Away, away with all these cobweb tissues of rights of discovery, exploration, settlement, contiguity etc. … The American claim is by the right of our manifest destiny to overspread and to possess the whole of the continent which Providence has given us for the development of the great experiment of liberty and federative self-government entrusted to us. It is a right such as that of the tree to the space of air and earth suitable for the full expansion of its principle and destiny of growth … It is in our future far more than in our past or in the past history of Spanish exploration … that our True Title is found.

KEY FIGURE

Martin Van Buren (1782–1862)

Van Buren was Democratic president 1837–41. Having lost the 1840 election, he retired to New York, re-emerging as the Free Soil Party's presidential candidate in 1848.

KEY TERM

Manifest destiny The USA's supposed right to take over North America.

? What arguments did O'Sullivan use in Source B to justify manifest destiny?

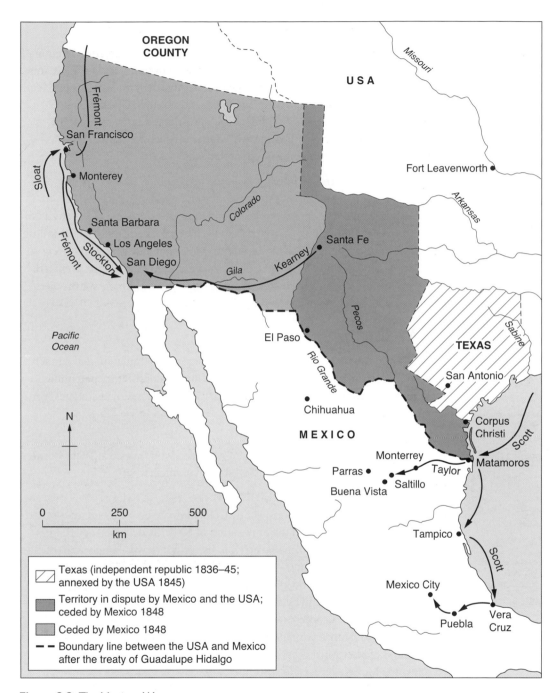

Figure 2.2 The Mexican War.

The outbreak of war

The USA's annexation of Texas angered Mexico, which still claimed sovereignty over the state. The fact that there were disputed boundaries between Texas and Mexico was a further problem that the USA now inherited. The barely concealed designs of Polk on California and New Mexico did not help US–Mexican relations. Efforts to reach some agreement were hindered by the situation in Mexico. Mexican governments came and went with such rapidity that it was difficult for the USA to know with whom to deal.

In 1845 Polk sent US troops into the disputed border area north of the Rio Grande River, hoping to provoke an incident that would result in war – a war which would lead to US annexation of California and New Mexico. In May 1846 Mexican troops duly ambushed a party of US troops in the disputed area, killing or wounding sixteen men. Polk declared that Mexicans had 'shed American blood on American soil' and asked Congress to declare war. Congress obliged. While most southerners and westerners supported the war, many northerners saw it as a southern war of aggression.

The Mexican War

Although the USA had a smaller army, it had twice the population and a much stronger industrial base than Mexico and thus far greater military potential. Mexican forces were poorly led and equipped. The USA's main advantages were as follows:

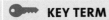

KEY TERM

West Point The main US military academy.

- superior artillery
- a pool of junior officers, most of whom had been well trained at **West Point**
- enthusiastic (mainly southern and western) volunteers
- naval supremacy.

In the summer of 1846, US troops, led by Colonel Kearney, marched unopposed into Santa Fe and proclaimed the annexation of New Mexico. Kearney then set off to California. By the time he arrived, the province was largely under US control. American settlers in California had proclaimed independence from Mexico. They were helped by John C. Frémont (see page 72), in the region on an exploratory expedition, and by a US naval squadron, conveniently stationed off the California coast. Kearney's arrival in California in December ended what little Mexican resistance remained. Polk hoped that Mexico would accept defeat and the loss of New Mexico and California. But General Santa Anna, once again in control in Mexico, refused to surrender.

The US war heroes were General Zachary Taylor and General Winfield Scott.

- Taylor won a series of victories over Santa Anna in 1846 and then defeated the Mexicans at the battle of Buena Vista in February 1847.
- Scott, with only 11,000 men, marched 260 miles (420 km) inland over difficult terrain, storming several fortresses before capturing Mexico City in September 1847.

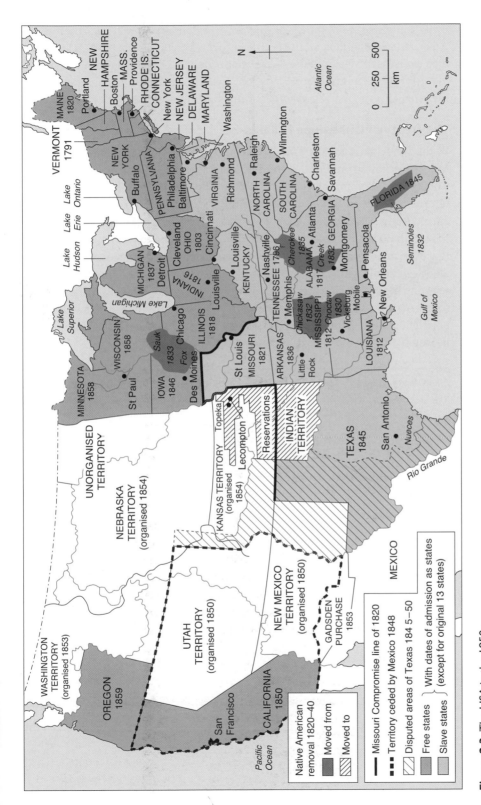

Figure 2.3 The USA in the 1850s.

By the autumn of 1847, the Mexican War was essentially over. It had cost the Americans $100 million and 13,000 dead soldiers (2000 died in battle; 11,000 died of disease). Mexican losses were approximately 25,000. The USA was now in a position to enforce peace. Some southerners called for the annexation of all Mexico. However, many northerners wanted to annex no territory whatsoever.

The Treaty of Guadalupe Hidalgo

By the Treaty of Guadalupe Hidalgo (February 1848), California and New Mexico (including present-day Nevada, Utah, most of Arizona, and parts of Colorado and Wyoming) were ceded to the USA (see Figure 2.3, page 45). In return for this huge area – two-fifths of the USA's present territory – the USA agreed to pay Mexico $15 million. Polk was unhappy with the treaty. Despite the fact that the USA had gained everything it had gone to war for, he thought that even more territory could have been gained. Spurred on by southerners, who saw the dizzying prospect of dozens of new slave states, Polk considered rejecting the treaty. However, given northern opinion and the fact that some southerners baulked at the notion of ruling Mexico's mixed Spanish and Indian population, he reluctantly accepted the treaty, which was ratified by the Senate in May 1848.

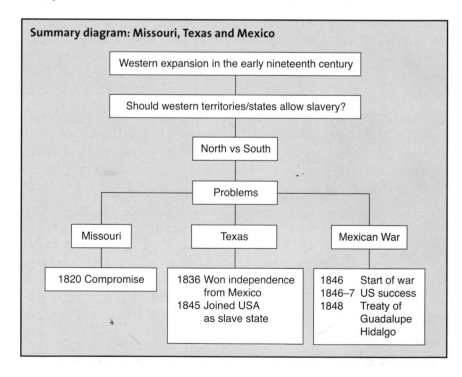

Summary diagram: Missouri, Texas and Mexico

Western expansion in the early nineteenth century

Should western territories/states allow slavery?

North vs South

Problems

Missouri · Texas · Mexican War

Missouri: 1820 Compromise

Texas: 1836 Won independence from Mexico; 1845 Joined USA as slave state

Mexican War: 1846 Start of war; 1846–7 US success; 1848 Treaty of Guadalupe Hidalgo

The impact of the Mexican War 1846–50

▶ *What was the main political impact of the Mexican War?*

Northerners and southerners were divided over the Mexican War before it began. They remained divided during it and were even more divided by the end of it. Anticipating winning territory from Mexico at the start of the war, American politicians could not agree whether states created from Mexican land would become slave or free.

The Wilmot Proviso

In August 1846, David Wilmot, a Democrat from Pennsylvania, added an amendment to a finance bill in the House of Representatives. By the terms of his **proviso**, slavery was to be excluded from any territory gained from Mexico.

Wilmot was not an abolitionist. Like many northern Democrats, he resented the fact that Polk seemed to be pursuing a pro-southern policy. While happy to fight the Mexican War, Polk had reneged on his promise to take the whole of Oregon. Instead, an agreement had been reached whereby Britain took the area north of the 49th parallel and the USA took southern Oregon. This made sense: the USA did well out of the deal and it would have been foolish to have fought both Mexico and Britain. But northern Democrats felt that Polk's agreement with Britain, coupled with his forceful action against Mexico, symbolised his pro-southern bias.

In supporting the proviso, northern Democrats hoped to keep black people out of the new territories and ensure that white settlers would not face competition from planters who would use slave labour. Concerned at the coming **mid-term elections**, northern Democrats were warning Polk of their unease with the direction of his policies.

After a bitter debate, the proviso passed the House of Representatives by 83 votes to 64. The voting was sectional: every southern Democrat and all but two southern Whigs voted against it. Most northerners voted for it. Senator Toombs of Georgia warned that if the proviso became law, he would favour disunion rather than 'degradation'. Failing to pass the Senate, the proviso did not become law. Nevertheless, for anti-slavery forces, the proviso became a rallying cry. Many northern state legislatures endorsed it. Most southern states denounced it.

 **KEY TERMS**

Proviso A term or condition.

Mid-term elections The whole of the House of Representatives and a third of the Senate are re-elected every two years. This means that there are major elections half way through a president's term of office.

SOURCE C

From a speech by James Hammond, a politician from South Carolina, 1846.

Enactment of the Wilmot Proviso will yield ten new free states. The North will then ride over us rough shod in Congress, proclaim freedom or something equivalent to it to our slaves and reduce us to the condition of Haiti … Our only safety is in equality of POWER. If we do not act now, we deliberately consign our children, not our posterity, but our children to the flames.

Were James Hammond's fears, as outlined in Source C, rational?

The Calhoun Doctrine

Northerners believed that Congress had the power to exclude slavery from the territories and should exercise that power. Southerners challenged the doctrine of Congressional authority to regulate or prohibit slavery in the territories. John C. Calhoun, an elder statesman from South Carolina, played a crucial role. He had first entered Congress in 1811. He had then been an out-and-out American nationalist, supporting increasing federal power at the expense of state rights. However, in the late 1820s he changed his mind and developed the doctrine of nullification. This had proclaimed the right of any state to overrule or modify any federal law deemed unconstitutional. The crisis over nullification came to a head in 1832–3 when South Carolina disallowed two tariff acts. President Jackson labelled this action treason and threatened to use force. South Carolina, unable to muster support from other southern states, pulled back from declaring secession and Jackson, in return, lowered tariffs.

Calhoun remained a force to be reckoned with. In February 1847 he issued a series of resolutions, known subsequently as 'The Platform of the South', in which he claimed that citizens from every state had the right to take their 'property' to any territory. Congress, he asserted, had no authority to place restrictions on slavery in the territories. If the northern majority continued to ride roughshod over the rights of the southern minority, the southern states would have little option but to secede.

The search for compromise

The problem of slavery expansion preoccupied the 30th Congress, which met in December 1847, to the exclusion of every other issue. Moderate politicians, aware that the issue could destroy the Union, sought a compromise. The preferred solution of some, including Polk, was to continue the 36°30′ line across the continent. Slavery would be banned in any territory gained from Mexico north of this line but would be allowed south of the line. This proposal, opposed by most northerners, failed to win enough support to pass through Congress.

Popular sovereignty

A more successful compromise idea was popular sovereignty – the view that settlers, not Congress, should decide whether a territory should or should not allow slaves. This was associated with two mid-western Democratic Senators: Lewis Cass and Stephen Douglas. Consistent with democracy and self-government, popular sovereignty seemed to offer something to both North and South.

- It met the South's wish for federal non-intervention and held out the prospect that slavery might be extended to some of the Mexican territories.
- It could be presented to the North as an exclusion scheme because it was unlikely that settlers in the new territories would vote for the introduction of slavery.

However, there were problems with the concept of popular sovereignty. First, it went against previous practice. In the past, Congress had decided on what should happen in the territories. Did popular sovereignty mean that it no longer had that power? There were also practical difficulties. The main problem was when exactly a territory should decide on the slavery question. Northern Democrats envisaged the decision being made early, as soon as the first territorial assembly met. Southern Democrats, keen to ensure that slaves were allowed into territories, saw the decision being made late, near the end of the territorial phase (see page 3) when settlers were seeking admission to the Union. In the interim, they envisaged that slavery would be recognised and protected.

Despite this ambiguity, popular sovereignty was supported by many Democrats. It was opposed by a few southerners who thought they had the right to take their 'property' anywhere they wanted, and by northerners who believed that slavery should not be allowed to expand under any circumstances, not even if most settlers wished it to expand.

The 1848 election

Although Polk had presided over an administration that had won the greatest area of territory in US history, he gained little credit for the Mexican War. Worn out by constant opposition, he decided not to seek a second term. The Democrats, rallying round the concept of popular sovereignty, nominated Lewis Cass of Michigan as their presidential candidate.

The Whigs nominated a hero of the Mexican War, Zachary Taylor. Taylor had no previous political experience. The fact that he was a Louisiana slave owner did not endear him to abolitionists. Nevertheless, many northern Whigs were prepared to endorse Taylor if only because he seemed a likely winner. To avoid a split between its northern and southern wings, the Whigs had no national platform on slavery expansion. This meant that they could conduct a two-faced campaign, running as an anti-slavery party in the North and as a pro-southern rights party in the South.

A new party, the Free Soil Party, was formed to fight the election. It included:

- northern Democrats who were alarmed at the southern dominance of the Democrat Party
- 'Conscience' Whigs who had no intention of campaigning for a southern slave owner
- Liberty Party supporters (see page 25).

The party supported the Wilmot Proviso and nominated Martin Van Buren as its presidential candidate.

KEY TERMS

Electoral college The body that elects the president. Each state has the same number of electoral college representatives as it has members of Congress. Electoral college representatives are selected by the party with the most votes in each state.

Mormons Members of a religious sect founded in the 1820s by Joseph Smith. In 1846–7 Brigham Young established a Mormon 'state' in Utah, centred on Salt Lake City.

Polygamy A state of marriage to more than one partner.

KEY FIGURES

Henry Clay (1777–1852)

A slaveholding Whig Senator from Kentucky. He had a reputation for being a master legislator and an eloquent orator, and for being able to find compromise solutions between northerners and southerners.

Daniel Webster (1782–1852)

A celebrated northern lawyer, Whig politician and orator. He had been secretary of state 1841–3.

The election result

The election was a triumph for Taylor, who won 1,360,000 votes (47.5 per cent of the total) and 163 **electoral college** votes. Cass won 1,220,000 votes (42.5 per cent) and 127 electoral college votes. Van Buren won 291,000 votes (ten per cent) but no electoral college votes. Taylor's victory was not sectional. He carried eight of the fifteen slave states and seven of the fifteen free states. Even so, sectional issues influenced the result. Throughout the election, the expansion of slavery had been the crucial issue. The fact that the Free Soil Party won ten per cent of the popular vote was some indication of northern opinion.

Congressional tension

The Congress, which met in December 1848, was dominated by debates over slavery. Northern representatives, who controlled the House, reaffirmed the Wilmot Proviso and condemned slave-trading in Washington, DC. Calhoun now issued his *Address to the People of the Southern States* – an effort to unite all southern Congressmen behind the 'Southern cause'. The *Address* was essentially a defence of slavery and an attack on northern aggression. Calhoun's tactic, however, failed. At this stage, most southern Whigs placed their trust in Taylor. Only 48 members of Congress, about one-third of slave state members, signed the address.

California and New Mexico

Few Americans had thought that California or New Mexico would speedily apply for statehood. But the discovery of gold in California touched off the 1848–9 gold rush. Within months, there were 100,000 people in California, more than enough to enable the area to apply for statehood. New Mexico had fewer people. However, thousands of **Mormons** had settled around Salt Lake City in 1846–7, hoping to establish their own state of Deseret. Now, as a result of the Mexican War, they found themselves under US jurisdiction. In early 1849 the non-slaveholding – but **polygamous** – Mormons drew up a constitution and sought admission to the Union. This was an additional problem. The key issue was whether California and New Mexico would be allowed to have slavery, given that slavery had been illegal in both Mexican-owned areas before 1848.

President Taylor

While Zachary Taylor was (and is) generally seen as a man of honesty and integrity, he was judged by most contemporaries (and by many historians since) as a political amateur who was prone to oversimplify complex problems. Although he was a southern slave owner, he was determined to act in a way that, he hoped, benefited the national interest. Surprisingly and perhaps foolishly, Taylor deliberately shunned the advice of **Henry Clay** of Kentucky and **Daniel Webster** of Massachusetts, the great Whig elder statesmen. He was far more influenced by the radical New York Senator **William Seward**. Few southern Whigs were happy with Seward's prominence.

Congress's sitting ended in March 1849. It would not meet again until December. Accordingly, Taylor, rather than Congress, had to deal with the problems of California and New Mexico. He determined to act decisively. Hoping that a quick solution to the problem might reduce the potential for sectional strife, he encouraged settlers in both California and New Mexico to frame constitutions and apply immediately for admission to the Union without first going through the process of establishing territorial governments. He was sure that people in both states would vote for free state constitutions. Taylor, who had no wish to see slavery abolished, believed that it would be best protected if southerners refrained from rekindling the slavery issue in the territories.

In 1849, California duly ratified a constitution prohibiting slavery and applied for admission to the Union. Taylor was also prepared to admit New Mexico, even though it did not have enough people to apply for statehood. There was a further problem with New Mexico: it had a major boundary dispute with Texas. Southerners supported Texas's claim, whereas northerners – and Taylor – supported New Mexico. A clash between the state forces of Texas and the US army suddenly seemed imminent.

Southern resentment

Having done much of the fighting against Mexico, southerners – Democrats and Whigs alike – were incensed that they were now being excluded from the territory gained. Many appreciated that the climate and terrain of the area made it inhospitable to slavery, so there was no great rush to take slaves into New Mexico or California. Nevertheless, southerners believed that neither territory should be admitted to the Union as a free state without compensation to the South. Some southerners went further. In October 1849, Mississippi issued a call to all slave states to send representatives to a convention to meet at Nashville in June 1850 to devise and adopt 'some mode of resistance to northern aggression'.

Taylor's hopes of resolving the sectional strife were dashed. Bitter divisions were reflected in Congress, which met in December 1849. Fistfights between Congressmen became commonplace. Debates over slavery expansion were equally fierce. Southerners also raised the issues of fugitive slaves, claiming (rightly) that many northern states were flouting the **Fugitive Slave Act of 1793** and frustrating slaveholders' efforts to catch runaways and return them to the South. The dispute between Texas and New Mexico added to the tension as more and more southerners began to talk of secession.

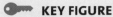

KEY FIGURE

William Seward (1801–72)

A former Whig governor of New York. Elected as a US senator in 1848, he alienated southerners by championing anti-slavery measures.

KEY TERM

Fugitive Slave Act of 1793 This provided for slaves who had escaped and fled into a different state to be returned to their owners. It was ignored by most northern states by the 1840s.

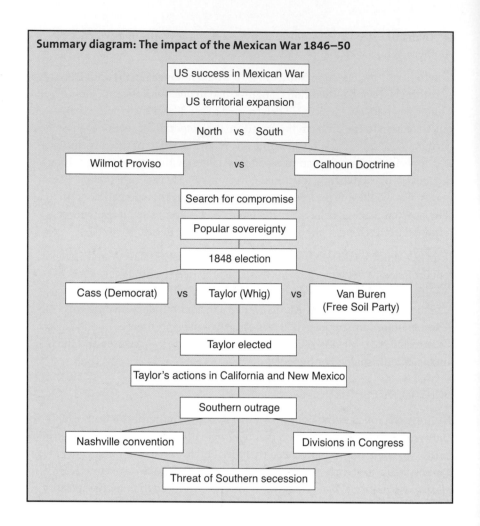

Summary diagram: The impact of the Mexican War 1846–50

US success in Mexican War

US territorial expansion

North vs South

Wilmot Proviso — vs — Calhoun Doctrine

Search for compromise

Popular sovereignty

1848 election

Cass (Democrat) vs Taylor (Whig) vs Van Buren (Free Soil Party)

Taylor elected

Taylor's actions in California and New Mexico

Southern outrage

Nashville convention — Divisions in Congress

Threat of Southern secession

5 The 1850 Compromise

▶ *How successful was the 1850 Compromise?*

Taylor was prepared to call (what he saw as) the southern bluff and, if need be, be ready to lead an army into the South to prevent secession. However, many politicians from mid-western states were worried by events and felt that the South had to be placated. Their leader was 73-year-old Henry Clay. With a reputation as a conciliator from previous crises, he seemed the ideal man to lead compromise efforts.

In January 1850, Clay offered the Senate a set of resolutions as a basis for a compromise:

● California was to be admitted as a free state.

- Utah (formerly the Mormon 'state' of Deseret) and New Mexico were to be organised as territories without any mention of, or restriction on, slavery.
- Slave-trading but not slavery itself should end in Washington, DC.
- A more stringent Fugitive Slave Act should be passed to placate the South (see page 51).
- In order to resolve the Texas–New Mexico dispute, Texas should surrender the disputed land to New Mexico. In return, Congress would assume the $10 million public debt that Texas still owed.

The Compromise debate

The next few months were marked by a series of epic speeches as Clay's proposals, rolled into a single 'omnibus' bill, were debated in Congress. Most of the 'old guard' politicians, many making their last major appearance on the public stage, contributed to the debates. So too did a number of men (for example, William Seward and Stephen Douglas) who were just beginning what were to be prestigious political careers.

Clay defended his proposals in a four-hour long speech in February 1850. He declared: 'I have seen many periods of great anxiety, of peril, and of danger in this country and I have never before risen to address any assemblage so oppressed, so appalled, and so anxious.' Warning the South against secession, he assured the North that nature would check the spread of slavery more effectively than a thousand Wilmot Provisos.

Calhoun would have spoken but he was seriously ill. His speech was thus read by Senator Mason of Virginia on 4 March. (Within a month of the speech Calhoun was dead.) Calhoun declared that the North was responsible for the crisis: northerners threatened slavery. If the threats continued, southern states would have no option but to leave the Union.

SOURCE D

From John C. Calhoun's speech to Congress, March 1850.

How can the Union be saved? There is but one way by which it can be, and that is by adopting such measures as will satisfy the States belonging to the Southern section, that they can remain in the Union consistently with their honor and their safety. But can this be done? Yes, easily; not by the weaker party, for it can of itself do nothing – not even protect itself – but by the stronger. The North has only to will it to accomplish it – to do justice by conceding to the South an equal right in the acquired territory, and to do her duty by causing the stipulations relative to fugitive slaves to be faithfully fulfilled – to cease the agitation of the slave question.

What was Calhoun hoping to achieve by his speech in Source D? **?**

On 7 March, 69-year-old Daniel Webster spoke in support of the Compromise. 'I wish to speak today', he declared, 'not as a Massachusetts man, not as a northern man, but as an American'. While moderates praised his speech, abolitionists denounced him for betraying the cause of freedom.

The conciliatory voices of Clay and Webster made few converts. With every call for compromise, some northern or southern speaker would rise and inflame passions. Moreover, Taylor made it clear that he opposed Clay's proposals. In his view, California should be admitted as a free state immediately, while New Mexico should also come in with all possible speed. Southerners would have to accept their medicine.

The Nashville convention

In June 1850, delegates from nine slave states met at Nashville. The fact that six slave states did not send delegates was disconcerting to those who supported secession, as was the fact that the convention displayed little enthusiasm for secession. The Nashville convention, therefore, had little impact.

The death of Taylor

In July, President Taylor died of gastroenteritis. (Daniel Webster was not alone in believing there would have been a civil war if Taylor had lived.) Vice-President Millard Fillmore now became president. Although a northerner, Fillmore was sympathetic to the South. His break with the policies of his predecessor was immediately apparent. There were wholesale cabinet changes (Webster, for example, became secretary of state) and Fillmore threw his weight behind the Compromise proposals. Nevertheless, on 31 July, Clay's bill was defeated, mainly because most northern Congressmen voted against it.

Douglas to the rescue

Senator Douglas now demonstrated his political skill. Known as the 'Little Giant' (he was less than 162 cm tall), Douglas replaced Clay as leader of the Compromise cause. Stripping Clay's bill down to its component parts, he submitted each part as a separate bill. This strategy was successful. Southerners voted for those proposals they liked; northerners did likewise. A few moderates, like Douglas himself, swung the balance. By September 1850, all the bits of the Compromise had passed:

- statehood for California
- territorial status for Utah and New Mexico, allowing popular sovereignty
- resolution of the Texas–New Mexico boundary dispute
- abolition of the slave trade in Washington, DC
- a new Fugitive Slave Act.

Political leaders hailed the Compromise as a settlement of the issues that threatened to divide the nation.

Compromise or armistice?

Historian David Potter (1976) questioned whether the Compromise was a compromise. He thought it was more an armistice. Most northern Congressmen had, after all, voted against the pro-slavery measures while most southern Congressmen had voted against the anti-slavery measures. The Compromise had skirted, rather than settled, the controversy over slavery in the territories, providing no formula to guide the future.

Many northerners believed that Congress had cravenly surrendered to southern threats. However, the North gained more than the South from the Compromise. The entry of California into the Union tilted the balance in favour of the free states. The resolutions on New Mexico and Utah were hollow victories for the South. The odds were that these areas would one day enter the Union as free states. The Fugitive Slave Act was the North's only major concession.

The end of the crisis

Most Americans seemed prepared to accept the Compromise. Across the USA, there were mass meetings to celebrate its passage. Southern secessionists' hopes foundered. In southern state elections in 1851–2 Unionist candidates defeated secessionists. The South had decided against secession – for now. But ominously for the future, many southerners had come to accept Calhoun's doctrine that secession was a valid constitutional remedy, applicable in appropriate circumstances. The hope was that those circumstances would not arise.

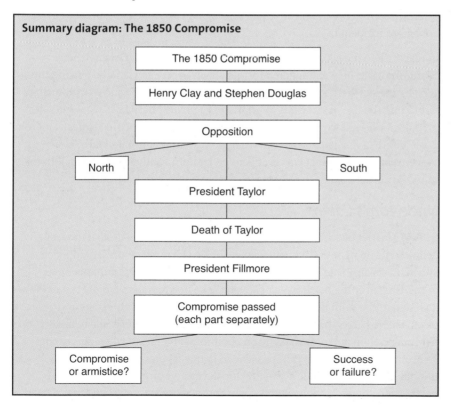

Summary diagram: The 1850 Compromise

- The 1850 Compromise
- Henry Clay and Stephen Douglas
- Opposition
  - North
  - South
- President Taylor
- Death of Taylor
- President Fillmore
- Compromise passed (each part separately)
  - Compromise or armistice?
  - Success or failure?

North–South problems 1850–3

▶ *How serious was sectional strife in the years 1850–3?*

In December 1851, President Fillmore announced that the Compromise was 'final and irrevocable'. Douglas resolved 'never to make another speech on the slavery question … Let us cease agitating, stop the debate and drop the subject.' While the remainder of Fillmore's administration was relatively tranquil, sectional problems remained.

The Fugitive Slave Act

KEY TERM

Posse A group of men called out by a sheriff or marshal to aid in enforcing the law.

The Fugitive Slave Act contained a number of features that were distasteful to moderates and outrageous to abolitionists. For example, it authorised federal marshals to raise **posses** to pursue fugitives on northern soil. Those who refused to join risked a $1000 fine. In addition, the law targeted not only recent runaways but also those who had fled the South decades earlier.

Efforts to return fugitive slaves inflamed feelings. In 1854, a Boston mob broke into a courthouse and killed a guard in an abortive effort to rescue the fugitive slave Anthony Burns. Troops had to escort Burns to Boston harbour, where a ship carried him back to slavery. The Burns affair was one of a number of well-publicised incidents.

In response to the act, vigilance committees sprang up in many northern communities to help endangered former slaves escape to Canada. During the 1850s, nine northern states passed personal liberty laws. By such techniques as forbidding the use of state jails to imprison fugitives, these laws were intended to make it difficult to enforce federal law. The fact that some free states went to great lengths to negate the act caused huge resentment in the South. However, overt resistance to the act was exaggerated by both southerners and abolitionists. In most northern states the law was enforced without much trouble.

Uncle Tom's Cabin

In 1851 Harriet Beecher Stowe began publishing *Uncle Tom's Cabin* in weekly instalments in an anti-slavery newspaper. The story, which presented a fierce attack on slavery, sold 300,000 copies in 1852 and a further 2 million copies in the USA over the next ten years. Even those northerners who did not read it were familiar with its theme because it was also turned into songs and plays. Stowe herself had little first-hand knowledge of slavery: she relied on her imagination and drew heavily on abolitionist literature when describing its brutalities. Although it is impossible to gauge its precise impact, the book undoubtedly aroused wide sympathy for slaves and probably pushed some northerners toward a more aggressively anti-slavery stance. In historian David Potter's view, northerners' attitude to slavery was 'never quite the same after *Uncle Tom's Cabin*'.

The 1852 election

The Democrats were confident of victory in 1852. Many Irish and German immigrants were now entitled to vote and were expected to vote Democrat. Moreover, Van Buren and his supporters, who had formed the core of the Free Soil Party (see page 49), had now returned to the Democrat fold. The Democrats chose Franklin Pierce of New Hampshire as their presidential candidate. Handsome, charming but somewhat lightweight, Pierce's main asset was that he was acceptable to all factions of the party. 'We "Polked" 'em in "44"', boasted the Democrat press: 'we'll Pierce 'em in "52".' The Democrats campaigned on a platform supporting the 1850 Compromise and popular sovereignty.

The Whigs were divided North against South, in terms of agreeing to a platform and choosing a candidate. While most northerners supported Mexican War hero General Winfield Scott (a southerner), most southern Whigs hoped to retain Fillmore (a northerner). Scott, who was finally nominated, was in many ways a good choice. Although politically inexperienced, he was a man of integrity and ability and the Whigs had twice won elections by nominating military heroes. Although the Whigs managed to agree on a leader, they could not agree on policies. Accordingly, their platform said virtually nothing.

Pierce won the election with 1,601,274 votes (51 per cent). He carried 27 states (254 electoral college votes). Scott won 1,386,580 votes (44 per cent) but carried only four states (42 electoral votes). John Hale, the Free Soil Party candidate, won 156,000 votes (five per cent), carrying not a single state. Many Whigs were stunned by the defeat. Whig Senator Alexander Stephens from Georgia moaned that 'the Whig Party is dead'.

President Pierce

Pierce was inaugurated President in March 1853. Although he was soon to prove himself weak and irresolute, he seemed to be in a strong position. The Democrats had large majorities in both Houses of Congress and the economy continued to boom. The Whig Party, seriously divided, was unable to mount much of a challenge and two of its best known leaders, Webster and Clay, died in 1852. Pierce intended to maintain the unity of his party by championing expansionist policies. Southerners had good reason for hoping that the USA would expand into Central America and/or Cuba, thus allowing the opportunity for slavery also to expand.

The Gadsden Purchase

In 1853, Pierce gave **James Gadsden** the authority to negotiate the purchase of 250,000 square miles (650,000 km²) of Mexican territory. Gadsden eventually agreed to purchase 54,000 square miles (140,000 km²). Southerners supported the acquisition of this territory, not because of its slavery potential, but because it would assist the building of a southern railway to the Pacific. Gadsden's treaty

 KEY FIGURE

James Gadsden (1788–1858)

A diplomat and railroad entrepreneur. In 1853 he was US minister to Mexico.

gained Senate approval only after a northern amendment slashed 9000 square miles (23,000 km²) from the proposed purchase.

Cuba

Pierce encountered serious opposition when he tried to acquire Cuba, the last remnant of Spain's American empire. In 1851 an American-sponsored **filibuster** expedition to try to overthrow the Spanish Cuban government had failed miserably. In 1853–4, Mississippi's former senator John Quitman planned an even greater expedition. Several thousand American volunteers were recruited and contact was made with Cuban rebels. In July 1853, Pierce met Quitman and, unofficially, encouraged him to go ahead with his plans. Pierce's main problem was northern opinion: northerners viewed filibustering as another example of southern efforts to expand slavery. Alarmed by northern reaction, Pierce forced Quitman to scuttle his expedition.

The Ostend Manifesto

Still hoping to obtain Cuba, Pierce authorised Pierre Soule, the US minister in Spain, to offer up to $130 million for the island. Events, however, soon slipped out of Pierce's control. In October 1854 the US ministers to Britain (Buchanan), France (Mason) and Spain (Soule) met in Belgium and issued the Ostend Manifesto. This stated that Cuba 'is as necessary to the North American Republic as any of its present members'. If Spain refused to sell, then the USA would be 'justified in wresting it from Spain'. Unfortunately for Pierce, details of the Ostend Manifesto were leaked and immediately denounced by northern politicians. Pierce repudiated the Manifesto and Soule resigned. The unsuccessful expansionist efforts angered northerners who believed that the South aspired to establish a Latin American slave empire. Many southerners did so aspire, and remained optimistic about their aspirations, throughout the 1850s.

? Why did many
southerners support
expansion in Central
America and the
Caribbean?

SOURCE E

A Virginian journalist, Edward A. Pollard, writing in 1859.

The path of our destiny on this continent lies in … tropical America [where] we may see an empire as powerful and gorgeous as ever was pictured in our dreams of history … an empire … representing the noble peculiarities of Southern civilisation … having control of the two dominant staples of the world's commerce – cotton and sugar … The destiny of Southern civilisation is to be consummated in a glory brighter even than that of the old.

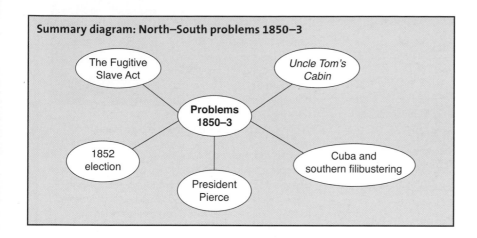

Summary diagram: North–South problems 1850–3

- The Fugitive Slave Act
- Uncle Tom's Cabin
- Problems 1850–3
- 1852 election
- Cuba and southern filibustering
- President Pierce

 7 # The problem of Kansas–Nebraska

▶ *Why did the Kansas–Nebraska Act cause such a storm?*

Nebraska, part of the Louisiana Purchase, was still largely unsettled in the early 1850s. Until Congress organised the area into a territory, land could not be surveyed and put up for sale. While northerners were keen to see Nebraska developed, southerners were less enthusiastic. Nebraska lay north of latitude 36°30′ and, by the terms of the Missouri Compromise (see page 41), new states in the area would enter the Union as free states. Southern politicians, therefore, made every effort to delay granting territorial status to Nebraska.

Douglas's motives

In January 1854, Senator Douglas introduced the Kansas–Nebraska bill into Congress. A man of talent, energy and (presidential) ambition, Douglas had long pushed – unsuccessfully – for Nebraska's becoming a territory. In order to get a Nebraska bill enacted Douglas knew that he needed the support of some southern senators. Douglas's bill, while avoiding all mention of the Missouri Compromise, was designed to appeal to the South:

- It repealed the Missouri Compromise, introducing popular sovereignty in its stead.
- It divided the Nebraska territory into two: Kansas, the area immediately west of Missouri; and Nebraska, the area west of Iowa and Minnesota. There was little chance of slavery taking hold in Nebraska, since the climate was too cold for plantation agriculture. But it seemed possible that it might spread to Kansas (see Figure 2.3, page 45).

Stephen Douglas

1813	Born in Vermont
1833	Settled in Illinois, where he practised law
1843	Elected to the House of Representatives
1847	Became a Senator for Illinois
1850	Helped to pass the Compromise
1854	Introduced the Kansas–Nebraska bill
1857	Denounced the Lecompton constitution and broke with President Buchanan
1858	Took part in a series of famous debates with Lincoln
1860	Nominated as Democratic candidate for the presidency
1861	Died of typhoid fever

Douglas was committed to popular sovereignty. Energetic and eloquent, the 'Little Giant' had presidential ambitions. These ambitions were not helped by the Kansas–Nebraska Act. In 1854 he was depicted as a traitor to the North. 'I could travel from Boston to Chicago by the light of my own effigy', said Douglas, referring to the fact that models of him were burned across the northern states.

Douglas represented Illinois. He thus frequently came into contact with Abraham Lincoln, who was his political opponent. The Democrats were usually successful in Illinois – good news for Douglas, bad news for Lincoln. In 1858 Douglas and Lincoln had a series of famous debates in the Illinois senatorial race (see pages 78–9). While securing Douglas's re-election, the debates served to boost Lincoln's reputation. Douglas stood against Lincoln in the presidential election of 1860 but was defeated (see page 89). Douglas venerated the Union. It is thus somewhat ironic that he figured prominently in many of the events leading to its disruption in 1861.

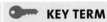

KEY TERM

Slave Power conspiracy
A northern notion that southerners were plotting to expand slavery. Those who believed in the conspiracy were never very specific about who exactly was conspiring.

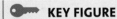

KEY FIGURE

Salmon Chase (1808–73)

A lawyer, Whig politician and leading abolitionist. He became secretary of the treasury in 1861 and was chief justice of the US Supreme Court from 1864 until 1873.

Douglas, a patriot who had no wish to heighten sectional tension, was confident that his bill would cause no great strain. Although, in theory, slavery could now expand northwards it was unlikely that it would do so. Douglas, a great believer in popular sovereignty, was happy to let the people of Kansas–Nebraska decide their own fate, and he was confident that they would not vote for slavery. Douglas did not want the settlement of the West to be stalled by sectional controversy. Such controversy could prevent the building of a northern transcontinental railway that would have to run through Kansas–Nebraska. Douglas had other motives. He believed there was political capital to be gained from his Kansas–Nebraska measure. It should enhance his reputation in Illinois, where many people (not least himself) stood to benefit financially from a transcontinental railway leading west from Chicago. Settlement of the Nebraska issue would also enhance his presidential ambitions.

'A hell of a storm'

Douglas believed he had succeeded in winning over the South without conceding much in return. However, he seriously miscalculated. His bill, far from healing tension, created a 'hell of a storm'. It was proof to many northerners that the **Slave Power conspiracy** was still at work. Abolitionists had a field day. One of the most effective pieces of abolitionist propaganda was a pamphlet, written by **Salmon Chase**, entitled *The Appeal of the Independent Democrats in Congress to the People of the United States*, published in January 1854:

'We arraign this bill as a gross violation of a sacred pledge; as a criminal betrayal of precious rights; as part and parcel of an atrocious plot to exclude from the vast unoccupied region immigrants from the Old World and free labourers from our own states and convert it into a dreary region of despotism, inhabited by masters and slaves.'

SOURCE F

From a sermon by an abolitionist preacher, Theodore Parker, delivered in February 1854.

The Slave Power has long been seeking to extend its jurisdiction. It has eminently succeeded. It fills all the chief offices of the nation; the Presidents are Slave Presidents; the Supreme Court is of Slave Judges, every one … In all that depends on the political action of America, the Slave Power carries the day. In what depends on industry, population, education, it is the North. The Slave Power seeks to extend its institutions at the expense of humanity. The North works with it … So the question is, shall we let Slavery into the two great territories of Kansas and Nebraska? That is a question of economy. Here it is. Shall men work with poor industrial tools, or with good ones? Shall they have the varied industry of New England and the North or the Slave labour of Virginia and Carolina? Shall their land be worth five dollars and a half as in South Carolina, or thirty dollars and a half as in Connecticut?

Why was Parker critical of the Kansas–Nebraska bill in Source F?

Initially, southerners had been apathetic about the Kansas–Nebraska bill. But the ferocity of northern attacks led to the passage of the bill suddenly becoming a symbol of southern honour. The result was a great Congressional struggle. After months of bitter debate (and presidential pressure on northern Democratic Congressmen), the bill became law in May 1854. Ninety per cent of southerner Congressmen voted for it; 64 per cent of northerner Congressmen voted against it. Northern Democrats splintered: 44 in the House voted for it; 43 voted against it. By failing to predict the extent of northern outrage generated by his act, Douglas weakened his party, damaged his presidential ambitions and helped to revive North–South rivalry.

Summary diagram: The problem of Kansas–Nebraska

The Kansas–Nebraska Act

Work of Stephen Douglas

Douglas's motives

Slave Power conspiracy?

North vs South

Congress divided

Whigs and Democrats divided

Chapter summary

In the early nineteenth century the USA expanded westwards. American settlers poured across the Appalachians in search of fertile land. Native Americans were the main losers. By 1840 many had been forced to leave their ancestral homes and move beyond the Mississippi. Western expansion was a crucial issue for southerners and northerners. Northerners were determined to prevent slavery's expansion. Southerners, fearing that slavery would be declared illegal by a northern-dominated Congress, were anxious that slavery should spread westwards. Problems arising from western expansion, resulting from the Mexican War (1846–8), aroused serious sectional confrontations. By 1849–50 some southerners supported seceding from the Union. The 1850 Compromise, largely the work of Stephen Douglas, contained the immediate danger. However, the Kansas–Nebraska Act (1854), also the work of Douglas, reignited sectional tensions.

Refresher questions

Use these questions to remind yourself of the key material covered in this chapter.

1 How did federal government action encourage western expansion?

2 What were the main economic factors encouraging western expansion?

3 Why were communication developments so important in opening up the West?

4 Why were Native Americans unable to hold on to their land?

5 Why was Missouri's entry to the Union a problem and how was the problem solved?

6 Why did Texas become a problem for the USA in 1835–6?

7 Why did the USA go to war with Mexico in 1846?

8 Why did US victory in the Mexican War cause problems?

9 Why and how did southerners oppose the Wilmot Proviso?

10 What were the main results of the 1848 presidential election?

11 How successful was the 1850 Compromise?

12 How serious was sectional strife in the years 1850–3?

13 Why did Senator Douglas introduce the Kansas–Nebraska Act?

14 Why did the Kansas–Nebraska Act cause such a storm?

Question practice

ESSAY QUESTIONS

1 Assess the reasons for so many Americans moving westwards in the period from 1803 to 1850.

2 'Misjudgements by politicians explain why the issue of western expansion divided North and South so sharply in the years 1845–54.' How far do you agree with this statement?

3 'Western expansion was a key factor in the deterioration of relations between the North and South by 1850.' Explain why you agree or disagree with this view.

4 To what extent did the Kansas–Nebraska Act revive tensions between North and South?

INTERPRETATION QUESTION

1 Read the interpretation and then answer the question that follows: 'There was really no compromise in 1850 – a truce perhaps, an armistice, certainly a settlement, but not a true compromise.' (David Potter, *The Impending Crisis 1848–1861*, Harper & Row, 1976.) Evaluate the strengths and limitations of this interpretation, making reference to other interpretations that you have studied.

SOURCE ANALYSIS QUESTIONS

1 With reference to Sources 1 and 2, and your understanding of the historical context, which of these two sources is more valuable in explaining why there was sectional tension in 1850?

2 With reference to Sources 1, 2 and 3, and your understanding of the historical context, assess the value of these sources to a historian studying the 1850 Compromise.

SOURCE I

From Henry Clay, in a speech to the Senate, February 1850.

We are told now, and it is rung throughout this entire country, that the Union is threatened with subversion and destruction. Well, the first question which naturally rises is, supposing the Union to be dissolved – having all the causes of grievance which are complained of – how far will a dissolution furnish a remedy for those grievances? If the Union is to be dissolved for any existing causes, it will be dissolved because slavery is threatened to be abolished in the District of Columbia and because fugitive slaves are not returned, as in my opinion they ought to be ... Mr President, I am directly opposed to any purpose of secession, of separation. I am for staying within the Union, and defying any portion of this Union to expel or drive me out of the Union.

SOURCE 2

From John C. Calhoun, in a speech to the Senate, March 1850.

What has caused this widely diffused and almost universal discontent? ... One of the causes is, undoubtedly, to be traced to the long-continued agitation of the slave question on the part of the North, and the many aggressions which they have made on the rights of the South ... There is another lying back of it – with which this is intimately connected – that may be regarded as the great and primary

---

cause. This is to be found in the fact that the equilibrium between the two sections, in the Government as it stood when the constitution was ratified and the Government put in action, has been destroyed. At that time, there was nearly a perfect equilibrium between the two … but as it now stands, one section has the exclusive power of controlling the Government, which leaves the other without any adequate means of protecting itself against its encroachments and oppression.

SOURCE 3

From Daniel Webster, a respected Whig politician, speaking in Congress, on 7 March 1850.

It is not to be denied that we live in the midst of strong agitations and are surrounded by very considerable dangers to our institutions and government … I speak today for the preservation of the Union … I shall bestow a little attention, Sir, upon these various grievances existing on the one side and on the other. I begin with complaints of the South and especially to one which has in my opinion just foundation; and that is that there has been found at the North, among individuals and among legislators, a disinclination to perform fully their constitutional duties in regard to the return of persons bound to service who have escaped into the free states. In that respect, the South, in my judgement, is right, and the North is wrong …. Peaceable secession! … Why, what would be the result? Where is the line to be drawn? What states are to secede? What is to remain American? What am I to be? An American no longer? Am I to become a sectional man, a local man, a separatist with no country in common with the gentlemen who sit around me here … Heaven forbid!

CHAPTER 3

The rise of the Republican Party

From the 1830s to the early 1850s, the Democrat and Whig Parties drew on national, not sectional, support. As long as voters placed loyalty to party ahead of sectional loyalty neither North nor South could easily be united one against the other. In the early 1850s the second party system collapsed. While the Democrat Party survived, the Whig Party disintegrated. The Republican Party, which drew support only from the North, emerged to challenge the Democrats. This chapter will focus on:

★ The collapse of the second party system

★ The 1856 presidential election

★ James Buchanan's presidency

Key dates

1856	May	The sack of Lawrence	1857	Lecompton constitution supported by Buchanan
	May	'Bleeding Sumner'		Dred Scott decision
			1858	Mid-term elections: Lincoln–Douglas debates
	Nov.	James Buchanan won presidential election	1859	John Brown's raid

1 The collapse of the second party system

▶ *Why did the second party system collapse and the Republican Party emerge?*

In the 1854 mid-term elections the Democrats, apparently blamed for sponsoring the Kansas–Nebraska Act (see pages 59–61), lost all but 23 of their (previously 91) free-state seats in Congress. Prior to 1854, the Whigs would have benefited from Democratic unpopularity in the North. By 1854, however, the Whig Party was no longer a major force in many free states.

The Whig collapse has often been seen as a direct result of the Kansas–Nebraska Act, which set southern against northern Whigs. However, while divisions over slavery certainly played a part in the Whig collapse, other factors were also important. Interestingly, Whig decline began well before the debates over Kansas–Nebraska. State and local elections in 1853 were a disaster for northern Whigs. This was largely because of the party's failure to deal with two related issues: immigration and Catholicism. These issues led to the rise of the Know Nothing movement. This occurred at the same time as the emergence of the Republican Party.

Catholic immigrants

Between 1845 and 1854, some 3 million immigrants entered the USA. Over a million of these were Irish Catholics, escaping the horrors of the **potato famine**. German immigrants, some of whom were Catholic, outnumbered the Irish. Many Germans had sufficient funds to buy land out west. The Irish, with fewer resources, tended to settle in northeastern cities, such as New York and Boston. Americans accused the Irish of pulling down wage levels and taking jobs from native-born workers. They also associated Irish immigrants with increased crime and welfare costs.

Fear of a **papal plot** to subvert the USA was deep-rooted among Protestant Americans. Many were horrified by the growth of Catholicism: between 1850 and 1854 the number of Catholic bishops, priests and churches almost doubled. Protestant Americans resented the growing political power of Catholic voters, claiming that the Irish voted as their political bosses, or their priests, told them. This was seen as a threat to democracy.

Whig failure

Given that most Irish and Germans voted Democrat, that party was unlikely to support anti-immigrant or anti-Catholic measures. But the Whig Party also failed to respond to **nativist** concerns. Indeed, in the 1852 election, the Whigs were actively pro-Catholic, hoping to capture the growing immigrant vote. This strategy failed: few Catholics were persuaded to vote Whig while some traditional Whig voters refused to vote for a party which was trying to appease Catholics. Many northerners began to look to new parties to represent their views. Disintegration of loyalty to the old parties in 1853 had little to do with sectional conflict between North and South; indeed, it occurred during a temporary lull in that conflict.

The Know Nothings

Concern about immigration and Catholicism resulted in the rise of the Know Nothing movement. (When asked questions about the order, members were supposed to reply, 'I know nothing', thereby giving the movement its name.) Know Nothings pledged to vote for no one except native-born Protestants. The

KEY TERMS

Potato famine In 1845–6 the Irish potato crop was hit by a devastating fungus, resulting in a serious famine. Millions of Irish people died or emigrated to Britain or the USA.

Papal plot A fear, mainly held by Protestants, that the Roman Catholic Church was conspiring to increase its influence.

Nativist Someone who is suspicious of immigrants and usually aggressively nationalistic.

movement had so much success that by 1854 it took on the characteristics of a political party, selecting its own candidates. Most Know Nothings wanted checks on immigration and a 21-year probationary period before immigrants could become full US citizens.

In 1854, the unpopularity of the Kansas–Nebraska Act, associated with the Democrats, helped the Know Nothings. With over a million members, the movement began to wield real political power. In 1854 it won 63 per cent of the vote in Massachusetts. In 1855, the order, which now called itself the American Party, took control of three more New England states and won large-scale support, mainly from ex-Whigs, in the South.

SOURCE A

From a speech in August 1855 by Abraham Lincoln, quoted in Mark E. Neely, Jr, *The Last Best Hope of Earth*, Harvard University Press, 1993, pp. 45–6.

I am not a Know Nothing. That is certain. How can anyone who abhors the oppression of negroes be in favour of degrading classes of white people? Our progress in degeneracy appears to me to be pretty rapid. As a nation, we began by declaring that 'all men are created equal'. We now practically read it 'all men are created equal except negroes'. When the Know Nothings get control, it will read 'all men are created equal, except negroes, and foreigners, and Catholics'. When it comes to this, I should prefer emigrating to some country where they make no pretence of loving liberty – to Russia for instance, where despotism can be taken pure, and without the base alloy of hypocrisy.

> How far do you think Lincoln's views in Source A were representative of northern public opinion? ?

The Republican Party

The northern electorate was not just concerned with anti-immigrant and anti-Catholic issues. The Kansas–Nebraska Act awakened the spectre of the Slave Power (see page 60) and many northerners were keen to support parties opposed to slavery expansion. In 1854, several anti-slavery coalitions were formed under a variety of names. The Republican name finally became the most popular.

By 1854–5 it was not clear whether the Know Nothings or Republicans would pick up the tattered Whig mantle in the North. In general, the Republicans were strongest in the mid-west; the Know Nothings in New England. However, in most free states the two parties were not necessarily in competition; indeed, they often tried to avoid a contest in order to defeat the Democrats. Many northerners hated both Catholicism and the Slave Power.

Given the Democrat reverses in the North in 1854, it was clear that there would be an anti-Democrat majority in the Congress, which met in December 1855. Whether the anti-Democrat Congressmen were more concerned with immigration or slavery expansion remained to be seen. At this stage, many Republicans were Know Nothings and vice versa. For those 'pure' Republicans who were opposed to nativism, the 1854 elections were a major setback. Given

Know Nothing strength, Republican success was far from inevitable. Indeed, most political observers expected the Know Nothings to be the Democrats' main opponents in 1856. Whereas the Republicans could never be more than a northern party, the Know Nothings drew support from both North and South.

The situation in Kansas 1854–6

After 1854, settlers began to move into Kansas. Their main concern was land. However, for politicians far more was at stake. Northerners thought that if slavery expanded into Kansas it might expand anywhere. Southerners feared that a free Kansas would be another nail in the slavery coffin. Senator Seward of New York threw down the gauntlet to the South: 'We will engage in competition for the virgin soil of Kansas and God give the victory to the side which is stronger in numbers as it is in right.' Senator Atchison of Missouri accepted the challenge: 'We are playing for a mighty stake; if we win we carry slavery to the Pacific Ocean; if we fail, we lose Missouri, Arkansas and Texas and all the territories; the game must be played boldly.'

A number of northerners and southerners tried to influence events in Kansas. The Massachusetts Emigrant Aid Company, for example, sponsored over 1500 northerners to settle in Kansas. However, pro-slavers seemed to be in the stronger position, given the proximity of Kansas to Missouri. Senator Atchison formed the Platte County Defensive Association that was pledged to ensure that Kansas became a slave state.

Elections in Kansas

In March 1855, Kansas elected its first territorial legislature which would decide on the subject of slavery; the elections were thus seen as crucial. 'There are 1100 coming over from Platte County to vote and if that ain't enough we can send 5000 – enough to kill every God-damned abolitionist in the Territory', declared Atchison. The fact that hundreds of pro-slavery Missourians did cross into Kansas to vote was probably a tactical mistake. In March 1855 the pro-slavers would probably have won the elections anyway. The Missourians simply cast doubt on the pro-slavery victory. When the legislature, which met at Lecompton, proceeded to pass a series of tough pro-slavery laws, northern opinion was outraged.

The Topeka government

'Free-state' or 'free-soil' settlers in Kansas, denying the validity of the pro-slavery legislature, set up their own government at Topeka. The free-staters were deeply divided, especially between 'moderates' and 'fanatics'. While the (minority) 'fanatics' held abolitionist views, the 'moderates' were openly racist, opposing slavery because it would result in an influx of black people. The Topeka government, dominated by moderates, banned black people, enslaved or free, from Kansas.

'Bleeding Kansas'

In May 1856 a pro-slavery posse, trying to arrest free-state leaders, 'sacked' the town of Lawrence, burning some buildings. This event was magnified out of all proportion by northern journalists. According to the first reports, dozens of free-staters were killed in the 'attack'. In reality there were no casualties (except a pro-slaver who died when a building collapsed on him).

The Lawrence raid sparked off more serious violence. The man largely responsible for this was John Brown, a fervent abolitionist. At Pottawatomie Creek, he and several of his sons murdered five pro-slavery settlers. Northern newspapers, suppressing the facts, claimed that Brown had acted in righteous self-defence. Overnight, he became a northern hero. In Kansas, his actions led to an increase in tension and a series of tit-for-tat killings. The northern press again exaggerated the situation, describing it as civil war.

With events seemingly drifting out of control, Pierce appointed a new governor, John Geary, who managed to patch up a truce between the warring factions. Nevertheless, events in Kansas, and the distorted reporting of them, helped to boost Republican fortunes. 'Bleeding Kansas' became a rallying cry for northerners opposed to what they perceived to be the Slave Power at work.

American Party problems

The American Party – the party of the Know Nothings – was the main anti-Democrat party in both the North and South in 1855. (In the South it was essentially the Whig Party under a new name.) Ironically, southern success was to be a major reason for the American Party's undoing. The Know Nothing order had won massive support in the North in 1854–5 because it had been able to exploit both anti-slavery and nativist issues. However, by 1856 the American Party, if it was to be a national party, had little option but to drop its anti-Kansas–Nebraska position. By so doing, it lost northern support. Other factors also damaged the party:

- The decline of immigration in the mid-1850s resulted in a decline of nativism.
- The failure of Know Nothing-dominated legislatures to make good their campaign promises enabled critics to claim that the movement not only knew nothing, it did nothing.
- Some Americans hated the secretive side of the movement.
- The very success of the American Party helped to tarnish its image as an authentic people's party: it attracted to it many of the 'old guard' politicians – the very people the Know Nothing order had been set up to help purge.

Events in Congress, which met in December 1855, weakened the American Party. Nativists split North and South. After a great struggle, **Nathaniel Banks**, an ex-Know Nothing but now a Republican, became Speaker of the House. The speakership contest helped to weld the Republicans into a more coherent party.

 KEY FIGURE

Nathaniel Banks (1816–94)

A major politician in the late 1850s. In 1856 he became speaker of the House of Representatives and in 1857 governor of Massachusetts. During the Civil War he became a – not very successful – general.

Republican policies

The Republican Party, which held its first national convention in February 1856, included abolitionists (like Charles Sumner), ex-Whigs (like William Seward), ex-Democrats (like David Wilmot) and ex-Know Nothings (like Nathaniel Banks). Not surprisingly, historians have different opinions about what the party stood for and why northerners supported it.

It is easier to say what Republicans were against than what they were for. Obviously they were against the Democrat Party. Almost all were also united in opposition to the Slave Power, which was seen as conspiring against northern interests. However, Republican leaders were not consistent in defining who was conspiring. Was it all or just some planters, all slaveholders or all southerners? Republicans also had different views about the nature of the conspiracy. Many were convinced that it sought to re-establish slavery in the North. Such fears were grossly exaggerated. Nevertheless, the idea of a Slave Power conspiracy was a Republican **article of faith**.

Moral aversion to slavery was certainly a moving force behind the Republican Party. Most Republicans had a moral antipathy to slavery. However, while almost all were opposed to slavery expansion, not all supported immediate abolition. Many were horrified at the prospect of thousands of emancipated slaves pouring northwards. Relatively few believed in black equality.

Early twentieth-century historians thought that the Republican Party represented the forces of emerging capitalism and that its main concern was the promotion of industrialisation, by measures such as high tariffs. Few historians now accept this thesis. Industrialisation was not a major concern of Republican voters in the 1850s, most of whom were farmers. The party itself was divided on many economic issues. Republican leaders were also divided on nativism. While some wanted to reach a compromise with – or steal the clothing of – the Know Nothings, others wanted no concessions to nativism.

'Bleeding Sumner'

A single event in Congress in May 1856 may have been even more important in helping Republican fortunes than the situation in Kansas. Following a speech in which Senator Sumner attacked southern Senator Butler, Congressman Preston Brooks entered the Senate, found Sumner at his desk and proceeded to beat him with his cane, which he shattered in the process. 'Bleeding Sumner' seems to have outraged northerners more than 'bleeding Kansas'. Here was clear evidence of the Slave Power at work, using brute force to silence free speech.

While Sumner became a northern martyr, Brooks became a southern hero. Resigning from Congress, Brooks stood for re-election and won easily. Scores of southerners sent him new canes to replace the one he had broken when beating Sumner.

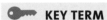

KEY TERM

Article of faith A central belief.

SOURCE B

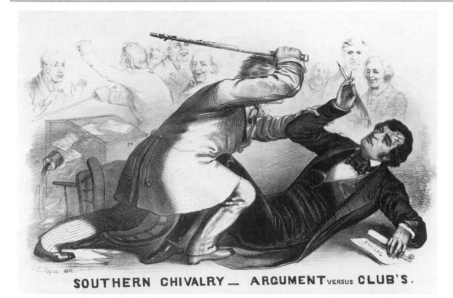

SOUTHERN CHIVALRY — ARGUMENT versus CLUB'S.

Why is this source useful to historians, even though it doesn't show what really happened?

A northern cartoon, from 1856, showing Preston Brooks caning Senator Charles Sumner. This 1856 northern cartoon shows southern senators enjoying the sight and preventing intervention by Sumner's friends. This did not actually happen!

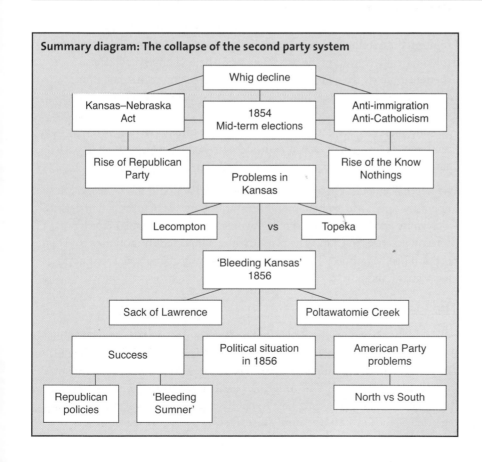

Summary diagram: The collapse of the second party system

```
                        Whig decline
                            |
  Kansas–Nebraska         1854            Anti-immigration
      Act           Mid-term elections    Anti-Catholicism
                            |
  Rise of Republican                      Rise of the Know
      Party           Problems in             Nothings
                        Kansas
                            |
        Lecompton        vs        Topeka
                            |
                    'Bleeding Kansas'
                         1856
                            |
    Sack of Lawrence              Poltawatomie Creek
                            |
   Success      Political situation    American Party
                     in 1856              problems
                            |
Republican    'Bleeding                North vs South
 policies      Sumner'
```

The 1856 presidential election

▶ *Why was the 1856 presidential election so important for the USA?*

While 'bleeding Kansas' and 'bleeding Sumner' helped the Republican cause, it was far from certain which party – Republican or American – would be the main threat to the Democrats in the 1856 presidential election.

American Party versus North American Party

The American Party held its national convention in February 1856. After a call to repeal the Kansas–Nebraska Act was defeated, many northern delegates left the convention. (After forming a splinter 'North American' Party, most drifted into the Republican Party.) The American Party went on to select ex-President Fillmore as its presidential candidate. This proved to be a serious mistake. Fillmore, more an old-fashioned Whig than a Know Nothing, was known to have pro-southern sympathies (as president in 1850 he had signed the Fugitive Slave Act, see page 56) and thus had limited appeal in the North.

John C. Frémont

Republican leaders decided that the party's best choice would be **John C. Frémont**. Born in the South, Frémont had had a colourful career as a western explorer. Relatively young (he was 43 in 1856), he had limited political experience. An ex-Know Nothing, he had been a (Democrat) senator for California for just seventeen days. A southern-born, ex-Know Nothing and ex-Democrat was a strange choice for Republican candidate. But the romance surrounding Frémont's career was likely to make him popular. Those who knew Frémont were aware that he was rash and egoistical. However, these flaws in character could easily be concealed from the voters.

The Republican platform declared that Congress had 'both the right and the imperative duty … to prohibit in the Territories those twin relics of barbarism – Polygamy and Slavery'. (The polygamy reference was a popular attack on Mormon practices in Utah.) The platform also supported the notion of a northern Pacific railroad. The Republican slogan was: 'Free Soil, Free Labour, Free Men, Frémont.'

The Democrats in 1856

President Pierce was so unpopular that he faced almost certain defeat. Douglas, the most dynamic Democrat, was tarnished by events in Kansas (see page 61). The Democrats thus nominated James Buchanan, a politician who had spent four decades in public service. A northerner, he sympathised with – and was thus acceptable to – the South. Given that his native state was Pennsylvania, regarded as the key **battleground state**, he was probably the Democrats'

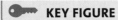 **KEY FIGURE**

John C. Frémont (1813–90)

A famous western explorer. He was also a national hero: many saw him (wrongly) as the 'Conqueror of California' in 1846. While he had assumed leadership of some US settlers in California, he had achieved very little, except getting in the way of the official US forces.

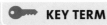 **KEY TERM**

Battleground state A state whose voters might well determine the outcome of the presidential election.

strongest candidate. The Democratic platform upheld the 1850 Compromise (see page 54) and endorsed popular sovereignty.

The 1856 campaign

The 1856 campaign generated great excitement. In the North, the contest was essentially between Buchanan and Frémont. In the South, it was between Buchanan and Fillmore. For the first time since 1849–50 there was widespread fear for the safety of the Union. If Frémont won, it was conceivable that many southern states would secede from the Union. Senator Toombs of Georgia declared that: 'The election of Frémont would be the end of the Union and ought to be.' Republicans, stressing that Frémont was young and vibrant, portrayed Buchanan as an old fogey and supporter of the South. The Democrats, claiming that they were the party of Union, attacked the Republicans for being rabid abolitionists who aimed to elevate blacks to equality with whites.

The 1856 result

In November, Fillmore obtained 871,731 votes (21.6 per cent) but only eight electoral college votes. Frémont won 1,340,537 votes (33.1 per cent in total) and 114 electoral votes. Buchanan, with 1,832,955 votes (45.3 per cent) and 174 electoral votes, became president. He won all but one southern state plus Pennsylvania, New Jersey, Indiana, Illinois and California. Frémont won the rest of the free states. The Democrats had cause for celebration. They had seen off the Fillmore challenge in the South and retained their traditional supporters – Catholics and mid-western farmers – in the North. Northern Democrats increased the number of seats they held in the House of Representatives to 53, although they were still outnumbered by 75 southern Democrats and 92 Republicans.

While Republicans were disappointed by the result, they too had cause for optimism. Their party had:

- trounced the American Party: the election indicated that northerners perceived the Slave Power to be a greater threat than the Catholic Church
- come close to capturing the presidency; if the party had carried Pennsylvania and Illinois, Frémont would have become president.

Republican pundits, confident that they could win over American Party supporters in the North, were soon predicting victory in the next presidential election in 1860. However, that victory was far from certain. Conceivably, the Republican Party could collapse as quickly as it had risen.

Summary diagram: The 1856 presidential election

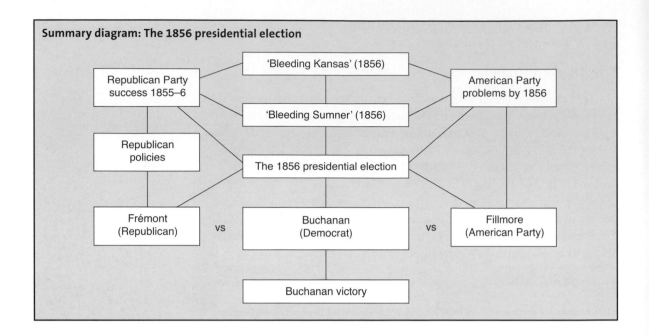

3 James Buchanan's presidency

▶ *How successful was President Buchanan?*

Buchanan's election, which had prevented a major rift in the USA, seemed cause for optimism. If the problem of Kansas could be solved, then sectional tension was likely to ease. No other territory in the immediate future was likely to be so contentious. Buchanan seemed 'safe'. He had served in both the House and the Senate, in the Cabinet, and as US minister in Russia and Britain. His position seemed strong. Both Houses of Congress and the Supreme Court were dominated by Democrats. However, from the start, many northerners feared that Buchanan was a tool of the Slave Power. His actions in 1857–8, particularly with regard to the Dred Scott case (see below) and Kansas, soon confirmed this fear. Ideologically attached to the South and aware of his dependence on southern support, Buchanan chose a pro-southern cabinet. (Four of his cabinet members were slave owners.) By the end of 1857, historian Kenneth Stampp has claimed that North and South had probably reached 'the political point of no return'. The events of 1857, according to Stampp, were decisive in preventing a peaceful resolution to sectional strife. Buchanan, in Stampp's view, must shoulder much of the blame – pursuing policies which:

- pushed most northerners into the Republican camp
- contributed to the fragmentation of the Democrat Party.

The Dred Scott case

Dred Scott was a slave who had accompanied his owner (an army surgeon) first to Illinois, then to the Wisconsin territory, before returning to Missouri. In the 1840s, with the help of anti-slavery lawyers, Scott went before the Missouri courts, claiming he was free on the grounds that he had resided in a free state and in a free territory. The Scott case, long and contentious, eventually reached the Supreme Court. By March 1857 the court – composed of five southerners (including Chief Justice Roger Taney) and four northerners – was ready to give judgment.

Buchanan referred to the case in his **inaugural address**. Claiming (not quite truthfully) that he knew nothing of the Supreme Court's decision, he said he was ready to 'cheerfully submit' to its verdict and urged all good citizens to do likewise. Two days later the decision was made public. The court decided (by seven votes to two) the following:

- Scott could not sue for his freedom. Black Americans, whether slave or free, did not have the same rights as white citizens.
- Scott's stay in Illinois did not make him free.
- Scott's stay in Wisconsin made no difference. The 1820 Missouri Compromise ban on slavery in territories north of 36°30′ was illegal. US citizens had the right to take their 'property' into the territories.

Northern reaction

Northerners were horrified. Here was further proof that Buchanan, the Supreme Court and the Democrat Party were involved in a Slave Power conspiracy. Republicans claimed that a whispered conversation between Taney and Buchanan on inauguration day proved that the president had been aware of the court's decision when he asked Americans to accept it. The northern press launched a fierce onslaught on the Supreme Court and some editors talked openly of defying the law. However, the judgment was easier to denounce than defy. In part, it simply annulled a law which had already been repealed by the Kansas–Nebraska Act (see page 59). The court's decision even had little effect on Scott: he was soon bought by the sons of one of his previous owners and set free. Nevertheless, the judgment was important. Many northerners saw it as an attempt to undermine:

- the Republican Party, which was committed to slavery's exclusion from the territories
- the concept of popular sovereignty – that territorial legislatures could prohibit slavery if they chose.

Problems in Kansas

In Kansas, Buchanan faced a situation which seemed to offer more in the way of hope than despair. Although there were still two governments (the official

KEY TERM

Inaugural address A new president's first speech, made after he has been sworn in as president.

pro-slave at Lecompton and the unofficial free state at Topeka), Governor Geary had restored order. It was obvious to Geary, and to other independent observers, that free-staters were now in the majority in Kansas. Given his declared commitment to popular sovereignty, all that Buchanan needed to do was ensure that the will of the majority prevailed. This would deprive the Republicans of one of their most effective issues.

In March 1857 Geary resigned, warning Buchanan that he should not support the pro-slavers. Buchanan now appointed Robert Walker, an experienced southern politician, in Geary's place. Walker accepted the job only after being assured by Buchanan that he would support fair elections. Arriving in Kansas in May, Walker quickly realised that most settlers opposed slavery. Accordingly, he decided that his aim should be to bring Kansas into the Union as a free, Democrat-voting state. Achieving that aim proved difficult. In February 1857 the Lecompton government had authorised the election (in June) of a convention to draw up a constitution that would set the territory on the road to statehood. Free-staters, suspecting that any election organised by the pro-slavers would be rigged, refused to get involved. Thus, only 2200 of the registered 9000 people entitled to vote did so and the pro-slavers won all the convention seats.

Pro-slaver success, while making a mockery of popular sovereignty, raised the expectations of southerners, who realised that the creation of a new slave state was now a distinct possibility. Meanwhile, elections for the Kansas territorial legislature were held in October. By now Walker had managed to convince free-staters that they should participate in the electoral process, promising that he would do all he could to see that the elections were fairly conducted. When the pro-slavers declared victory, Walker set about investigating charges of fraudulence. The charges were soon confirmed. Hundreds of fictitious people had been recorded as voting for the pro-slavers. Walker overturned enough results to give the free-staters a majority in the legislature.

The Lecompton constitution

The constitutional convention was now the last refuge of the pro-slavers. Few thought that the convention represented majority opinion in Kansas. Yet it proceeded to draft a pro-slavery Lecompton constitution. While agreeing to allow a referendum on its proposals, it offered voters something of a spurious choice:

- They could accept the pro-slavery constitution as it was.
- They could accept another constitution which banned the future importation of slaves but guaranteed the rights of slaveholders already in Kansas.

While Walker denounced the convention's actions as a 'vile fraud' and urged Buchanan to repudiate them, southerners urged the president to endorse them. The ultimatum – 'Lecompton or disunion' – rang out in southern newspapers. Buchanan, determined to maintain his southern support and possibly genuinely believing that anti-slavery forces were to blame for all the troubles in Kansas, decided to reject Walker's advice. Walker, in consequence, resigned in December. That same month Kansas voted on the Lecompton constitution. In fact, most free-staters abstained in protest. The pro-slave returns showed 6143 for the constitution with slavery and 569 for it without slavery. In his annual message to Congress, Buchanan endorsed the actions of the Lecompton convention, claiming that the question of slavery had been 'fairly and explicitly referred to the people'.

Buchanan versus Douglas

Buchanan's decision to support the Lecompton constitution was a huge blunder. By the end of 1857 everyone knew that most people in Kansas were opposed to slavery. Even some southerners were embarrassed by the fraud perpetrated by the pro-slavers. Had Buchanan accepted Walker's advice, he might not have lost much southern support. By accepting the Lecompton constitution, he gave the Republicans massive political ammunition. More importantly, he enraged northern Democrats who were committed to popular sovereignty. In an impassioned speech in the Senate, Douglas attacked both Buchanan and the Lecompton constitution. Southern Democrats immediately denounced Douglas as a traitor. The Democrat Party, like almost every other American institution, was now split North and South. A titanic Congressional contest followed, with Douglas siding with the Republicans. While the Senate passed the Lecompton constitution, the real battle was in the House. Despite huge **patronage pressure**, enough northern Democrats opposed Buchanan, ensuring that the constitution was defeated by 120 votes to 112.

Buchanan now accepted that Kansas should vote again on the measure. The new vote, conducted as fairly as possible in August 1858, resulted in a free-state victory: 11,300 voted against the Lecompton constitution while only 1788 voted for it. Kansas now set about drawing up a free-state constitution. It finally joined the Union in January 1861 as a free state.

The Panic of 1857

In 1857, US industry was hit by depression, later called the Panic of 1857. Mainly caused by the economic situation in Europe, it resulted in mass northern unemployment. Buchanan, believing the government should not involve itself in economic matters, did nothing. Inevitably, he and his party were blamed by northerners for their seeming indifference. Republican economic proposals – internal improvement measures and higher protective tariffs – were blocked by Democrats in Congress. The depression, albeit short-lived (it was over by 1859), helped the Republicans in the 1858 mid-term elections.

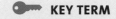 **KEY TERM**

Patronage pressure Using the offer of government jobs and offices effectively to bribe Congressmen.

The 1858 elections

The 1858 mid-term elections came at a bad time for northern Democrats, with the party split between those who supported Buchanan and those who supported Douglas. Given that Douglas had to stand for re-election as senator for Illinois, national attention focused on the Illinois campaign. The Republicans chose Abraham Lincoln to run against Douglas.

Abraham Lincoln

Born in a log cabin and with little formal schooling, Lincoln in many ways epitomised the American dream. Able and ambitious, he won the first of four terms as an Illinois state legislator in 1834. A loyal Whig (his hero was Henry Clay), he was elected to the House of Representatives in 1846, where he spoke in opposition to the Mexican War (see page 44). Defeated in 1848, he returned to Illinois, resumed his successful law practice and for a few years took less interest in politics.

The Kansas–Nebraska Act brought Lincoln back into politics. He hoped at first that the act would bring new life to the Whigs. Once it was clear that the future lay with the Republicans, he committed himself to the Republican cause. Previously, his main political concern had been economic matters. Now his speeches became more anti-slavery and anti-Slave Power. Although he had not much of a national reputation in 1858, he was well known in Illinois. Douglas respected Lincoln, commenting: 'I shall have my hands full. He is the strong man of the party – full of wit, facts, dates – and the best stump speaker with his droll ways and dry jokes, in the west. He is as honest as he is shrewd.'

The Lincoln–Douglas debates

Douglas agreed to meet Lincoln for seven open-air, face-to-face debates. These debates, which ran from August to October 1858, drew vast crowds. While visually different – Lincoln was a gawky 6 feet 4 inches tall (193 cm), Douglas a foot shorter (at 163 cm) – both men were gifted speakers. The debates were confined almost exclusively to three topics: race, slavery and slavery expansion. By today's standards, Lincoln and Douglas do not seem far apart. This is perhaps not surprising: both men were moderates and both were fighting for the middle ground. Both considered blacks to be inferior to whites. Lincoln declared: 'I am not, nor ever have been in favour of bringing about in any way the social and political equality of the white and black races – that I am not nor ever have been in favor of making voters or jurors of negroes, nor of qualifying them to hold office, nor to intermarry with white people.' Even the difference between Lincoln's free-soil doctrine (see page 68) and Douglas's popular sovereignty, in terms of practical impact, was limited: neither man doubted that popular sovereignty would keep slavery out of the territories. However, the two did differ in one key respect. Douglas never once said in public that slavery was morally wrong. Lincoln may not have believed in racial equality but he did

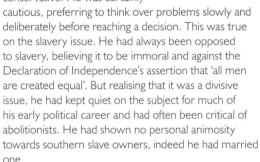

Abraham Lincoln

1809	Born in Kentucky
1831	Moved to Illinois and over the next few years experienced a host of jobs: shop worker, postmaster and surveyor
1832	Volunteered to fight in the Black Hawk Indian War but saw no action
1837	Moved to Springfield, Illinois's state capital, and became a lawyer
1842	Married Mary Todd, daughter of a Kentucky slaveholder
1846	Elected to the House of Representatives
1856	Joined the Republican Party
1858	Challenged Douglas for election as senator for Illinois
1860	Elected president
1862	Issued the Emancipation Proclamation (see page 187)
1864	Re-elected president
1865	Assassinated

Lincoln was complex and enigmatic. On the one hand he was a calculating politician, often non-committal and evasive. On the other, he was a humane, witty man who never seemed to worry much about his own bruised ego. Historians continue to debate whether he was moderate, radical or conservative. He was certainly cautious, preferring to think over problems slowly and deliberately before reaching a decision. This was true on the slavery issue. He had always been opposed to slavery, believing it to be immoral and against the Declaration of Independence's assertion that 'all men are created equal'. But realising that it was a divisive issue, he had kept quiet on the subject for much of his early political career and had often been critical of abolitionists. He had shown no personal animosity towards southern slave owners, indeed he had married one.

When he was chosen by the Republicans to run against Douglas in 1858 he determined to remind Illinois voters of the gulf separating him from his opponent. In his acceptance speech in June 1858, Lincoln declared: 'A house divided against itself cannot stand. I believe this government cannot endure permanently half slave and half free. I do not expect the Union to be dissolved – I do not expect the house to fall – but I do expect it will cease to be divided. It will become all one thing or all the other.'

believe that blacks and whites shared a common humanity: 'If slavery is not wrong', he said, 'then nothing is wrong.' He did not expect slavery to wither and die immediately. He did not suppose that 'the ultimate extinction would occur in less than a hundred years at the least', but he was convinced that 'ultimate extinction' should be the goal. If slavery did not expand, he believed it would eventually die.

SOURCE C

From Senator Douglas's opening speech, 21 August 1858, quoted in Harold Holzer, editor, *The Lincoln–Douglas Debates*, HarperCollins, 1993, p. 53.

Mr Lincoln here says that our government cannot endure permanently in the same condition in which it was made by its framers. It was made divided into free States and slave States. Mr Lincoln says it has existed for near eighty years thus divided; but he tells you that it cannot endure permanently on the same principle and in the same conditions relatively in which your fathers made it … .

What points does Senator Douglas make in Source C against Lincoln's view that 'a House divided against itself cannot stand'?

Why can't it exist upon the same principles upon which our fathers made it? Our fathers knew when they made this government that in a country as wide and broad as this – with such a variety of climate, of interests, of productions as this – that the people necessarily required different local laws and local institutions in certain localities from those in other localities. Hence they provided that each State should retain its own Legislature and its own sovereignty, with the full and complete power to do as it pleased within its own limits in all that was local and not national. One of the reserved rights of the States was that of regulating the relations between master and slave.

The Illinois result

Lincoln won some 125,000 popular votes to Douglas's 121,000. However, Douglas's supporters kept control of the Illinois legislature and it was the legislature which appointed the state's senators. Thus, Douglas was re-elected as senator. This was a significant triumph for Douglas, ensuring that he would be in a strong position to battle for the presidential candidacy in 1860. However, during the debates with Lincoln, Douglas had said much that alienated southerners, not least his stressing of the **Freeport Doctrine**. Although Lincoln had lost, he had emerged from the Illinois election as a Republican spokesman of national stature.

The 1858 results

The 1858 elections were a disaster for the northern Democrats. Helped by the collapse of the American Party, Republicans won control of the House of Representatives. The Republican share of the vote in the crucial states of Pennsylvania, Indiana, Illinois and New Jersey rose from 35 per cent in 1856 to 52 per cent in 1858. If the voting pattern was repeated in 1860 the Republicans would win the presidency. Southerners were naturally alarmed. Their fears were heightened by the actions of John Brown.

John Brown's raid

John Brown had risen to fame – or infamy – in Kansas (see page 69). Now in his late fifties, Brown was still determined to do something decisive for the anti-slavery cause. Some thought he was mad. (There was a history of insanity in his family.) However, many abolitionists believed that Brown was a man of moral conviction. The fact that he was able to win financial support from hard-headed northern businessmen is testimony to both his charisma and the intensity of abolitionist sentiment.

On the night of 16 October 1859, Brown and eighteen men (including three of his sons) left their base in Maryland and rode to the federal **arsenal** at Harper's Ferry. Brown's aim was to seize weapons, retreat to the Appalachians and spark a slave revolt. The fact that it was impossible to inform the slaves in advance

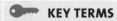

KEY TERMS

Freeport Doctrine A view that voters in a territory could exclude slavery by refusing to enact laws that gave legal protection to owning slaves, thus effectively invalidating the Dred Scott ruling.

Arsenal A place where military supplies are stored or made.

of his intentions was a major – but by no means the only – flaw in Brown's plan. In retrospect what is remarkable is that the raid was kept secret. Brown's main financial backers – the 'Secret Six' – although not certain of his precise goal, were aware of his broad intentions. Politicians who had heard rumours of Brown's plan refused to take them seriously.

Brown captured the arsenal with remarkable ease. A few slaves were induced or compelled to join Brown and a number of hostages were taken. Then things began to go wrong. A train pulled into Harper's Ferry, shots were fired by one of Brown's men, and the first person to die was a black baggage master. Rather than flee, Brown took refuge in the arsenal's fire-engine house. Virginia and Maryland **state militia** units and a detachment of troops, led by Colonel Robert E. Lee, quickly converged on the town. A 36-hour siege followed, with Brown threatening to kill the hostages and Lee attempting to persuade Brown to give himself up. On 18 October, Lee ordered the fire-engine house to be stormed. In the ensuing struggle Brown was wounded and captured along with six of his men. Ten of his 'army' were killed (including two of his sons). Seven other people also died.

The results of the raid

Brown was tried for treason. Refusing a plea of insanity, he determined to die a martyr's death, by so doing helping the anti-slavery cause rather more than his raid had done. Found guilty, he was executed on 2 December 1859. In his last letter he wrote: 'I, John Brown am now quite certain that the crimes of this guilty land will never be purged away but with Blood.'

Brown's raid was a crucial event. Coming on the eve of the 1860 presidential election, it raised sectional tensions to new heights. Most southerners were appalled at what had happened. Their worst fears had been realised. An abolitionist had tried to stir up a slave revolt. Aware that Brown had considerable financial support, they suspected that most northerners sympathised with his action. While some northerners did indeed regard Brown as a hero, northern Democrats condemned Brown out of hand, as did many leading Republicans. Few southerners were reassured. Most saw Republicans and abolitionists (like Brown) as one and the same. 'The Harper's Ferry invasion has advanced the cause of disunion more than any other event that has happened since the formation of its government', said one Richmond newspaper.

Sectional tension 1859–60

Over the winter of 1859–60, in the wake of John Brown's raid, there were rumours of slave insurrection in many southern states. Local vigilante committees were set up and **slave patrols** strengthened. Dozens of slaves, suspected of planning revolt, arson or mass poisoning, were rounded up and some were **lynched**. Southern state governments purchased additional weapons and southern militia units drilled rather more than previously.

 **KEY TERMS**

State militia All able-bodied men of military age (in most states) could be called up to fight in an emergency. By the 1850s most militias were shambolic; many men did not bother turning up for drill practice.

Slave patrol Armed men who rode round slave areas, especially at night, to ensure that there was no disorder.

Lynched Put to death without the usual forms of law.

When Congress met in December 1859, both Houses divided along sectional lines. Northern and southern politicians exchanged insults and accusations, carrying inflammatory rhetoric to new heights of passion. Southerners opposed all Republican measures: **free homesteads**, higher tariffs and a Pacific railroad. Northerners blocked all pro-southern proposals, such as the purchase of Cuba.

Buchanan, who had sought to avoid controversy, had failed. Far from easing tension, his policies had helped to exacerbate the sectional rift. His presidency must thus be regarded as one of the great failures of leadership in US history.

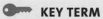

KEY TERM

Free homesteads The Republicans hoped to provide 160 acres (65 hectares) of land to farmers who settled in the West.

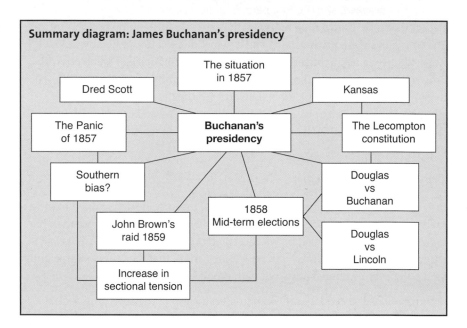

Summary diagram: James Buchanan's presidency

- The situation in 1857
- Dred Scott
- Kansas
- The Panic of 1857
- **Buchanan's presidency**
- The Lecompton constitution
- Southern bias?
- Douglas vs Buchanan
- John Brown's raid 1859
- 1858 Mid-term elections
- Douglas vs Lincoln
- Increase in sectional tension

Chapter summary

The Whig Party's collapse in the early 1850s led to the rise of the Know Nothings and the Republican Party. Events in 'Bleeding Kansas' ensured that the Republicans emerged as the main opponent of the Democrats. The election of Democrat James Buchanan as president in 1856 averted a serious sectional crisis. But Buchanan's poor leadership, especially with regard to Kansas, alienated northerners, helping to ensure Republican success in the 1858 mid-term elections – elections marked by the debates between Abraham Lincoln and Stephen Douglas. John Brown's raid on Harper's Ferry in 1859 served only to raise sectional tensions to new heights.

Refresher questions

Use these questions to remind yourself of the key material covered in this chapter.

1 Why did the second party system collapse?

2 Why did the Know Nothings win so much support?

3 How did events in Kansas help the Republicans?

4 Why did the Republicans emerge as the Democrats' main rivals?

5 What were the main aims of the Republicans?

6 Why did James Buchanan win the 1856 presidential election?

7 What were Buchanan's main mistakes in 1857–8?

8 What issues divided Lincoln and Douglas in the 1858 mid-term elections?

9 How significant was John Brown's raid on Harper's Ferry?

10 Why was sectional tension so high in 1860?

 Question practice

ESSAY QUESTIONS

1 Which of the following was the greater threat to the Union in the years 1854–61? a) The Kansas–Nebraska Act. b) The Dred Scott decision. Explain your answer with reference to both a) and b).

2 How successful was President Buchanan?

3 'Events in Kansas from 1854 to 1858 were of significant importance in increasing sectional tension in the USA.' Explain why you agree or disagree with this view.

4 How important was John Brown's raid in bringing about the Civil War?

INTERPRETATION QUESTION

1 Read the interpretation and then answer the question that follows. 'By the end of 1857 both North and South had probably reached the political point of no return.' (K. Stampp, OUP, 1990). Evaluate the strengths and limitations of this interpretation, making reference to other interpretations that you have studied.

SOURCE ANALYSIS QUESTIONS

1 With reference to Sources 1 and 2, and your understanding of the historical context, which of these two sources is more valuable in explaining why there was sectional tension in the late 1850s?

2 With reference to Sources 1, 2 and 3, and your understanding of the historical context, assess the value of these sources to a historian studying the problem of slavery in the territories.

SOURCE 1

From the Kansas–Nebraska Act, May 1854. Congress passes the act to organise the territories of Kansas and Nebraska.

Part of the Act of Congress of 1820, preparing for the admission of Missouri into the Union, is inconsistent with the principle of non-intervention by Congress in the matter of slavery in the states and territories set out in the legislation of 1850 known as the Compromise Measures. It was the true intent of

---

the Compromise of 1850 neither to legislate slavery into any territory or state, nor to exclude it, but to leave the people perfectly free to regulate their domestic institutions in their own way, subject only to the Constitution of the United States.

SOURCE 2

From the third Lincoln–Douglas debate at Jonesboro, Illinois, September 1858. Lincoln replies to Douglas on the issue of slavery in the territories.

The Supreme Court has decided in the case of Dred Scott that any Congressional prohibition of slavery in the territories is unconstitutional. It has also decided that the Constitution of the USA expressly recognizes slaves as property, and that no person shall be deprived of his property. Hence the court reaches the conclusion that to pass an Act of Congress by which a man who owned a slave on one side of a line would be deprived of him if he took him across the other side is to pass an Act that deprives him of his property. I understand that Senator Douglas agrees most firmly with that decision. The difficulty is this: how is it possible for any power to exclude slavery from the territories unless it defies that decision? The proposition that slavery cannot enter a new country without police regulation is false.

SOURCE 3

From the *Charleston Mercury*, February 1860. A southern newspaper argues that northern political interference has prevented slavery from entering the new territories.

What has been the policy pursued in Kansas? Has the territory had a fair chance of becoming a slave state? Has the principle of equal protection to slave property been carried out by the government there? On the contrary, has not every device been used to hinder the South and to expel or prohibit her sons from colonizing there? In our opinion, had the principle of equal protection to Southern men and property been rigorously observed, Kansas would undoubtedly have come into the Union as a slave state.

CHAPTER 4

The 1860 election, secession and civil war

In early 1860 southerners who claimed that the South would be better off going its own way were still a minority. However, by February 1861 seven southern states had seceded from the Union and formed the Confederacy. By April 1861 the Confederacy was at war with the Union. To explain how and why this happened, this chapter will focus on the following:

★ The 1860 presidential election

★ Secession

★ The creation of the Confederacy

★ The search for compromise

★ The problem of Fort Sumter

The key debate on *page 107* of this chapter asks the question: Why did civil war break out in 1861?

Key dates

1860	Nov.	Lincoln elected president	1861	March	Lincoln inaugurated as president
	Dec.	South Carolina seceded			
1861	Jan.	Mississippi, Florida, Alabama, Georgia and Louisiana seceded		April	Confederate forces opened fire on Fort Sumter
	Feb.	Texas seceded		April–June	Virginia, Arkansas, North Carolina and Tennessee seceded
	Feb.	Confederacy established			

1 The 1860 presidential election

▶ *Why did Lincoln win the 1860 election?*

The events of the 1850s had brought a growing number of southerners to the conclusion that the North had deserted the true principles of the Union. In southern eyes, it was the North, not the South, that was 'peculiar'. It was the North that had urbanised, industrialised and absorbed large numbers of immigrants while the South had remained agricultural, Anglo-Saxon and loyal to its roots. Southerners suspected that most northerners held abolitionist views and the prospect of a Republican triumph in 1860 filled them with outrage and dread. It was not merely that a Republican victory might threaten slavery. More fundamentally, southerners believed that the North was treating the South as its inferior, not least because it sought to prohibit slavery in the territories. Submission to the Republicans, declared Mississippi Senator Jefferson Davis, 'would be intolerable to a proud people'. If a Republican did become president, then plenty of southerners were prepared to consider the possibility of secession.

The Democratic convention

If the Republicans were to be defeated in 1860 it seemed essential that the rifts within the Democrat Party should be healed. Douglas, determined to run for president, made some efforts to build bridges to the South in 1859–60. Rationally, he was the South's best hope: he was the only Democrat who was likely to carry some free states – essential if the Democrats were to win the election. But Douglas's stand against the Lecompton constitution (see page 77) alienated him from most southerners.

Events at the Democrat convention, which met in April 1860 in Charleston, South Carolina, showed that the party, never mind the country, was a house divided against itself. From Douglas's point of view, Charleston, situated in the most **fire-eating** of the southern states, was an unfortunate choice for the convention. Townspeople, many of whom crowded into the convention hall, made clear their opposition to Douglas. Nevertheless, delegates were appointed according to the size of a state's population, ensuring that northern Democrats outnumbered southerners. When northerners blocked a proposal which would have pledged the party to protect the rights of slaveholders in the territories, some 50 delegates from the **lower South** walked out of the convention.

Unable to reach consensus on policy, the Democrats found it equally impossible to nominate a candidate. Although Douglas had the support of more than half the delegates, he failed to win the two-thirds majority which Democrat candidates were required to achieve. The convention thus agreed to reconvene at Baltimore in June.

Douglas versus Breckinridge

When some of the southern delegates who had left the Charleston convention tried to take their seats at Baltimore, the convention, dominated by Douglas's supporters, preferred to take pro-Douglas delegates from the lower South. This led to another mass southern walk-out. With so many southern delegates gone, Douglas won the Democratic nomination. The southern delegates now set up their own convention and nominated the current Vice-President John Breckinridge of Kentucky on a platform that called for the federal government to protect slavery in the territories.

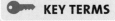

KEY TERMS

Fire-eating/fire-eaters Southerners who wanted to leave the Union.

Lower South The deep southern states: Alabama, Louisiana, Georgia, Texas, Florida, South Carolina and Mississippi.

The Democratic split is often seen as ensuring Republican success. However, even without the split, the Republican Party, which simply had to carry the North, was odds-on favourite to win. The Democrat schism may actually have weakened the Republicans. The fact that Douglas could now campaign in the North without having to try to maintain a united national Democrat Party probably helped his cause.

The Republican convention

The Republican convention met in May at Chicago in the Wigwam, a huge wooden building that could hold over 10,000 people. The delegates found it easier to agree on a platform than a candidate. While opposed to any extension of slavery, the Republicans declared that they had no intention of interfering with slavery where it already existed. Their platform condemned John Brown's raid as 'the gravest of crimes' and called for the following:

- higher protective tariffs
- free 160-acre homesteads for western settlers
- a northern transcontinental railway.

Lincoln becomes the Republican candidate

William Seward, governor of New York for four years and a senator for twelve, was favourite to win the Republican presidential nomination. However, the fact that he had been a major figure in public life for so long meant that he had many enemies. Although he was actually a pragmatic politician who disdained extremism, he was seen as holding militant abolitionist views on slavery. Moreover, he had a long record of hostility to nativism. His nomination, therefore, might make ex-Know Nothings think twice about voting Republican. Although there were several other potential candidates, Seward's main opponent turned out to be Abraham Lincoln. Lincoln had several things in his favour:

- He came from Illinois, a battleground state whose voters might decide the outcome of the 1860 election.
- His debates with Douglas in 1858 had enhanced his reputation.
- In 1859–60 he had made dozens of speeches across the North, gaining friends and making himself known.
- Given that it was difficult to attach an ideological label to him, he was able to appear to be all things to all men.
- His lack of administrative experience helped his reputation for honesty.
- The fact that the convention was held in Chicago (in Illinois) allowed his campaign managers to pack the Wigwam with his supporters.

On the first ballot, Seward won 173 votes: a majority but not the 233 votes needed for an absolute majority. Lincoln won 102 votes, well behind Seward but more than twice the votes of anyone else. With the race now clearly between

Seward and Lincoln, the votes of other candidates drifted to Lincoln. The second ballot was very close. By the third ballot there was an irresistible momentum in Lincoln's favour, helped in part by the sheer noise in the Wigwam. Lincoln's campaign managers almost certainly made secret deals with delegates from Pennsylvania and Indiana, probably to the effect that Lincoln would appoint Simon Cameron and Caleb Smith, leading politicians from Pennsylvania and Indiana, respectively, to his cabinet. These deals helped Lincoln to win the Republican nomination on the third ballot.

SOURCE A

From a newspaper article in the *Cincinnati Commercial* by Murat Halstead, a famous northern journalist, in May 1860.

I left the city [Chicago] on the night train on the Fort Wayne and Chicago road. The train consisted of eleven cars, every seat full and people standing in the aisles and corners. I never before saw a company of persons so prostrated by continued excitement. The Lincoln men were not able to respond to the cheers which went up along the road for 'Old Abe'. At every station where there was a village, until after two o'clock, there were tar barrels burning, drums beating, boys carrying rails, and guns, great and small, banging away. The weary passengers were allowed no rest, but plagued by the thundering jar of cannon, the clamour of drums, and glare of bonfires, and the whooping of the boys, who were delighted with the idea of a candidate for the Presidency who thirty years ago split rails on the Sangamon River … and whose neighbors named him 'honest'.

> ? What does Source A show about northern enthusiasm for Lincoln's candidacy in May 1860?

The Constitutional Unionist Party

The – new – Constitutional Unionist Party mounted a challenge for the presidency. Composed mainly of ex-Whigs, its main strength lay in the upper South. The party nominated John Bell of Tennessee as its presidential candidate. Its platform was the shortest in US political history: 'The Constitution of the Country, the Union of the States and the Enforcement of the Laws of the United States.' Essentially, the party wanted to remove the slavery question from the political arena, thus relieving sectional strife.

The campaign

In the North, the main fight was between Lincoln and Douglas. Bell and Breckinridge fought it out in the South. Douglas was the only candidate who actively involved himself in the campaign. At some personal risk, he campaigned in the South, warning southerners of the dangerous consequences of secession.

Throughout the campaign, Lincoln remained at home in Springfield, conferring with Republican chiefs, but saying nothing. Perhaps he should have made some effort to reassure southerners that he was not a major threat to their section.

However, he could hardly go out of his way to appease the South: this would have done his cause no good in the North. Moreover, it is difficult to see what he could have said to allay southern fears, given that the very existence of his party was offensive to southerners. Although Lincoln, Bell and Breckinridge kept silent this did not prevent their supporters campaigning for them. Republicans, flooding the North with campaign literature, held torchlight processions and carried wooden rails, embodying the notion that Lincoln was a self-made man who had once split wood for rails. Republican propaganda concentrated on the Slave Power conspiracy.

Southern Democrats stereotyped all northerners as 'Black Republicans' set on abolishing slavery. Most of Breckinridge's supporters did not draw attention to the fact that they might support secession if Lincoln triumphed. In some northern states the three anti-Republican parties tried to unite. However, these efforts at 'fusion' were too little and too late and were bedevilled by the bitter feuds that existed between the supporters of Breckinridge, Douglas and Bell.

The election results

In November, 81 per cent of the electorate voted. Bell won 593,000 votes (39 per cent of the southern vote) carrying the states of Virginia, Kentucky and Tennessee. Breckinridge, with 843,000 votes (45 per cent of the southern vote) won eleven of the fifteen slave states. Douglas obtained 1,383,000 votes – mainly from the North – but won only two states, Missouri and New Jersey. Lincoln won 1,866,000 votes – 40 per cent of the total. Although he got no votes at all in ten southern states, he won 54 per cent of the free-state vote, winning every state, except New Jersey. With a majority of 180 to 123 in the electoral college, he became president. Even if the opposition had combined against him in every free state, Lincoln would still have triumphed.

Breckinridge, the most popular southern candidate, won less than half the vote in the slave states as a whole. Not that this made any difference. Lincoln would have won the election if the South had voted solidly for Breckinridge or for anyone else. It was in the North where Lincoln had to be challenged. Douglas came close in Illinois, Indiana and California: if Douglas had carried these states Lincoln would not have won the election.

Why did northerners vote for Lincoln?

Northerners voted for Lincoln because he seemed to represent their section. A vote for Lincoln was a vote against the Slave Power. While not wishing to get rid of slavery immediately, most northerners had no wish to see it expand. Slavery and the Slave Power, however, were not the only concerns of northerners. Nativism had not disappeared with the Know Nothings' demise. Although the Republican Party took an ambiguous stand on nativist issues, anti-Catholic northerners had little option but to vote Republican, if only because the Democrat Party remained the home of Irish and German Catholics. Many northerners approved the Republican economic proposals. The corruption issue was also important. In June 1860 a House investigative committee had found corruption at every level of Buchanan's government. This had tarnished the Democrat Party. 'Honest Abe' Lincoln, by contrast, had a reputation for integrity.

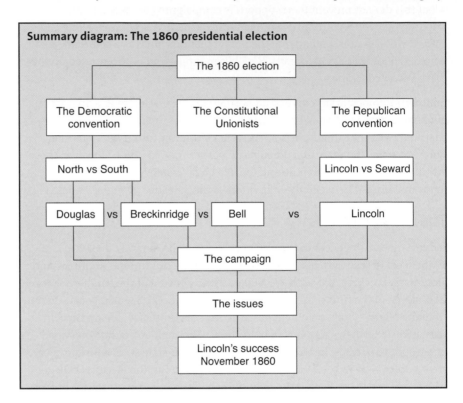

Summary diagram: The 1860 presidential election

The 1860 election

The Democratic convention — The Constitutional Unionists — The Republican convention

North vs South — Lincoln vs Seward

Douglas vs Breckinridge vs Bell vs Lincoln

The campaign

The issues

Lincoln's success November 1860

2 Secession

▶ *Why and how did the lower South states secede?*

Rationally, there were excellent reasons why Lincoln's victory should not have sparked southern secession:

- Lincoln had promised that he would not interfere with slavery in those states where it existed.
- Even if Lincoln harboured secret ambitions to abolish slavery, there was little he could do: his party did not control Congress or the Supreme Court.
- Secession would mean abandoning an enforceable Fugitive Slave Act: slaves would be able to flee to the North.
- Secession might lead to civil war, which would threaten slavery far more than Lincoln's election.

Few southerners regarded things so calmly. Most were outraged that a northern anti-slavery party had captured the presidency. Lincoln was depicted as a rabid abolitionist who would encourage slave insurrections. He would certainly stop slavery expansion. Southerners feared they would thus be encircled by more free states and that, ultimately, slavery would be voted out of existence.

For more than a generation, southerners had seen themselves as the aggrieved innocents in an unequal struggle that unleashed more and more northern aggressions on southern rights. They believed they had been denied their fair share of the western territories and unfairly taxed through high tariffs to subsidise northern industry. Honour demanded that a stand be taken against the latest outrage, the election of Lincoln. Across the South there was a strange mixture of moods – hysteria, despondency and elation. Fire-eaters, who had agitated for years for the cause of southern independence, capitalised on the mood. Long on the fringe of southern politics, they now found themselves supported by 'mainstream' politicians.

Problems for the secessionists

Secession was not inevitable. There was still much Unionist sympathy in the South. Nor was there any great southern organisation that might organise a secessionist movement. Southerners were loyal to their state rather than to the 'South'. There had never been a southern nation. Nor was the South united. Virtually every state was rife with tensions, often between small farmers and planters.

There was not even unity on the best political strategy to adopt. While some believed that Lincoln's election was grounds enough for secession, others thought it best to wait until he took hostile action against the South. 'Immediate' secessionists feared that if they forced the issue, they might destroy the unity they were seeking to create. How to force the issue was another problem. If individual states acted alone, there was the danger that they would receive no support, as South Carolina had found in the 1832 Nullification Crisis (see page 48). Yet trying to organise a mass move for secession might ensure nothing happened, as in 1849–50 (see page 54).

South Carolina secedes

Events moved with a rapidity few had foreseen. On 10 November, South Carolina's state legislature called for elections to a convention to meet on 17 December to decide whether the state would secede. This move created a chain reaction across the lower South. In Texas, Governor Sam Houston, who opposed disunion, delayed proceedings but only by a few weeks.

Individual states committed themselves, initially, to individual action. However, it was clear that southerners were also committed to joint action. There was liaison between the southern states at various levels but particularly between southern congressmen. When Congress met in early December, 30 representatives from nine southern states declared: 'We are satisfied the honour, safety and independence of the southern people are to be found only in a southern Confederacy – a result to be obtained only by separate state secession.'

Separate state secession was not long in coming. On 20 December, the South Carolina convention voted 169 to nil for secession. The state defended its action, claiming that: 'A geographical line has been drawn across the Union, and all the States north of that line have united in the election of a man to the high office of President of the United States whose opinions and purposes are hostile to Slavery.'

South Carolina sent commissioners to other southern states to propose a meeting, in Montgomery, Alabama on 4 February 1861, to create a new government.

SOURCE B

South Carolina's Declaration of Causes of Secession, 24 December 1860.

And now the State of South Carolina having resumed her separate and equal place among nations, deems it due to herself, to the remaining United States of America, and to the nations of the world, that she should declare the immediate causes which have led to this act … .

We affirm that these ends for which this [United States] Government was instituted have been defeated; and the Government itself has been destructive of them by the action of the non-slaveholding States. Those States have assumed the right of deciding upon the propriety of our domestic institutions; and have denied the rights of property established in fifteen of the States and recognised by the Constitution; they have denounced as sinful the institution of Slavery; they have permitted the open establishment among them of societies, whose avowed object is to disturb the peace of and eloin [legally remove] the property of the citizens of other States. They have encouraged and assisted thousands of our slaves to leave their homes; and those who remain, have been incited by emissaries, books and pictures, to servile insurrection.

> According to Source B, why did South Carolina secede?

Secession spreads

Over the winter of 1860–1, the election of delegates for conventions that would decide on secession took place across other southern states. Voters generally had a choice between 'immediate secessionists' and 'cooperationists'. While the standpoint of the immediate secessionists was clear, the cooperationists represented a wide spectrum of opinion. Some were genuine secessionists but believed the time was not yet right to secede; others were Unionists, opposed to secession. Historians find it hard to determine the exact distribution of voters along this spectrum. The situation is even more confused because some candidates, running as independents, committed themselves to no position.

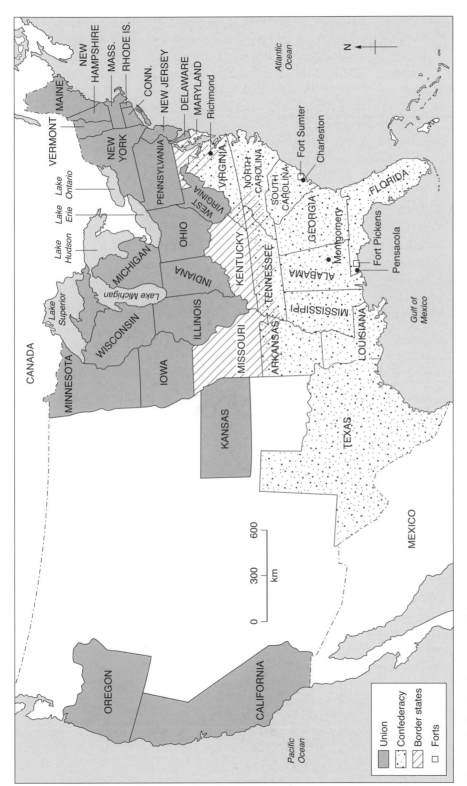

Figure 4.1 The Confederate and Union states.

- In Mississippi there were 12,000 votes for candidates whose positions were not specified and whose views remain unknown; 12,218 voted for cooperationist candidates; 16,800 voted for immediate secession. On 9 January 1861 the Mississippi convention supported secession by 85 votes to 15.
- On 10 January, a Florida convention voted 62 to seven for secession – but cooperationists won over 35 per cent of the vote.
- Alabama voted to secede by 61 votes to 39 on 11 January. The secessionists won 35,600 votes, the cooperationists 28,100 votes.
- Secessionist candidates in Georgia won 44,152 votes, cooperationists 41,632. The Georgia convention voted to secede on 19 January by 208 votes to 89.
- In Louisiana, secessionists won 20,214 votes, the cooperationists 18,451. On 26 January the Louisiana convention voted to secede by 113 votes to 17.
- A Texas convention voted (on 1 February) for secession by 166 votes to eight. Texas then had a **referendum** to ratify the convention's action. Secession was approved by 44,317 votes to 13,020.

KEY TERM

Referendum A vote on a specific issue.

A Slave Power conspiracy?

Republicans saw events in the South as a continuation of the Slave Power conspiracy. They claimed that a few planters had conned the electorate into voting for secession, to which most southerners were not really committed.

The debate about whether secession was led by an aristocratic clique or was a genuinely democratic act has continued. Slaveholders certainly dominated politics in many lower South states. Texas apart, no state held a referendum on the secession issue. Areas with few slaves tended to vote against disunion. Conversely, secession sentiment was strongest wherever the percentage of slaves was highest. According to historian David Potter, 'To a much greater degree than the slaveholders desired, secession had become a slave owners' movement.' Potter believed that a secessionist minority, with a clear purpose, seized the momentum and, at a time of excitement and confusion, won mass support.

Nevertheless, Potter conceded that the secessionists acted democratically and in an 'open and straightforward' manner. By no means all the secessionists were wealthy planters. (Nor did all wealthy planters support secession.) Many non-slaveholders supported secession. While it is true that secessionists opposed efforts by cooperationists to submit the secession ordinances to a popular referendum, this would probably have been superfluous. The southern electorate had made its position clear in the convention elections. There was no conspiracy to thwart the will of the majority. Moreover, many cooperationists were quite prepared to support secession.

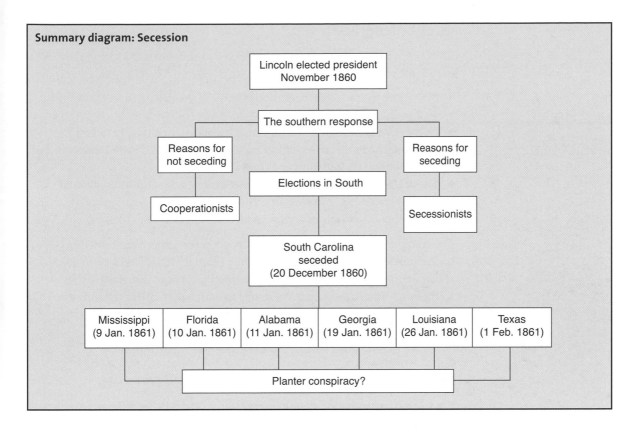

Summary diagram: Secession

Lincoln elected president November 1860

The southern response

Reasons for not seceding

Reasons for seceding

Elections in South

Cooperationists

Secessionists

South Carolina seceded (20 December 1860)

| Mississippi (9 Jan. 1861) | Florida (10 Jan. 1861) | Alabama (11 Jan. 1861) | Georgia (19 Jan. 1861) | Louisiana (26 Jan. 1861) | Texas (1 Feb. 1861) |

Planter conspiracy?

③ The creation of the Confederacy

▶ *Why did the upper South states not join the Confederacy in February 1861?*

Few Americans expected war in early 1861. Most northerners believed that the seceded states were bluffing or thought that an extremist minority had seized power against the wishes of the majority. Either way, the seceded states would soon be back in the Union: the southern bluff would be called or the Unionist majority would assert itself. In contrast, most southerners thought that the North would not fight to preserve the Union. Americans in the **border states** were confident that a compromise could be arranged which would bring the seceded states back into the Union. These hopes and expectations were not to be realised. By April 1861 the United States were no longer united; they were at war. Was this the fault of blundering politicians? Or was the rift between North and South so great that war was inevitable?

 **KEY TERM**

Border states The states between the North and the deep South (for example, Kentucky, Maryland, Tennessee, Delaware and Missouri). These states supported slavery but were not committed to secession.

The Confederacy

On 4 February 1861, 50 delegates of the seceded states met at Montgomery to launch the Confederate government.

- Chosen by the secession conventions, most of the delegates were lawyers or well-to-do planters.
- Of the 50, 49 were slave owners and 21 owned at least twenty slaves.
- Almost all had extensive political experience. Thirty had been Democrats and the remaining twenty were ex-Whigs.
- The delegates comprised a broad cross-section of the South's traditional political leadership. Almost half the delegates were cooperationists who had been either opponents or at best lukewarm supporters of secession.

The convention, desperate to win the support of the upper South, tried to project a moderate and united image. On 8 February it adopted a provisional constitution. The next day, sitting now as the Provisional Congress of the Confederate States, it set up a committee to draft a permanent constitution. This was approved in March and quickly ratified by all seven Confederate states. Closely modelled on the US Constitution, the main differences were features that more closely protected slavery and guaranteed state rights.

Jefferson Davis and the Confederate government

On 9 February the convention unanimously elected Senator Jefferson Davis of Mississippi as provisional president. He seemed a good appointment. Educated at West Point, he had served with distinction in the Mexican War and had been a successful secretary of war. Although a champion of southern rights, he was by no means a fire-eater. Alexander Stephens, from Georgia, a leading cooperationist, became vice-president. Davis's cabinet was made up of men from each Confederate state.

On 18 February, Davis took the oath of office as president. In his inaugural speech he asked only that the Confederacy be left alone. Although he expected the North to oppose secession, he was confident that the Confederacy would survive. His main concern was the fact that no states from the upper South had yet joined the Confederacy. The seven original Confederate states comprised only ten per cent of the USA's population and had only five per cent of its industrial capacity.

The Provisional Congress quickly got down to business:

- It passed major pieces of financial legislation.
- It adopted the Stars and Bars as the national flag.
- It set about raising an army.

SOURCE C

From a speech by Alexander Stephens, Vice-President of the Confederacy, 21 March 1861.

The new Constitution has put at rest forever all the agitating questions relating to our peculiar institutions – African slavery as it exists among us – the proper status of the negro in our form of civilization. This was the immediate cause of the late rupture and present revolution ...

Our new Government's ... foundations are laid, its cornerstone rests, upon the great truth that the negro is not equal to the white man; that slavery, subordination to the superior race, is his natural and moral condition. This, our new Government, is the first, in the history of the world, based upon this great physical, and moral truth.

To what extent are Stephens' views, as expressed in Source C, likely to have appealed to southern whites in 1861?

The upper South

In January 1861, the state legislatures of Arkansas, Virginia, Missouri, Tennessee and North Carolina all called elections for conventions to decide on secession. The results of these elections proved that the upper South was far less secessionist inclined than the lower South. In Virginia, only 32 immediate secessionists won seats in a convention with 152 members. Tennessee and

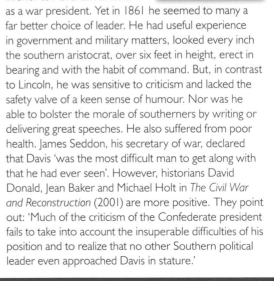

Jefferson Davis

1808	Born in Kentucky
1825	Graduated from West Point
1835	Resigned from the army after marrying Zachary Taylor's daughter Sarah against her father's wishes. Sarah died three months after their marriage
1835–45	Planter at Brierfield, Mississippi
1845	Married Varina Howell and elected to Congress
1846	Fought in the Mexican War: helped to win the battle of Buena Vista
1847	Elected to the US Senate
1853–7	Secretary of war
1861	Became Confederate president
1865	Captured by Union troops; imprisoned
1867	Released from prison
1889	Died

Historians differ sharply in their evaluation of Jefferson Davis as leader of the Confederacy. Most agree that he was inferior to Abraham Lincoln as a war president. Yet in 1861 he seemed to many a far better choice of leader. He had useful experience in government and military matters, looked every inch the southern aristocrat, over six feet in height, erect in bearing and with the habit of command. But, in contrast to Lincoln, he was sensitive to criticism and lacked the safety valve of a keen sense of humour. Nor was he able to bolster the morale of southerners by writing or delivering great speeches. He also suffered from poor health. James Seddon, his secretary of war, declared that Davis 'was the most difficult man to get along with that he had ever seen'. However, historians David Donald, Jean Baker and Michael Holt in *The Civil War and Reconstruction* (2001) are more positive. They point out: 'Much of the criticism of the Confederate president fails to take into account the insuperable difficulties of his position and to realize that no other Southern political leader even approached Davis in stature.'

North Carolina had referendums, which opposed conventions being held. Arkansas voted for a convention but delegates rejected secession. Secessionists made no headway in Maryland, Delaware, Missouri or Kentucky.

A number of reasons have been put forward to explain why the upper South states did not vote immediately for secession:

- Importantly, these states had a smaller stake in slavery than the lower South. Less than 30 per cent of the upper South's population was black. Nearly half of Maryland's black people were already free.
- Many non-slaveholders questioned how well their interests would be served in a planter-dominated Confederacy.
- The upper South had close ties with the North and thus had more reason to fear the economic consequences of secession.

In many respects, the upper South voting came as no surprise: its voters had supported Bell and Douglas in 1860, not Breckinridge. Nevertheless, most people in the upper South distrusted Lincoln. The legislatures of Virginia and Tennessee made it clear that they would oppose any attempt to force the seceding states back into the Union. If it came to the crunch, there would be many in the upper South who would put their southern affiliations before their American loyalties.

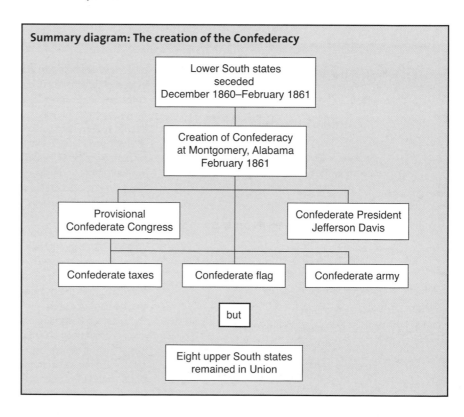

Summary diagram: The creation of the Confederacy

Lower South states seceded December 1860–February 1861

Creation of Confederacy at Montgomery, Alabama February 1861

Provisional Confederate Congress

Confederate President Jefferson Davis

Confederate taxes

Confederate flag

Confederate army

but

Eight upper South states remained in Union

The search for compromise

▶ *Could a compromise have been found in 1860–1?*

Buchanan continued as president until March 1861. Blaming the Republicans for the crisis, his main concern was not to provoke war. He thus took no action as federal institutions across the lower South – forts, customs houses and post offices – were taken over by the Confederate states. However, he determined not to recall the federal garrisons at Fort Sumter and Fort Pickens. This was to have major repercussions.

Buchanan has been criticised by historians for not doing more to seek a compromise. In fairness, it is difficult to see what he could have done, given that Republicans did not trust him and the lower South was set on leaving the Union.

Congressional efforts

Congress met in December. Both the House and the Senate set up committees to explore plans of conciliation. The House Committee, with 33 members, proved to be too cumbersome. The Senate Committee of thirteen, on which Kentucky unionist John Crittenden played a leading role, was more effective. It recommended a package of proposals that was known as the Crittenden Compromise:

- The Missouri Compromise line (see page 41) should be extended to the Pacific. Slavery would be recognised south of 36°30′ in all present territories, as well as those 'hereafter acquired'.
- A constitutional amendment would guarantee that there would be no interference with slavery in those states where it already existed.
- Congress would be forbidden to abolish slavery in Washington, DC.

Republicans, whose strength in Congress had grown significantly as southerners withdrew, rejected the proposals, which seemed to smack more of surrender than compromise.

The Virginia peace convention

In February 1861, a peace convention met in Washington, DC, at the request of Virginia, to see if it could find measures that would bring the seceded states back into the Union. Attended by 133 delegates, it included some of the most famous names in US politics but no Confederate delegates. After three weeks of deliberation, the convention supported proposals similar to those of Crittenden. These proposals were ignored by Congress and by the Confederacy. 'Given the momentum of secession and the fundamental set of Republicanism', observed historian David Potter (1976), 'it is probably safe to say that compromise was impossible from the start'.

Northern opinion

Up to 1860, slavery had been the main issue dividing North from South. That had now been replaced by secession. There were some, like newspaper editor Horace Greeley, who thought that the 'erring' Confederate states should be allowed to 'go in peace'. However, most northerners were unwilling to accept the USA's dismemberment. The great experiment in self-government must not collapse. 'The doctrine of secession is anarchy', declared a Cincinnati newspaper. 'If the minority have the right to break up the Government at pleasure, because they have not had their way, there is an end of all government.'

Few Republicans, however, demanded the swift despatch of troops to suppress the 'rebellion'. There was an appreciation that such action might have a disastrous impact on the upper South. The best bet seemed to be to avoid provocation, hoping that the lower South would see sense and return to the Union.

Lincoln's position

Lincoln maintained a strict silence. However, in a letter written on 1 February 1861 to William Seward (soon to be his secretary of state), he made it clear that he was ready to compromise with the South on a number of issues such as the Fugitive Slave Act and slavery in Washington, DC. He was even prepared to make some concessions with regard to New Mexico, given that the 1850 Compromise specifically allowed settlers there to decide on the issue. However, Lincoln's general position with regard to slavery expansion was clear (see Source D).

? What does Source D reveal about Lincoln's willingness to compromise?

SOURCE D

From a letter sent by Lincoln to Seward, 1 February 1861.

I say now … as I have all the while said, that on the territorial question – that is, the question of extending slavery under the national auspices – I am inflexible. I am for no compromise which assists or permits the extension of the institution on soil owned by the nation. And any trick by which the nation is to acquire territory, and then allow some local authority to spread slavery over it, is as obnoxious as any other. I take it that to effect some such result as this, and to put us again on the highroad to a slave empire, is the object of all these proposed compromises. I am against it. As to fugitive slaves, District of Columbia, slave trade among the slave States and whatever springs of necessity from the fact that the institution is amongst us, I care but little, so that what is done be comely and not altogether outrageous. Nor do I care much about New Mexico, if further extension were hedged against.

Lincoln believed that he had won the 1860 election on principles fairly stated and was determined not to concede too much to the South. Like many Republicans, he exaggerated the strength of Union feeling in the South; he thought, mistakenly, that secession was a plot by a small group of planters. His hope that inactivity might allow southern Unionists a chance to rally and overthrow the extremists was naive. This probably made little difference. Even with hindsight, it is difficult to see what Lincoln could have done before he became president that would have significantly changed matters.

Lincoln's cabinet

Lincoln's seven-man cabinet was more a cabinet of all factions than of all talents. Some of its members were radical, others conservative. Some represented the east, others the west. (Lincoln would have liked to appoint a 'real' southerner but there was no obvious candidate.) Some were ex-Whigs, others ex-Democrats. Four had been competitors for the 1860 Republican nomination. Not one had been friendly with Lincoln pre-1861; they knew little about him and he knew even less about them.

- Seward became secretary of state. He expected, and was expected, to be the power behind the throne.
- Salmon Chase, secretary of the treasury, was seen as the main radical spokesman in the cabinet.
- Gideon Welles became secretary of the navy.
- The appointments of Caleb Smith, from Indiana, as secretary of the interior and Simon Cameron, from Pennsylvania, as secretary of war were seen as 'debt' appointments in return for support for Lincoln's presidential nomination.
- Attorney General Edward Bates and Postmaster General Montgomery Blair completed the cabinet.

Some doubted that Lincoln would have the personality to control such an unlikely 'team'. However, Lincoln trusted to his political skill to make the separate elements pull together.

Lincoln arrives in Washington, DC

Lincoln set out from Springfield to Washington, DC in February 1861. Instead of travelling directly to the capital, he stopped at various towns to make set speeches. This was probably a mistake: there was relatively little he thought he could say before his inauguration and thus he said little – to the disappointment of many who heard him.

Nearing Baltimore, Lincoln was warned of an assassination plot. Heeding the advice of his security advisers, he abandoned his planned journey and slipped into Washington, DC anonymously, 'like a thief in the night' according to his critics. This cast doubts about his courage to face the crisis ahead. In addition, neither his western accent nor his social awkwardness inspired much confidence. Over the next few days Lincoln met mobs of office seekers and endless delegations, as well as Congressmen and members of his cabinet. Meanwhile, he worked hard on his inauguration speech. The speech was looked over by several people, including Seward, who persuaded Lincoln to soften a few phrases.

Lincoln's inauguration

Lincoln became president on 4 March 1861. His inaugural speech was conciliatory but firm. He said that he would not interfere with slavery where it already existed. Nor would he take immediate action to reclaim federal property or appoint federal officials in the South. However, he made it clear that, in his view, the Union was unbreakable and that secession was illegal. He thus intended to 'hold, occupy and possess' federal property within the seceded states. He ended by saying:

> *In your hands, my dissatisfied fellow countrymen, and not in mine, is the momentous issue of civil war. The government will not assail you. You can have no conflict without being yourselves the aggressors. You have no oath registered in heaven to destroy the government, while I shall have the most solemn one to 'preserve, protect, and defend' it … We are not enemies, but friends. We must not be enemies. Though passion may have strained, it must not break, our bonds of affection.*

Most Republicans liked his firm tone. Border state Unionists and many northern Democrats approved of his attempts at conciliation. Unfortunately, the speech had no effect whatsoever in the Confederate states. They had no wish to rejoin the Union.

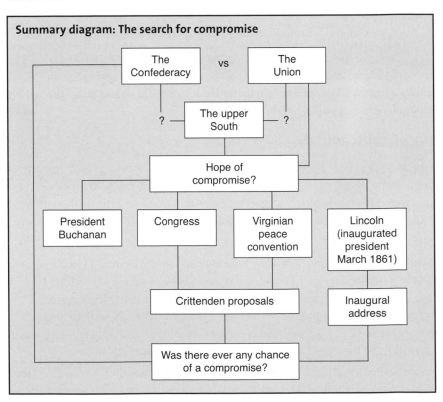

Summary diagram: The search for compromise

The problem of Fort Sumter

▶ *Why did Fort Sumter precipitate the outbreak of war?*

Over the winter, the Confederacy had taken over most of the (virtually unmanned) forts in the South. There were two exceptions: Fort Pickens and Fort Sumter. Both forts were on islands. Pickens, off Pensacola, Florida, was well out of range of shore **batteries** and could easily be reinforced by the federal navy. Sumter, in the middle of Charleston harbour, was a more serious problem. Its garrison, numbering less than a hundred men, was led by Major Robert Anderson, an ex-Kentucky slaveholder.

In January 1861 Buchanan sent a supply ship to Sumter. As it approached the fort, South Carolina batteries opened fire and its captain hastily put about. Anderson decided not to return fire and war was thus avoided. Secessionists from other states, fearing that South Carolina's actions might provoke a conflict before the South was ready, warned the state to cool down. A truce (of sorts) was agreed. South Carolina would make no efforts to seize the fort and Buchanan would send no further aid to Sumter.

Lincoln and the problem of Fort Sumter

By March 1861, Fort Sumter had become the symbol of national sovereignty for both sides:

- If the Confederacy was to lay claim to the full rights of a sovereign nation it could hardly allow a 'foreign' fort in the middle of one of its main harbours.
- Lincoln had declared in his inaugural speech that he intended to hold on to what remained of federal property in the South. Retention of Sumter was thus a test of his credibility.

Lincoln had spoken as he did at his inauguration, believing that time was on his side. But within hours of his speech, he learned that the Sumter garrison would run out of food in six weeks. Lincoln sought the advice of his general-in-chief, 74-year-old Winfield Scott. Sumter's evacuation, Scott informed Lincoln, was 'almost inevitable': it could not be held without a large fleet and an army of 25,000 soldiers, neither of which the USA possessed. On 15 March Lincoln brought the matter before his cabinet. Most favoured withdrawal. Putting off making an immediate decision, Lincoln sent trusted observers to Charleston to assess the situation.

Seward was the chief spokesman for the policy of masterly inactivity. If the upper South was not stampeded into joining the Confederacy by a coercive act, Seward argued, the 'rebel' states would eventually rejoin the Union. Fearing that conflict between the federal government and the Confederacy might unite the entire South, he urged Lincoln to make some effort to appease the Confederacy. While Lincoln hesitated, Seward, on his own initiative, sent assurances to Confederate leaders that Sumter would be abandoned.

 **KEY TERM**

Batteries Units of artillery.

SOURCE E

A contemporary painting from 1861 showing Fort Sumter under attack.

SOURCE F

A contemporary photograph showing Confederate forces occupying Fort Sumter immediately after its surrender. Note the Confederate flag, the 'stars and bars', flying from the makeshift flagpole.

> ? How useful are Sources E, F and G to modern historians in understanding what happened at Fort Sumter?

SOURCE G

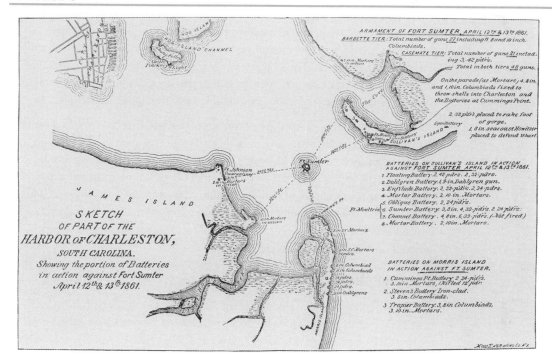

A contemporary map of Charleston harbour, with Fort Sumter in the centre.

At the end of March, following a report from Scott advising that both Sumter and Pickens should be abandoned, Lincoln called another cabinet meeting to discuss the crisis. By now, the fact-finding mission to Charleston had returned and reported finding no support for the Union whatsoever, quashing hopes that Union sentiment would prevail. Moreover, northern newspapers were demanding that Sumter be held. Heedful of northern opinion, most of the cabinet now favoured resupplying Sumter and protecting Pickens.

Lincoln acts

Lincoln determined to send ships to reprovision, but not reinforce, both forts. Seward, who had thought Sumter's evacuation a foregone conclusion, had miscalculated. He now suggested that Lincoln should delegate power to him, evacuate Sumter, and provoke a war against France and Spain which might help to reunite to the nation. Lincoln made it clear that he had no intention of delegating power, abandoning Sumter or fighting more than one war at a time.

On 4 April, Lincoln informed Anderson that a relief expedition would soon be coming and that he should try to hold out. Two days later he sent a letter to South Carolina's governor telling him that he intended to resupply Sumter. A small naval expedition (three ships and 500 men) finally left for Charleston on 9 April.

It has been claimed that Lincoln deliberately manoeuvred the Confederacy into firing the first shots. More likely, he was simply trying to keep as many options open as possible. He hoped to preserve peace, but was willing to risk, and possibly expected, war. By attempting to resupply Sumter, he was passing the buck to Jefferson Davis. The Confederate leader had to decide what to do. If he gave the orders to fire on unarmed boats carrying food for hungry men, this was likely to unite northern opinion and possibly keep the upper South loyal.

Davis's cabinet met on 9 April. Most members thought that the time had come to take action. The fact that the Union flag was still flying on the fort was an affront to southern honour. Moreover, a crisis might bring the upper South into the Confederacy. Thus, Davis issued orders that Sumter must be taken before it was resupplied. General Beauregard, commander of Confederate forces in Charleston, was to demand that Anderson evacuate the fort. If Anderson refused, then Beauregard's orders were to 'reduce' Sumter, battering it into submission with his heavy artillery.

The first shots of the war

On 11 April, Beauregard demanded Sumter's surrender. Anderson, who had once been Beauregard's tutor at West Point, refused. Negotiations dragged on for several hours but got nowhere. And so, at 4.30a.m. on 12 April, Confederate guns opened fire. Over the next 33 hours the Confederate and Sumter batteries exchanged some 5000 rounds of artillery fire. Extraordinarily there were no deaths. On 13 April, with fires raging through the fort, Anderson surrendered. His troops were allowed to march out and were evacuated to Washington, DC.

The attack on Sumter electrified the North. In New York, a city which had previously tended to be pro-southern, 250,000 people turned out for a Union rally. 'There can be no neutrals in this war, only patriots – or traitors', thundered Senator Douglas. On 15 April, Lincoln issued a **call to arms**. Lincoln asked for 75,000 men for 90 days to put down the 'rebellion'. On 19 April he ordered a blockade of the Confederacy, intending to prevent it trading with Britain and Europe. This action implied that the conflict was more a war than a rebellion. It is rare that a country blockades itself.

Secession: the second wave

Given that Lincoln called on all Union states to send men to put down the rebellion, the upper South states now had to commit themselves. Virginia's decision was crucial. Its industrial capacity was as great as the seven original Confederate states combined. If it opted to remain in the Union, the Confederacy was unlikely to survive for long. However, most Virginians sympathised with the Confederacy. A state convention voted by 88 votes to 55 to support its southern 'brothers'. A referendum in May ratified this decision, with Virginians voting by 128,884 votes to 32,134 to secede. Richmond, Virginia's capital, now became the Confederate capital. In May, Arkansas and North Carolina joined

KEY TERM

Call to arms A presidential order calling up troops and putting the USA on a war-footing.

the Confederacy. In June, Tennessee voted by 104,913 votes to 47,238 to secede. However, support for the Confederacy in the upper South was far from total:

- West Virginia seceded from Virginia and remained in the Union.
- East Tennessee was pro-Unionist.
- Four slave states – Delaware, Maryland, Missouri and Kentucky – did not secede.

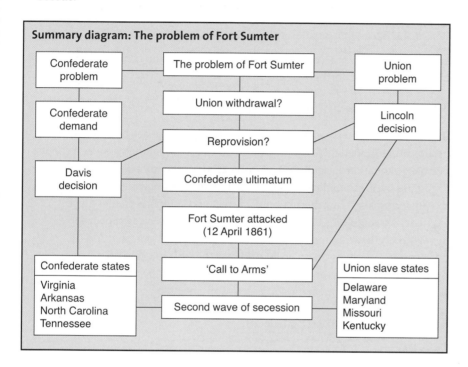

Summary diagram: The problem of Fort Sumter

6 Key debate

▶ *Why did civil war break out in 1861?*

In March 1865, Lincoln, in his second inaugural address, presented a succinct explanation of how and why the war came:

On the occasion corresponding this four years ago all thoughts were anxiously directed to an impending civil war …

One eighth of the whole population was coloured slaves, not distributed generally over the Union, but localised in the southern part of it. These slaves constituted a peculiar and powerful interest. All knew that this interest was somehow the cause of the war. To strengthen, perpetuate, and extend this interest was the object for which the insurgents would rend the Union even by war, while the government claimed no right to do more than to restrict the territorial enlargement of it.

For 50 years after the war, few northern historians dissented from this view. However, Jefferson Davis saw things differently. He insisted in his memoirs that the southern states had fought solely:

> *for the defense of an inherent, unalienable right … to withdraw from a Union which they had, as sovereign communities, voluntarily entered … The existence of African servitude was in no way the cause of the conflict, but only an incident.*

This explanation was accepted by many southerners, who continued to view the conflict as a war of northern aggression.

The progressive interpretation

In the 1920s, 'progressive' historians, convinced that clashes between interest groups underpinned most events in history, claimed that the war was a contest between plantation agriculture and **industrialising capitalism**. According to progressives, economic issues (such as the tariff) were what really divided the power-brokers – northern manufacturers and southern planters. The Confederacy could thus be seen as fighting for the preservation of a stable, **agrarian civilisation** in the face of the grasping ambitions of northern businessmen. Perhaps it was no coincidence that this interpretation emerged during much the same period as ***Gone With the Wind*** became one of the most popular literary and cinematic successes of all time.

The revisionist interpretation

EXTRACT 1

From 'A Blundering Generation' by James G. Randall, in *The Causes of the Civil War*, edited by Kenneth M. Stampp, Touchstone, 1991, p. 124.

Let one take all the factors traditionally presented – the Sumter maneuver, the election of Lincoln, abolitionism, slavery in Kansas, pre-war objections to the Union, cultural and economic differences, etc. – and it will be seen that only by a kind of false display could any of these issues or all of them together, be said to have caused the war if one omits the elements of emotional unreason and overbold leadership. If one word or phrase were selected to account for the war, that word would not be slavery, or economic grievance, or state rights, or diverse civilizations. It would have to be such a word as fanaticism (on both sides), misunderstandings, misrepresentation, or perhaps politics.

By the 1940s, revisionist historians denied that sectional conflicts, whether over slavery, state rights or industry versus agriculture, were genuinely divisive. The differences between North and South, wrote revisionist historian Avery Craven, were 'no greater than those existing at different times between East and West'. In the revisionist view, far more united than divided the two sections: sectional

KEY TERMS

Industrialising capitalism
A society in which industry and big business are developing.

Agrarian civilisation An advanced and sophisticated society based on farming.

Gone With the Wind
A novel, written by Margaret Mitchell (a southerner), published in 1936. It sold over 10 million copies and was soon made into a successful film. Both book and film suggested that the pre-war South was a civilised society.

quarrels could and should have been accommodated peacefully. Far from being irrepressible, the war was brought on by extremists on both sides: rabble-rousing abolitionists and fire-eaters. The passions they aroused got out of hand because politicians, lacking the skill of previous generations, failed to find a compromise. The result was an unnecessary war.

The importance of slavery

EXTRACT 2

From 'The Inevitability of Violence' by Arthur Schlesinger, Jr, in *The Causes of the Civil War*, edited by Kenneth M. Stampp, Touchstone, 1991, p. 164.

The problem [of slavery] in America was peculiarly recalcitrant. The schemes for gradual emancipation got nowhere. Neither internal reform nor economic emancipation contained much promise for a peaceful solution. The hard fact, indeed, is that the revisionists have not tried seriously to describe the policies by which the slavery problem could have been peacefully resolved. They have resorted instead to broad affirmations of faith; if only the conflict could have been staved off long enough, then somehow, somewhere, we could have worked something out. It is legitimate, I think, to ask how? where? what? – at least, if these affirmations of faith are to be used as the premise for castigating the unhappy men who had the practical responsibility for finding solutions and failed.

> Which one of Extracts 1 and 2 provides the more convincing interpretation of the cause of the Civil War?

Historians have now come full circle. The progressive and revisionist schools are currently dormant, if not dead. Lincoln's view that slavery was 'somehow' the cause of the war is generally accepted. While the Confederacy might claim its justification to be the protection of state rights, in truth, it was one state right – the right to preserve slavery – that impelled the Confederate states' separation. Slavery defined the South, permeating almost every aspect of its life. The market value of the South's 4 million slaves in 1860 was $3 billion – more than the value of land and cotton. Slavery, moreover, was more than an economic system. It was a means of maintaining racial control and white supremacy. While only a quarter of southern whites owned slaves in 1860, the vast majority of non-slaveholding whites supported slavery.

The rise of militant abolitionism increased North–South tension. Although abolitionists did not get far with their message of racial equality, the belief that slavery was unjust and obsolete entered mainstream northern politics. Convinced that a Slave Power conspiracy was at work, northerners came to support a Republican Party pledged to stop slavery expansion. Convinced that a Slave Power conspiracy was at work, northerners came to support the Republican Party, which was pledged to stop slavery expansion. For many southerners the election of Lincoln was the last straw – an affront to their honour.

The importance of nationalism

In 1861, most northerners fought to save the Union, not to end slavery. Confederate states fought to create a new nation. Thus, nationalism became the central issue. Pre-1860 most southerners saw themselves as loyal Americans; fire-eaters were a distinct minority. The creation of the Confederacy was a refuge to which many southerners felt driven, not a national destiny that they eagerly embraced. The Civil War did more to produce southern nationalism than southern nationalism did to produce war. In so far as there was a sense of southern-ness in 1861, it had arisen because of slavery.

Who was to blame?

With hindsight, it is clear that southerners got things wrong. Slavery was not in immediate peril in 1860–1. There was little Lincoln could do to threaten it, even if he was so inclined. In fact, he was prepared to make some concessions to the South. From November 1860 to April 1861 Lincoln acted reasonably and rationally.

The same cannot be said for southerners and their leaders. The South did not have to secede. The maintenance of slavery did not require the creation of a southern nation. For much of the pre-war period most southerners regarded the fire-eaters as quasi-lunatics. In the emotionally charged atmosphere of 1860–1, lunatic ideas – not so much the lunatics themselves – took over the South. Secession was a reckless decision. Some southerners at the time realised that it would mean war – and that war would probably result in Confederate defeat and the end of slavery. The North, so much stronger in terms of population and industry, was always likely to win. The fact that this was not obvious to most southerners is symptomatic of the hysteria that swept the South in 1860–1. Southerners picked the quarrel. They fired the first shots. And they suffered the consequences.

Chapter summary

Southerners deeply resented the election of Republican presidential candidate Abraham Lincoln in November 1860. In December 1860, South Carolina seceded from the Union; six other states, Mississippi, Florida, Alabama, Georgia, Louisiana and Texas, followed South Carolina's action. In February 1861 these states created the Confederacy, headed by Jefferson Davis. Politicians in the North and upper South desperately sought a compromise, to no avail. Abraham Lincoln was prepared to make some concessions to the South but the Confederate states had no wish to rejoin the Union. The Confederacy's attack on Fort Sumter led to the outbreak of civil war in April 1861. Four more states – Virginia, Arkansas, North Carolina and Tennessee – now joined the Confederacy. Lincoln, a committed Unionist, was determined to bring the Confederate states back into the Union fold.

Refresher questions

Use these questions to remind yourself of the key material covered in this chapter.

1 Did Democratic division make Republican success inevitable?

2 Why did the Republicans choose Lincoln?

3 Why did Lincoln win in November 1860?

4 Why did the lower South states secede?

5 How did the lower states secede?

6 Was secession a Slave Power conspiracy?

7 Why did the upper South states not join the Confederacy in February 1861?

8 Could and should a compromise have been found in 1860–1?

9 To what extent was Lincoln prepared to compromise?

10 Why was Fort Sumter a problem?

11 Did Lincoln deliberately manoeuvre the Confederacy into war?

12 Why did four upper South states now secede?

13 Who was to blame for the Civil War?

 Question practice

ESSAY QUESTIONS

1 'The election of a Republican president was the main reason for the outbreak of the Civil War.' Explain why you agree or disagree with this view.

2 How successful was Lincoln in his handling of events from November 1860 to April 1861?

3 Assess the reasons why the lower South seceded in early 1861 and the upper South did not.

4 How important was slavery in causing the Civil War?

INTERPRETATION QUESTION

1 Read the interpretation and then answer the question that follows: 'If it existed at all, the power to halt the progress of secession in 1861 rested with the Republicans, but they were not ready to make the kind of dramatic and concerted effort that the crisis demanded.' (David Potter, *The Impending Crisis 1848–1861*, Harper & Row, 1976.) Evaluate the strengths and limitations of this interpretation, making reference to other interpretations that you have studied.

SOURCE ANALYSIS QUESTIONS

1 With reference to Sources 1 and 2 on **page 112**, and your understanding of the historical context, which of these two sources is more valuable in explaining why it proved impossible to reach a compromise between North and South in early 1861?

2 With reference to Sources 1, 2 and 3 on **page 112**, and your understanding of the historical context, assess the value of these sources to a historian studying the causes of the Civil War.

SOURCE 1

Part of the Confederate President's inauguration speech, delivered on 18 February 1861 in Montgomery.

We have entered upon the career of independence, and it must be inflexibly pursued. Through many years of controversy with our late associates of the Northern States, we have vainly endeavored to secure tranquility and obtain respect for the rights to which we were entitled. As a necessity, not a choice, we have resorted to the remedy of separation, and henceforth our energies must be directed to the conduct of our own affairs and the perpetuity of the Confederacy which we have formed. If a just perception of mutual interest shall permit us peaceably to pursue our separate political career, my most earnest desire will have been fulfilled. But if this be denied to us and the integrity of our territory and jurisdiction be assailed, it will but remain for us with firm resolve to appeal to arms and invoke the blessing of Providence on a just cause.

SOURCE 2

Part of President Abraham Lincoln's inauguration speech, delivered on 4 March 1861 in Washington, DC.

Plainly, the central idea of secession is the essence of anarchy. A majority, held in restraint by constitutional checks and limitations, and always changing easily, with deliberate changes of popular opinions and sentiments, is the only true sovereignty of a free people. Whoever rejects it does of necessity, fly to anarchy or to despotism. Unanimity is impossible: the rule of a minority, as a permanent arrangement, is wholly inadmissible; so that, rejecting the majority principle, anarchy, or despotism in some form, is all that is left …

I am loth to close. We are not enemies, but friends. We must not be enemies. Though passion may have strained, it must not break our bonds of affection. The mystic chords of memory, stretching from every battle-field, and patriot grave, to every living heart and hearthstone, all over this broad land, will yet swell the chorus of the Union, when again touched, as surely they will be, by the better angels of our nature.

SOURCE 3

From the *Boston Transcript*, March 1861. A northern newspaper questions the motives for secession, and fears the consequences.

Alleged grievances in regard to slavery were originally the causes for the separation of the cotton states; but the mask has been thrown off, and it is apparent that the people of the principal seceding states are now in favour of commercial independence. They dream that the centers of traffic can be changed from Northern to Southern ports. The merchants of New Orleans, Charleston and Savannah are possessed with the idea that New York, Boston and Philadelphia may be deprived in the future of their mercantile greatness by a revenue system verging upon free trade. If the Southern Confederation is allowed to carry out a policy by which only a very low duty is charged on imports, no doubt the business of the chief Northern cities will be seriously injured.

CHAPTER 5

War on the home and foreign fronts

With fewer people, far less industry and a less well-developed railway system, the odds were stacked heavily against the Confederacy. To fight – never mind to win – the war, southerners would need to make far greater sacrifices than northerners. The Union was always favourite to win. However, 'big battalions' do sometimes lose wars. Resources by themselves do not win wars; they need efficient management. How effective was the Union war effort? How well did the Confederacy manage the war? Did it lose the war at home rather than on the battlefield? Or did it lose it on the diplomatic front? This chapter will consider these questions by examining the following themes:

★ The Confederate war effort

★ Confederate opposition to the war

★ The Union war effort

★ Union opposition to the war

★ The international situation

Key dates

1861		*Trent* affair	1862	**July**	Introduction of the Internal Revenue Act in the Union
1862	**Feb.**	Legal Tender Act			
	April	Introduction of conscription by the Confederacy	1863	**July**	New York draft riots
	May	Homestead Act		**Sept.**	Laird rams crisis

1 The Confederate war effort

▶ *How effective was the Confederate war effort?*

The Confederacy had to create a new government from scratch. The key man was President Jefferson Davis. He remains a controversial figure. His vice-president, Stephens, thought him 'weak, timid, petulant, peevish, obstinate' and blamed him for practically everything that went wrong in the war. Historian David Potter (1960) saw Davis's performance as the most important reason why the Confederacy lost the war, claiming that if Davis and Lincoln had reversed roles, the Confederacy might well have won. It may be that these judgements are too harsh.

The case against Jefferson Davis

Certainly Davis had his failings. One of these was his inability to establish good working relationships with many of his colleagues. He quarrelled with military commanders and leading politicians and found it hard to work with men who enjoyed less than his full approval. Perhaps the high turnover in his cabinet is proof of his inability to cement firm relationships. In the course of the war he appointed no fewer than four secretaries of state and six secretaries of war.

Davis has also been blamed for meddling in the affairs of subordinates. Finding it hard to prioritise and to delegate, he got bogged down in detail. Indecision is seen as another of his failings; lengthy cabinet meetings often came to no conclusion. While some contemporaries accused Davis of having despotic tendencies, historians have criticised him for exercising his powers too sparingly. He has also been blamed for failing to communicate effectively. At a time when the Confederacy needed revolutionary inspiration, he is seen as being too conservative.

The case for Jefferson Davis

Davis did and does have his defenders. In 1861, unlike Lincoln, he came to the presidency with useful military and administrative experience. He had, from the outset, a more realistic view of the situation than most southerners. He never underestimated the Yankees (northerners) and expected a long struggle. Robert E. Lee praised Davis and said he could think of no one who could have done a better job. The fact that Davis appointed Lee says much for his military good sense. Despite later accusations, he did not overcommand his forces. To generals he trusted, like Lee, he gave considerable freedom.

Although he had long been a state rights advocate, Davis supported tough measures when necessary, even when these ran contrary to concerns about state rights and individual liberty. He promoted the Conscription Act in April 1862 (the first national conscription measure in US history), imposed **martial law** in areas threatened by Union invasion, supported the **impressment of supplies** needed by southern troops, and urged high taxes on cotton and slaves.

As the war went on, he forced himself to become a more public figure, making several tours of the South to try to rekindle flagging faith. He probably did as much as anyone could to hold together the Confederacy. Few have questioned his dedication to the rebel cause or the intense work he put into a difficult job, the stress of which increasingly took its toll. Far from his performance contributing to Confederate defeat, it may be that his leadership ensured that the Confederacy held out for as long as it did.

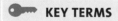 **KEY TERMS**

Martial law The suspension of ordinary administration and policing and, in its place, the exercise of military power.

Impressment of supplies Confiscation of goods.

Davis's cabinet

In all, Davis made sixteen appointments to head the six cabinet departments. Judah Benjamin accounted for three of these as he was appointed, in succession, to justice, war and state. A brilliant lawyer, he owed his survival to his ability and to his close relationship with Davis; no other adviser had his ear so often or so influentially. Benjamin, Stephen Mallory (navy) and John Reagan (postmaster general) served in the cabinet from start to finish.

The high turnover in the war and state departments resulted not from feuds between Davis and his secretaries, but from criticisms in the Confederate Congress that sometimes forced Davis to accept resignations. Benjamin was usually prepared to take the blame for events, if by so doing he sheltered Davis. Davis's cabinet met frequently and deliberated for hours. He usually heeded the advice he was given. For the most part he left his secretaries to get on with running their departments, involving himself only in the detailed decision making of the war department.

Most of the secretaries were capable men and government operations functioned reasonably smoothly for much of the war. The war department, with over 57,000 civilian employees at its height, was easily the largest office. The longest serving war secretary was James Seddon (November 1862–February 1865). Energetic and clear-thinking, Seddon, aided by Assistant Secretary John Campbell, oversaw the myriad details of running the war.

The Confederate Congress

Congressmen in the Provisional Congress (which met in 1861–2) were selected by their state legislatures. After this, there were two popularly elected Congresses, the first from 1862 to 1864, the second from 1864 to 1865, each consisting of a House and Senate.

Of the 267 men who served as Confederate Congressmen, about a third had sat in the US Congress. There was no two-party system. Men who had once been political enemies tried to present a united front. It may be, however, that the absence of an 'official' opposition resulted in less channelling of political activity and more squabbling. Davis, moreover, had no party organisation to mobilise support or to help him to formulate legislative policy and guide bills through Congress.

The Confederate Congress often found itself on the horns of a dilemma. While wanting to pass measures that would ensure victory, it was aware of its 'sacred heritage' to preserve state rights. These two principles often clashed.

In 1861–2 most Congressmen rallied round Davis; not to do so smacked of treason. Accordingly, the administration's measures, even those seen as draconian and anti-state rights, passed almost intact. However, as morale deteriorated under the impact of military setbacks, inflation and terrible casualty lists, opposition grew, both inside and outside Congress. This was reflected in the 1863 Congressional elections. Almost 40 per cent of the members of the second Congress were new to that body and many were opposed to Davis. His opponents defy easy categorisation. Some held extreme state rights views; others simply disagreed with the way the war was being waged. A small minority wanted peace. Not surprisingly, the 'opposition' never formed a cohesive voting block. Thus, there was no major rift between Congress and Davis.

State rights

To wage a successful war, the Confederacy needed the full cooperation of all its states. It also needed a central government strong enough to make the most of the South's resources. Some state leaders were not keen to concede too much power to the Confederate capital, Richmond. Appealing to the principle of state rights (for which they had seceded), they resisted many of the efforts of Davis's administration to centralise the running of the war effort. Governors Joseph Brown of Georgia and Zebulon Vance of North Carolina are often blamed for not working for the common cause. Brown, for example, opposed conscription and exempted thousands of Georgians from the draft by enrolling them in bogus state militia units.

In reality, however, most state governments cooperated effectively with Davis (see below). All the 28 men who served as state governors, including Brown and Vance, were committed to the Confederacy. As commanders-in-chief of their states, they had more power in war than in peace and were not averse to using this power. They initiated most of the necessary legislation at state level, **impressing** slaves and even declaring martial law. As a result, they often found themselves vying more with their own state legislatures than with Richmond. Usually they got their legislatures to comply with their actions.

'Died of democracy'?

In 1862 Davis boasted that, in contrast to the Union, 'there has been no act on our part to impair personal liberty or the freedom of speech, of thought or of the press'. Protecting individual rights might seem an important aim (albeit an unusual one for a state whose cornerstone was slavery). However, historian David Donald has claimed that concern for individual liberties cost the South the war. Unwilling to take tough action against internal dissent, Donald thinks the Confederacy 'died of democracy'. Donald's argument is not convincing. The notion that Davis could have created a government machine that could have suppressed **civil liberties** – and that if it had done so it might have triumphed – is nonsense. Davis, like most southerners, was fighting for what he saw as traditional American values; he could not easily abandon those values. Such action would have alienated the public whose support was essential.

Donald's supposition that the Confederacy allowed total individual freedom is also mistaken. In 1862 Congress authorised Davis to declare martial law in areas

KEY TERMS

Impressing Forcing into government service.

Civil liberties The rights of individuals.

threatened by the enemy and, given the widespread opposition to conscription, allowed him to suspend the **writ of habeas corpus** in order that **draft evaders** might be apprehended. Nor was there total freedom of speech. Although there was no specific legislation, public pressures that had long stifled discussion about slavery generally succeeded in imposing loyalty to the Confederacy. Opposition newspapers could find their presses destroyed by **vigilantes**. In short, it is unlikely that the preservation of basic freedoms, in so far as they were preserved, had more than a marginal impact on the Confederacy's demise.

Voluntary associations

Much of what was achieved in the Confederacy was due more to local initiative than to government orders:

- Men who led the local community were likely to lead either on the battlefield or on the home front. Planters often organised and outfitted regiments with their own money.
- In 1861 most states relied on local communities to supply the troops with basic necessities.
- Clergymen played an important role, preaching and writing in defence of the Confederacy.
- Women's groups made clothing, flags and other materials for the troops, and tried to feed the poor and help orphans.

Financing the war

The Confederacy was always likely to find it difficult to finance a long war. It had few **gold reserves** and the Union blockade made it difficult to sell cotton and to raise money from tariffs. Taxes on income, profits and property, levied in 1863, were unpopular, difficult to administer and failed to bring in sufficient revenue. While generally supporting the Confederate government, most state governments (which actually raised the taxes) were often reluctant to send money to Richmond. Rather than tax their citizens, states often borrowed money or printed it in the form of state notes to pay their dues, thus worsening **inflationary pressures**.

In 1863, in an effort to feed southern troops, Congress passed the Impressment Act, allowing the seizure of goods to support the armies at the front line, and the Taxation-in-kind Act, authorising government agents to collect ten per cent of produce from all farmers. Davis, while accepting the unfairness of the measures, thought them justified by 'absolute necessity'. He may have been right. Taxation-in-kind did help to supply rebel armies during the final two years of the war.

Only eight per cent of the Confederacy's income was derived from taxes. This meant it had to raise money in other ways. In February 1861, Congress allowed Treasury Secretary Christopher Memminger to raise $15 million in bonds and stock certificates. Guaranteed with cotton, there were initially many buyers,

KEY TERMS

Writ of habeas corpus The right of a prisoner to know why he or she has been arrested.

Draft evaders Those who avoided conscription.

Vigilantes Self-appointed and unofficial police.

Gold reserves Gold bullion held by a country. This gold usually underpins the country's currency.

Inflationary pressure An undue increase in the quantity of money in circulation. The result is that the value of money goes down.

SOURCE A

To what extent is Source A likely to be a reliable source of evidence for food prices in the Confederacy?

Extract from the *Richmond Dispatch* newspaper, July 1863

The Results of Extortion and Speculation. – The state of affairs brought about by the speculating and extortion practiced upon the public cannot be better illustrated than by the following grocery bill for one week for a small family, in which the prices before the war and those of the present are compared:

1860		1863	
Bacon, 10 lbs. at 12$\frac{1}{2}$c	$1.25	Bacon, 10 lbs. at $1	$10.00
Flour, 30 lbs. at 5c	1.50	Flour, 30 lbs. at 12$\frac{1}{2}$c	3.75
Sugar, 5 lbs. at 8c	.40	Sugar, 5 lbs. at $1.15	5.75
Coffee, 4 lbs. at 12$\frac{1}{2}$c	.50	Coffee, 4 lbs. at $5	20.00
Tea (green), $\frac{1}{2}$ lb. at $1	.50	Tea (green), $\frac{1}{2}$ lb. at $16	8.00
Lard, 4 lbs. at 12$\frac{1}{2}$c	.50	Lard, 4 lbs. at $1	4.00
Butter, 3 lbs. at 25c	.75	Butter, 3 lbs. at $1.75	5.25
Meal, 1 pk. at 25c	.25	Meal, 1 pk. at $1	1.00
Candles, 2 lbs. at 15c	.30	Candles, 2 lbs. at $1.25	2.50
Soap, 5 lbs. at 10c	.50	Soap, 5 lbs. at $1.10	5.50
Pepper and salt (about)	.10	Pepper and salt (about)	2.50
Total	$6.55	Total	$68.25

Inflation in Richmond 1860–3.

both within the Confederacy and abroad. But after 1863, when the tide of battle turned against the Confederacy, European financiers – and southerners – were reluctant to risk loaning money to what seemed like a lost cause.

Given that the Confederacy was able to raise only one-third of its war costs through taxes, bonds and loans, Memminger had little option but to print vast amounts of Treasury paper money. Individual states, towns, banks and railway companies also issued paper notes. The result was serious inflation (see Source A above). By 1865 prices in the eastern Confederacy were over 5000 times the 1861 levels. This led to widespread suffering. Memminger's efforts to slow down inflation proved inadequate. Attempts to fix prices, for example, encouraged hoarding, thus exacerbating shortages of vital produce. Massive inflation and a spiralling debt forced Memminger to resign in 1864. His successor, George Trenholm, tried to reduce the amount of money in circulation but by 1864–5 the Confederacy's financial situation was desperate. Given that inflation helped to erode southern morale, it is not surprising that Memminger has often been singled out for blame. In fairness, it is hard to see what else he could have done. Shortages of basic commodities, resulting from the breakdown of the railway system and from the blockade, meant that inflation was inevitable.

The economic impact of the war

In many respects, Davis's government acted forcefully to place the South's economy on a war footing and to expand its industrial base. This effort is usually known as '**Confederate socialism**'. It was not totally successful. Nor should it be exaggerated. Short of trained personnel, Richmond was not up to the task of carrying out many of its ambitious schemes. In the final analysis, most of what was achieved was the result of private initiative, not Confederate order. Davis's government mainly confined its activities to the military sphere. Even here, private enterprise was crucial. The Tredegar Ironworks at Richmond, the South's main ordnance producer, remained in private control.

Government efforts to manage the economy

Before the war most southerners took the view that economic development was beyond the proper scope of the central government's powers. But after 1861 officials intruded into almost every aspect of economic life as regulations multiplied to manage conscription, manufacturing and transportation. The result was that the Richmond government played a much greater role in economic matters than Lincoln's government did in the North.

The **Ordnance Bureau**, ably led by Josiah Gorgas, a northerner who stayed loyal to his southern wife rather than to Pennsylvania, played a crucial role. By 1863 there were enough arsenals, factories and gunpowder works in the South to keep its armies supplied with the basic tools of war. The War Department also assumed increasing control over the South's railway system. Companies were required to share spare parts and rolling stock. Railway schedules were regulated. **Draft exemptions** were issued to ensure that railway companies had skilled workers.

Steps were taken to regulate foreign trade. In 1863 a law required all blockade-runners to carry, as at least one-third of their cargo, cotton out and war supplies in. In 1864 the importation of luxury goods without a special permit was banned. **Blockade running** was remarkably successful. Hundreds of ships – some state owned, some Confederate government owned, but most owned by private individuals from the Confederacy and Britain (where most were built) – were involved. The most popular routes were from Nassau in the Bahamas to Charleston and from Bermuda to Wilmington. Given the advantage of surprise and speed, blockade-runners stood a 75 per cent chance of success – a success rate which continued until the final months of the war. Overall, the South imported 60 per cent of its small arms, 75 per cent of its **saltpetre** and nearly all its paper for making cartridges.

State governments played an important economic role. Most tried to regulate the distribution of scarce goods, such as salt. Successful efforts were also made

KEY TERMS

Confederate socialism
The Richmond government's attempts to control the Confederate economy.

Ordnance Bureau
The government agency responsible for acquiring war materials.

Draft exemptions Workers in key industries, such as the railways, did not have to serve in the armed forces.

Blockade running
Attempts by ships to avoid the Union navy's blockade of Confederate ports.

Saltpetre Potassium nitrate – an essential ingredient of gunpowder.

to ensure that farmers shifted from cotton to food production. There was a reduction in the cotton crop, from over 4 million bales in 1861 to only 300,000 bales in 1864.

Confederate government economic failure

There were steps that the Confederate government could have taken to limit the economic effects of the war:

- More could have been done to supervise the railway system which, handicapped by shortages of materials and labour, slowly collapsed. Thus, raw materials destined for factories and foodstuffs bound for armies or towns were often left at depots for want of transport.
- Cotton might have been used to better effect, especially early in the war. The embargo on cotton exports, supported if not officially sanctioned by Davis, had two aims: to ensure that planters turned to food production, and to create a cotton scarcity that might lead to foreign recognition (see page 136). More food was produced but the embargo failed to have much impact on Britain (see page 135). Had cotton been exported in 1861 (when the Union blockade was weak), money from the proceeds could have been used to buy vital war supplies. Instead, southern agents in Europe were handicapped by a lack of funds and often outbid by Union competitors.
- The Confederate government could have taken action sooner to control shipments on the blockade-runners. Before 1863, many blockade-runners were more concerned with making money than with helping the Confederacy, often bringing in luxury goods rather than essentials. By the time Davis's government got its blockade-running act together, many southern ports had been captured.
- Given that many plantations turned to food production, which was less labour intensive than cotton growing, more slaves could have been impressed into government service and used for non-combat labour. Although slaves were impressed by state governments, planter political power ensured that Congress did not authorise Confederate impressment of slaves until 1863–4.

By 1865 the Confederate economy was near collapse. Machinery was wearing out and could not be replaced. Sources of raw materials were lost as Union forces took over large areas of the South. The breakdown of the railway system, much of which was destroyed by Union armies, proved decisive in the Confederacy's final demise.

The social impact

The Confederacy succeeded in mobilising about 900,000 men – over 40 per cent of its white males of fighting age. This had important implications for all aspects of southern life, particularly on the role of women and slaves.

Confederate women

The war had a negative effect on the lives of most southern women:

- Wives of ordinary farmers had to work even longer hours to provide enough food for their families. They also had to practise strict domestic economy to conserve scarce resources.
- Wives of planters had to manage plantations and control restless slaves. In towns, women took over jobs that had been done by men.
- Most women lost loved ones – husbands, sons, fathers and brothers.

Without female support, the Confederacy would soon have collapsed. By mid-1862 it is true that fewer women were willingly sending their men off to war. Some attempted to prevent their being drafted or even encouraged desertion. Nevertheless, until the winter of 1864–5, when the Confederacy was on the point of collapse, most women seemed to have remained committed to the rebel cause for which they were willing to accept huge sacrifice.

The impact of the war on slavery

The war affected the institution of slavery (see pages 193–4). Although there was no slave revolt, many slaves fled their plantations whenever it was safe to do so. Historian James Roark (1977), claims that, 'Slavery did not explode; it disintegrated … eroded plantation by plantation, often slave by slave, like slabs of earth slipping into a southern stream.' By 1864–5, slave owners sometimes had to negotiate with their slaves in order to get them to work.

Demoralisation

Shortages of basic commodities, inflation and impressment had a demoralising effect on all parts of the South. Some areas were also devastated by Union troops. Sherman's marches through Georgia and the Carolinas in 1864–5 (see pages 170–2) left a huge swathe of destruction.

Refugees flooded the South as whites fled contesting armies. In an effort to tackle the problem of refugees, and poverty in general, Confederate and state governments, local and town authorities, plus private charities and wealthy individuals became involved in huge relief efforts. Yet by the winter of 1864–5 the scale of the problem was so great that it overwhelmed the relief activities.

Summary diagram: The Confederate war effort

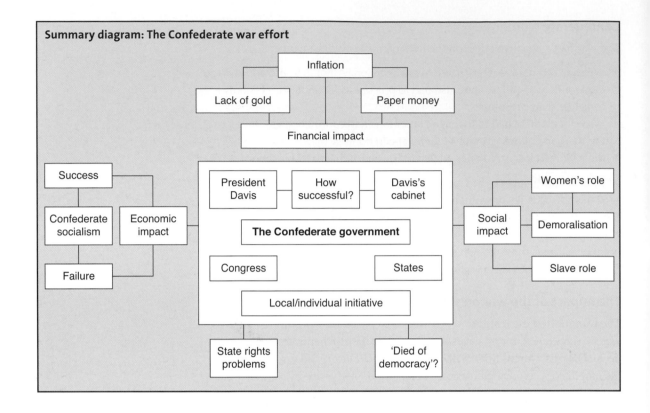

2 Confederate opposition to the war

▶ *Did internal opposition bring about Confederate defeat?*

Many non-slaveholders in upland areas of the South opposed secession from the start. There was so much support for the Union in East Tennessee and West Virginia that both areas effectively seceded from the Confederacy. This was a substantial drain on southern manpower; worse still was the fact that some 60,000 white men from these areas, and a further 30,000 from other southern states, joined the Union army. Nevertheless, most white southerners rallied to the Confederate cause in 1861; pro-Union sympathisers were a small minority.

Opposition grew as the war progressed. The introduction of conscription in 1862 was a major cause. Lukewarm southerners now faced a choice of military service or overt opposition. As the war ground on, organised resistance to conscription intensified, especially in the mountain regions of North Carolina and Alabama. Armed men joined together to help one another in eluding the enrolment officers and to fight them off when necessary. Bands of draft evaders and deserters dominated some areas of the South.

'A rich man's war and a poor man's fight'?

Conscription may have fuelled class conflict. Many ordinary farmers resented the fact that rich southerners could avoid military service by either hiring substitutes or exempting themselves because they held a managerial role on a plantation with twenty slaves or more. In reality, few wealthy southerners shirked military duty; indeed, they were more likely to fight and die than poor southerners. But the perception of 'a rich man's war and a poor man's fight' rankled. Significant numbers of non-slaveholders became restive and critical of the (perceived) planter-led government.

It may be that the opposition was not essentially 'class' based. It was strongest in upland areas where there had been limited support for secession. It is thus difficult to separate regional from class divisions. In truth, most – non-slaveholding – southerners remained committed to the Confederate cause until the end. Hatred of slaveholders and class resentment were not the main reasons why the loyalty of 'plain folk' to the Confederacy wavered. Southerners' will to fight faded only after they had been battered into submission by a stronger military force.

Confederate morale in 1863

From an Alabama newspaper, 1863

Wives! Mothers! Beware what you write. A thoughtless and imprudent letter may lead to discontent, desertion.

A southern wife to her soldier-husband in 1863

Our son is lying at death's door ... He is raving distracted. His earnest calls for Pa almost breaks my heart. John come if you can.

A letter received by a soldier in the 64th North Carolina Volunteers, 1863

The people is all turning Union here since the Yankees has got Vicksburg. I want you to come home as soon as you can.

A woman, writing to the governor of North Carolina in 1863

A crowd of we Poor women went to Greenesborough yesterday for something to eat as we had not a mouthful of meet nor bread in my house what did they do but put us in gail in plase of giving us aney thing to eat.. I have 6 little children and my husband is in the armey and what am I to do?

Confederate effort and morale

Southern morale seems to have been high in the first two years of the war, helped by a good harvest in 1861 and military success. However, defeats, huge casualties and growing hardship on the domestic front damaged morale.

There was an understandable, if not necessarily justified, loss of faith in the Confederate leadership. Certainly Davis's government made mistakes. But arguably it was no more mistake prone than Lincoln's government. Nor were southerners less dedicated than Yankees. Most fought hard and long for their new nation, enduring far more hardship than northerners. Although ultimately not equal to the challenge, the Confederacy's efforts on the home front were, in most respects, better than might have been expected. The bitter truth was that most of its domestic problems were insurmountable.

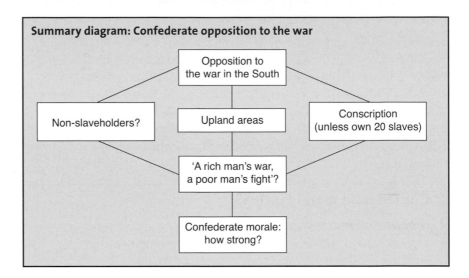

Summary diagram: Confederate opposition to the war

Opposition to the war in the South

Non-slaveholders?

Upland areas

Conscription (unless own 20 slaves)

'A rich man's war, a poor man's fight'?

Confederate morale: how strong?

③ The Union war effort

▶ *How effective was Lincoln's administration?*

Unlike the Confederacy, the Union did not have to start a government apparatus from scratch. How well the Union managed the war would largely depend upon the effectiveness of President Abraham Lincoln. Lincoln is usually regarded as one of the USA's greatest presidents. Contemporaries would have been staggered by this opinion. So unpopular was he in the summer of 1864 that it seemed he would not be re-elected president. How good a leader was he?

The case against Lincoln

Pre-1861 Lincoln had had little administrative experience. He was to prove himself a poor bureaucrat and his small staff did not provide much assistance. Accordingly, the machinery of government often became clogged. Moreover, it is possible to depict Lincoln as essentially a devious politician – a man who spent hours each day dealing with political matters rather than devoting time to the war effort. Arguably, he deserves little credit for foreign policy (handled by Seward), financial measures (handled by Chase) or economic matters (which were left to Congress). It is even debatable to what extent Lincoln deserves his reputation as the 'Great Emancipator' (see pages 184–9).

Lincoln can also be accused of meddling and incompetence, especially in military matters. His choice of commanders of the army of the Potomac down to 1863 – McDowell, McClellan, Pope, McClellan (again), Burnside and Hooker – was uninspired.

Democrats accused Lincoln of acting tyrannically. In 1862 he suspended the writ of habeas corpus: anyone could be imprisoned by military authority, for impeding conscription, or affording aid or comfort to the enemy. A horde of petty functionaries could decide who was loyal and who was not. Some were overzealous; others simply settled old scores. Over 40,000 people were subject to arbitrary arrest.

Arguably, Lincoln had an easier task than Davis. The Union was always favourite to win regardless of who was president. Cynics might claim that it was his assassination (see page 197), rather than his leadership, which assured Lincoln's reputation.

The case for Lincoln

It is far easier to praise Lincoln than to criticise him. Most historians recognise his resilience, his diligence, his tenacity, his honesty, his sense of humour, his unassuming style and his deceptive simplicity. He made a profound impression on those who knew him well, not least the members of his own cabinet. Generally, he selected able men and delegated well, playing his hunches, and giving those men who were successful free rein. Perhaps Lincoln's most important role was in shaping national strategy. With a mystical faith in the Union, he was determined to fight to the end to preserve it. One of his strengths was his ability to articulate the Union's war aims (see Source B).

SOURCE B

From Lincoln's second message to Congress, 1 December 1862, quoted in Mark E. Neely Jr, *The Last Best Hope of Earth*, Harvard University Press, 1993, p. 158.

Fellow-citizens, we cannot escape history. We of this Congress and this administration, will be remembered in spite of ourselves … The fiery trial through which we pass will light us down in honour or dishonour to the latest generation … We know how to save the Union. The world knows we do know how to save it. … In giving freedom to the slave, we assure freedom to the free – honourable alike in what we give, and what we preserve. We shall nobly save or meanly lose the last, best hope of earth. Other means may succeed; this could not fail. The way is plain, peaceful, generous, just – a way which, if followed, the world will forever applaud, and God must forever bless.

What does Source B show regarding
a) Lincoln's powers of oratory and b) his war aims?

Lincoln was certainly a consummate politician, keeping in touch with public opinion. The time devoted to matters of patronage and party organisation was time well spent. It ensured that there were many loyal men within both his party and the government, a fact that served him well in 1864.

Lincoln's man-management skills ensured that he did not really alienate any member of his cabinet. Historian James McPherson writes: 'The President's unique blend of firmness and deference, the iron fist of decision clothed in the velvet glove of humour and tact, enabled him to dominate his subordinates without the appearance of domination.' Lincoln's main preoccupations throughout his presidency were military matters and race; he rarely focused hard on other issues. There was no need, for example, to involve himself in economic matters. The Republican-controlled Congress enacted the party's economic programme – a programme that he fully supported. He generally worked well with Congress. His views tended to represent the middle ground but he kept open lines of communication with both the radical and conservative wings of his party. Sensitive to the pulse of public opinion, he was concerned with what might – rather than what should – be achieved. His exquisite sense of political timing and his awareness of what was politically possible helped the Union to win the war and free the slaves.

As commander-in-chief, Lincoln did not shirk responsibility. Taking the view that waging war was essentially an executive function, he believed that he must use his powers to best effect. Where no precedent existed, he was prepared to improvise, stretching the authority of his office beyond any previous practice. In April 1861, for example, he called for troops, proclaimed a blockade of the South and ordered military spending of $2 million without Congressional approval.

Lincoln and civil liberty

Lincoln was totally committed to 'government of the people, by the people, for the people'. Nevertheless, he was willing to suspend civil liberties, including both freedom of speech and freedom of the press. Inevitably, he came into conflict with both Congress and the Supreme Court over the legality of some of his actions. This does not seem to have unduly worried him. His main concern was to win the war. Arguably, Lincoln's vigorous policies in 1861 helped to keep the border states in the Union. Military rather than political goals were foremost in his mind when he allowed the restriction of civil liberties. Most of those imprisoned without trial came from states such as Missouri, which had many southern sympathisers. Given the grim reality of **guerrilla war**, martial law was essential.

Elsewhere, moderation was usually the norm. Many of those arrested – Confederate defectors, blockade-runners, draft dodgers – would have been arrested whether the writ of habeas corpus had been suspended or not. Moreover, those who were arbitrarily arrested usually found themselves being arbitrarily released. Relatively few were brought to trial. Arrests rarely involved

KEY TERM

Guerrilla war Warfare by which small units harass conventional armies.

Democrat politicians or newspaper editors. Overall, Lincoln remained faithful to the spirit, if not always the letter, of the Constitution. Later generations have generally approved – even applauded – the way in which he tackled difficult issues of civil liberties.

Lincoln and military matters

Despite some initial insecurity about military matters, Lincoln was very much involved in the conduct of the war, cajoling, praising and urging his generals forward. Some historians think that he showed considerable military talent, with an ability to concentrate on the wider issues rather than getting bogged down in matters of detail. As early as January 1862 he said: 'I state my general idea of this war to be that we have the greater numbers and the enemy has the greater facility of concentrating forces upon points of collision; that we must fail, unless we can find some way of making our advantage an overmatch for his; and that this can only be done by menacing him with superior forces at different points, at the same time.' To Lincoln's chagrin, Union generals proved unable to carry out such a strategy until 1864–5.

Some of Lincoln's appointments, if not wise militarily, made sense politically. Appointing generals who represented important ethnic, regional and political constituencies ensured that the North remained united. Ultimately his military appointments gave the Union the winning team of Grant and Sherman (see pages 165–72).

Conclusion

For four years Lincoln stuck at his job. He worked hard – from 7a.m. to 11p.m. most days – granting favours, distributing jobs, corresponding with friends and enemies, giving or listening to advice, accepting or rejecting proposals. Although often severely depressed, he kept going even when the war was going badly. Nothing kept him from his work, not even his own personal tragedies. (His youngest son died in 1862 and his wife was mentally unstable thereafter.) He learned from his mistakes and revealed real qualities of leadership.

Lincoln's cabinet

Lincoln's cabinet was far more stable than that of Davis, with most of the secretaries remaining at their posts for most of the war. Lincoln bothered little with the cabinet as such. He used the rare meetings as a sounding board to discuss the timing or language of statements he was about to issue or to get approval for actions he was about to take. The secretaries usually saw Lincoln individually rather than *en masse*. Within their departments, cabinet members performed well, working hard themselves and keeping their subordinates hard at work.

Secretary of State Seward was regarded as Lincoln's right-hand man. Salmon Chase, secretary of the treasury, was the main radical spokesman in the cabinet.

SOURCE C

The last photograph of Lincoln (April 1865).

? Compare the photograph in Source C with the photograph of Lincoln on page 79. How do you explain Lincoln's change of appearance?

? Given that Carpenter was not present when Lincoln read out the Emancipation Proclamation to his cabinet, how useful is Source D to historians?

Lincoln's first secretary of war, Simon Cameron, had a reputation for corruption before the war and this reputation quickly grew. In 1862 he was replaced by Edwin Stanton, an ex-Democrat, who proved himself efficient and incorruptible. Once a severe critic of Lincoln, Stanton became one of his closest advisors. Gideon Welles, secretary of the navy, served the Union well throughout the war. Postmaster Montgomery Blair came from one of the best known political families in the Union. On the conservative wing of the party, his father continued to own slaves until 1865. Caleb Smith, secretary of the interior, and Bates, the attorney general, played minor roles.

SOURCE D

An illustration after Francis Carpenter's famous painting of Lincoln and his cabinet. Treasury Secretary Chase stands to the left of Lincoln (who is reading the Emancipation Proclamation). Secretary of State Seward sits with legs crossed.

Congress

Depleted by the loss of its southern members, Congress was controlled by the Republicans throughout the war. In 1861 the House of Representatives had 105 Republicans, 43 Democrats and 28 'Unionists'. Of the 48 Senators, 31 were Republican. The Republicans retained control after the 1862 mid-term elections. Given the Republican dominance, Congress generally cooperated with Lincoln. While there was some conflict over the boundaries of executive and legislative power, Congress loyally provided the means for Lincoln to conduct the war.

Radical Republicans, the most energetic wing of the party, often blamed Lincoln for failing to prosecute the war more vigorously or to move against slavery more rapidly. However, the radicals were not a disciplined group. Nor did they always oppose Lincoln. When he wanted their support, he usually got it.

State government

State governments provided invaluable assistance to Lincoln, especially in raising troops. Most states were Republican controlled. Those that did fall under Democrat control did little to hinder the Union war effort.

Voluntary associations

Neither the federal nor state governments had the apparatus or traditions to manage all aspects of the war. Voluntary organisations helped to fill the gaps. The United States Sanitary Commission, for example, did much to help the Army Medical Bureau. Sanitary commissioners prowled Union camps and hospitals, insisting on better food and conditions. Thousands of women were the mainstay of the commission, knitting, wrapping bandages and raising funds.

Financing the war

In 1861 the Union (unlike the Confederacy) had an established Treasury, gold reserves and an assured source of revenue from tariffs. Nevertheless, northern financial structures were not ready for war, and over the winter of 1861–2 the whole northern banking system seemed near to collapse. Secretary Chase kept the Treasury afloat by raising loans and issuing bonds, in which ordinary citizens, as well as bankers, were encouraged to invest. One million northerners ended up owning shares in the national debt. Two-thirds of the Union's revenue was raised by loans and bonds. One-fifth was raised by taxes. An income tax, the first in US history, was enacted in 1861 and imposed a three per cent tax on annual incomes over $800. Far more important (it brought in ten times as much as the income tax) was the Internal Revenue Act (1862). This basically taxed everything.

Congress also approved an inflationary monetary policy. In 1862 the Legal Tender Act authorised the issuing of $150 million in paper currency, not redeemable in gold or silver. Ultimately 'greenback' notes to the value of $431 million were issued. The Legal Tender Act provided the Treasury with resources to pay its bills and restored investors' confidence sufficiently to make possible the sale of $500 million of new bonds. Linked to these measures were attempts to reform the banking system. Chase's ideas finally bore fruit in the 1863 and 1864 National Banking Acts. While the new national banks pumped paper money into the economy, a tax of ten per cent on state bank notes ensured that the Union was not awash with paper money. Inflation, over the course of the war, was only 80 per cent.

The economic impact of the war

After 1861, the Republicans were able to pass economic legislation, previously held up by Democratic opposition. The 1862 Homestead Act, for example, offered 160-acre (65-hectare) farms out west, free of charge, to settlers who worked on them for five years. Higher tariffs not only provided the government with extra revenue but also protected US industry from foreign competition. Generous railway subsidies were meted out. The most important railway development was the decision to build a transcontinental line from Omaha to San Francisco (see page 243).

By twentieth-century standards there was little assertion of federal power in the management of the wartime economy. There was no rationing, no attempt to control prices, wages and profits, and no central control of the railways. Although the US government was now a huge customer, businessmen made their own decisions and controlled their own production.

Union economic success

The northern economy, with its abundant raw materials, ready capital and technological expertise, was able to ensure that Union armies were well equipped and that civilians did not go short of basic commodities. It was not certain in 1861 that northern industry would meet the challenge. The loss of southern markets threatened disaster. However, the overall effect of the war, especially the need to feed, equip and arm the Union forces, is often seen as stimulating economic growth.

Production gains were especially notable in war-related industries such as canned food, shipbuilding and munitions. Railways made great profits. For the first time their full carrying capacity was utilised. The increased money supply ensured that manufacturers found it easier to pay off debts and secure loans for investment and expansion. The shortage of labour may have encouraged the introduction of new machinery in some industries. The war may also have resulted in businessmen adopting wider horizons and thinking in terms of millions (of bullets, boots, and so on) rather than thousands. Some men made fortunes from the war. Huge profits encouraged further expansion.

Farmers also benefited. Union forces had to be fed and there was a growing demand from abroad, particularly from Britain. Exports of wheat, corn, pork and beef doubled. The Union states grew more wheat in 1862–3 than the USA as a whole had grown in the previous record year of 1859, despite the fact that many farm boys were serving in the Union armies. The growth in production was due, in part, to the increased use of farm machinery, but mainly because more land was brought under cultivation – over 1 million hectares (2.5 million acres) between 1862 and 1864.

Union economic problems

The war's effects were not all positive:

- Some industries, not least the New England cotton mills, suffered hard times.
- The fact that so much of the labour force was drawn into the army may have slowed down industrial and agricultural growth.

- The war probably reduced immigration by some 1.3 million people, nearly twice the number lost by both sides in the war.
- According to some estimates, the combined effect of loss in immigration and military deaths reduced the population by 5.6 per cent from what it would have been without the war.
- Economic growth in the 1860s was slower (some claim) than in any other decade in the nineteenth century.
- If there was a shift to **mass production**, this was arguably a trend that was well under way before the war and one that was not particularly affected by it.

Conclusion

The North's economy grew, in spite, if not because, of the war. In March 1865, a New York newspaper reported: 'There never was a time in the history of New York when business prosperity was more general, when the demand for goods was greater … than within the last two or three years.' According to historian Peter Parish, 'The abiding impression [of the northern economy] is one of energy and enterprise, resilience and resource … The war was not the soil in which industrial growth took root, nor a blight which stunted it, but a very effective fertiliser.'

The social impact

In many ways life for most northerners during the war went on as usual. However, the fact that regiments were often made up of men from a single town or county could mean sudden calamity for a neighbourhood if that regiment suffered heavy casualties. The fact that so many men of military age left their homes to fight meant there were more job opportunities for women, who worked as teachers, in industry and in government service. However, the war did not bring women much closer to political or economic equality. They were not given the vote and after 1865 returned to their old roles.

There is some evidence that during the war the rich became richer while the poor became poorer. Some working men saw their real earnings drop as prices rose faster than wages. The result was labour unrest and some violent, albeit small-scale, strikes. However, some workers enjoyed rising wages resulting from a shortage of labour. Many working-class families also benefited from bounties and wages paid to soldiers who sent millions of dollars home. Overall, therefore, it is unlikely that there was a major rise in class tension.

In some areas, the war led to an increase in racial tensions. Some northerners resented fighting a war to free the slaves. Anti-black feeling was also fanned by job competition and the employment of black **strike breakers**. In 1863 there were race riots in a number of northern cities: Chicago, Buffalo and Boston. The most serious was in New York (see below).

The war initially led to a reduction in immigrant numbers: 92,000 in 1861–2 compared with 154,000 in 1860. But by 1863 there were over 176,000 immigrants

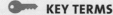

KEY TERMS

Mass production Making large quantities of goods by a standard mechanised process.

Strike breakers Workers employed to do the work of those on strike.

and by 1865 nearly 250,000; this was proof of the North's booming economy and also of the government's success in publicising opportunities and encouraging immigrants. Some immigrants, attracted by the high bounties, volunteered for the Union army. Others, by filling key jobs, helped the economy. The war may have helped the process of assimilation and possibly tamed anti-immigrant feeling. However, the assimilation process should not be exaggerated. Ethnic rivalry remained strong after 1865.

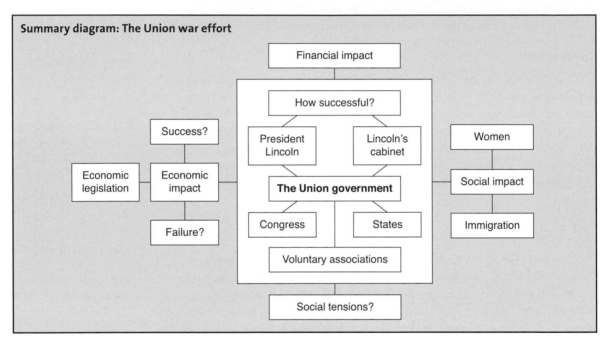

Summary diagram: The Union war effort

4 Union opposition to the war

▶ *How serious was internal opposition to the Union war effort?*

In 1861, leading northern Democrats like Senator Douglas called on all northerners to rally round Lincoln. Lincoln, aware of the need to maintain unity, promoted Democrats to his cabinet and to high military command. Some **War Democrats** threw in their lot totally with Lincoln. But as the war went on, Democratic opposition increased. Democrats disliked:

- the way the war was being handled
- Republican economic policies
- Lincoln's arbitrary measures
- efforts to end slavery.

Reflecting and exploiting northern racist views for all they were worth and capitalising on war weariness, the Democrats had some success in the 1862 mid-term elections.

 KEY TERM

War Democrats Those Democrats who were determined to see the war fought to a successful conclusion.

The Copperheads

Although many Democrats saw the conflict as a Republican war, most still wanted to restore the Union; pro-Confederate northerners were a small minority. This was not the way that many Republicans saw it. In the west, Republicans labelled their Democratic opponents 'Copperheads' (after a poisonous snake) and claimed that they belonged to subversive, pro-southern secret societies which planned to set up a Northwest Confederacy that would make peace with the South. Republican leaders realised that charges of treason could be used to discredit the Democrat party as a whole and could serve as an excuse to organise Union Leagues, which were Republican-led societies pledged to defend the Union.

SOURCE E

An 1863 cartoon from *Harper's Weekly* — a northern paper which supported Lincoln.

> What is the cartoon in Source E intending to depict?

Clement Vallandigham

Democrat dissent reached its height in early 1863 when Union military failures fostered a sense of defeatism. Some Democrats thought that the time had come to make peace. Clement Vallandigham, campaigning to become governor of Ohio, denounced the war and called on soldiers to desert. He was seeking to be made a martyr and a martyrdom of sorts duly followed. On the orders of General Burnside (whose political finesse was no more subtle than his military judgement, see page 159), Vallandigham was arrested in the middle of the night. Tried by a military tribunal, he was found guilty of treason and sentenced to imprisonment for the rest of the war. This led to a chorus of protest from outraged Democrats. Even some Republicans were appalled that a civilian had been tried and sentenced by a military court merely for making a speech.

Lincoln, while not liking what Burnside had done, saw no alternative but to support him. By discouraging enlistment and encouraging desertion, Vallandigham had broken the law. 'Must I shoot a simple-minded soldier-boy who deserts, while I must not touch a hair of a wiley agitator who induces him to desert?', mused Lincoln. 'I think that in such a case, to silence the agitator, and save the boy is not only constitutional, but withal a great mercy.' However, Lincoln was anxious to avoid making Vallandigham a martyr. Accordingly, he decided to banish him to the Confederacy for the duration of the war. Soon tiring of the South, Vallandigham moved to Canada, where he continued to conduct his campaign for governor of Ohio. But the upturn in Union military fortunes after July 1863 undermined his peace platform. Along with other pro-peace Democrats, he lost his election contest in 1863.

The New York draft riots

The most serious internal violence came in New York in July 1863. The New York riots followed the enforcement of the 1863 Conscription Act. New York's Democrat Governor, Horatio Seymour, whipped up opposition to the draft. When the names of the first draftees were drawn, a mob of mostly Irish workers attacked the recruiting station. The mob then went on the rampage, venting its fury on black people, who were blamed for the war. For several days New York was in chaos. Economic, ethnic, racial and religious factors all played a part in causing the riots. Lincoln moved quickly, sending in 20,000 troops to restore order. At least 120 people – mainly rioters – died in the process.

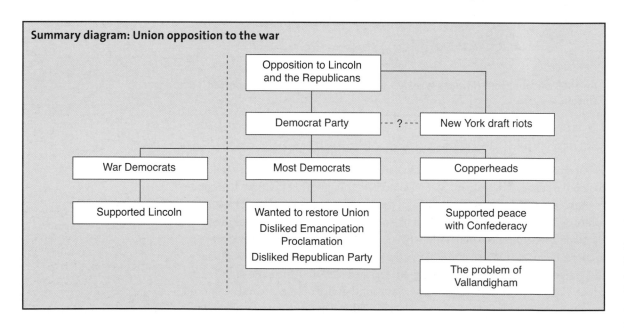

Summary diagram: Union opposition to the war

The international situation

▶ *Why did Britain not intervene in the war?*

Britain, given its great naval, economic, financial and imperial strength (including possession of Canada) was the key European power. Only Britain could mount a serious challenge to the Union. Realising from the outset that the Confederacy's best hope of success lay in Britain joining the war on its side, Jefferson Davis tried to secure British support. In May 1861, Confederate commissioners were sent to London and gained an informal interview with British Foreign Secretary Lord Russell. The Russian minister in Washington, DC was convinced that, 'England will take advantage of the first opportunity to recognise the seceded states.' In the event, neither Britain nor any other foreign power recognised the Confederacy, never mind intervened on its behalf.

Britain's attitude to the war

Prime Minister Lord Palmerston and Foreign Secretary Russell knew that there were good reasons for supporting the Confederacy:

- Britain's immediate and long-term self-interest might well be served by the break-up of the USA.
- An independent Confederacy would have strong economic links with Britain, providing raw cotton in return for manufactured goods.
- Cotton was an issue of immediate concern. In order to prevent economic hardship at home, it might be necessary for Britain to break the Union blockade to acquire southern cotton.
- Many Britons sympathised with the Confederacy and thought the North had no right to force people back into an unpopular Union.
- Given that four slave states remained in the Union, slavery did not seem to be a crucial issue. Indeed, Lincoln's administration insisted for most of 1861–2 that the war was not a crusade to abolish slavery. This made it easier for influential newspapers, such as *The Times*, to support the Confederacy.

However, there were many good reasons for not getting involved in the war:

- Conflict with the Union might result in the loss of Canada.
- War would certainly result in the loss of valuable markets and investments in the North.
- British opinion was far from united. Aware that slavery lay at the heart of the conflict, many Britons supported the Union.
- The **Crimean War** (1854–6) had indicated the difficulties of fighting a war thousands of miles from home.

Not surprisingly, Palmerston believed that Britain's best policy was neutrality.

 KEY TERM

Crimean War In 1854, Britain and France went to war against Russia to protect Turkey. Most of the war was fought in the area of Russia known as the Crimea.

British neutrality

One immediate problem was whether Britain should recognise the Confederacy as a sovereign state. Lincoln's administration made it clear that the conflict was a rebellion. Thus, recognition of the Confederacy was tantamount to a declaration of war against the USA. However, in legal terms the situation was confused because Lincoln had proclaimed a blockade against the Confederacy. A blockade was an instrument of war. If a state of war existed, Britain could make a reasonable case for recognising the Confederacy.

In May 1861, the British government adopted a compromise position. While declaring its neutrality and not recognising the Confederacy as a sovereign state, Britain recognised its **belligerent status**. Under international law belligerents had the right to contract loans and purchase arms in neutral nations. However, Britain's neutrality proclamation prevented the Confederacy fitting out its warships in British ports. It also recognised the Union blockade. Having declared itself neutral, Britain made every effort to remain so.

Confederate actions

In 1861, southerners believed that Britain would be forced to recognise the Confederacy and break the blockade because of its need for cotton. In order to tighten the screw, an unofficial cotton embargo was introduced. While the Confederate Congress did not establish a formal embargo, local 'committees of public safety' halted the export of cotton. The *Charleston Mercury* summed up the argument in June 1861: 'the cards are in our hands and we intend to play them out to the bankruptcy of every cotton factory in Great Britain and France or the acknowledgement of our independence'. Unfortunately for the Confederacy, the embargo ploy failed. European warehouses were full of cotton purchased in 1859–60, and so there was no immediate shortage. The cotton embargo thus backfired. Southerners failed to sell their most valuable commodity at a time when the blockade was at its least effective. Moreover, the embargo angered Europeans: 'To intervene on behalf of the South because they have kept cotton from us would be ignominious beyond measure', declared Russell. Nevertheless, the British government did consider breaking the Union blockade. 'We cannot allow some millions of our people to perish to please the northern states', said Palmerston. British and French diplomats discussed the possibility of joint action to lift the blockade. In the event, the talks were not followed by action.

The Confederacy did its best. Agents were sent across the Atlantic to establish contacts with sympathetic British MPs. In an attempt to influence British opinion, the Confederacy also set up a newspaper, the *Index*, devoted to presenting the rebel case. Confederate purchasing agents had spectacular successes purchasing British armaments. It is difficult to see what more the Confederacy could have done.

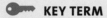

KEY TERM

Belligerent status
Recognised legally as waging war.

Union diplomacy

Northern politicians and diplomats, from Lincoln downwards, deserve some praise for their dealings with Britain:

- Charles Francis Adams, the US minister in London, employed every means at his disposal to ensure the strict maintenance of British neutrality.
- Secretary of State Seward displayed skilful statesmanship.
- Lincoln usually left policy to Seward. Only when there was a serious crisis (for example, the *Trent* affair) did he interfere.

The *Trent* affair

In November 1861, James Mason and John Slidell, **Confederate commissioners** to Britain and France, respectively, left Cuba for Europe in the *Trent*, a British steamer. Soon after leaving Havana, the *Trent* was stopped by Captain Wilkes, commanding the USS *San Jacinto*. Wilkes forcibly removed Mason and Slidell from the British ship. This action created a wave of anger in Britain: 'You may stand for this but damned if I will', Palmerston told his cabinet. Russell demanded that Mason and Slidell should be released and the USA must make a public apology. To back up the threat, the British fleet prepared for action and soldiers were sent to Canada. Britain also stopped the export of essential war materials to the Union.

The *Trent* affair posed a serious dilemma for Lincoln. While there was a danger of war if his government did not satisfy Britain, Union opinion would be outraged if he cravenly surrendered. Wilkes had become something of a national hero, so much so that the House of Representatives had passed a resolution

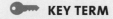

KEY TERM

Confederate commissioners Men representing the Confederate government.

?

Why is Source F supportive of Secretary of State Seward?

SOURCE F

A cartoon published in New York at the height of the *Trent* affair. In the cartoon, US Secretary of State Seward (beside the American eagle) returns the Confederate commissioners Slidell and Mason (in boat) to Europe. His act appeases Lord Russell (foot on the British lion) and frustrates Jefferson Davis (far right), who had hoped that Britain would enter the war as a Confederate ally.

praising his action. A compromise was eventually found. The US government, while not apologising for Wilkes's action, admitted that he had committed an illegal act and freed Mason and Slidell.

British mediation?

The closest the Confederacy came to getting British recognition was in the autumn of 1862 after its triumph at Second Manassas (see page 158). French Emperor Napoleon III's proposal that Britain and France should attempt to mediate in the conflict was seriously considered by Palmerston and Russell (see Source G below). Given that mediation meant recognition of the Confederacy, Britain and France might easily have found themselves at war with the Union. However, the failure of Lee's Maryland invasion (see pages 158–9) convinced Palmerston that it would be unwise to intervene.

Even after Lincoln's Emancipation Proclamation, some members of Palmerston's cabinet still wanted to take action. In October 1862, Chancellor of the Exchequer William Gladstone claimed that 'Jefferson Davis and other leaders have made an army, and are making, it appears, a navy, and they have made what is more than either, they have made a nation.' Supported by Gladstone, Russell prepared a memorandum arguing for mediation. Palmerston rejected the idea.

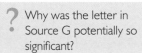

Why was the letter in Source G potentially so significant?

SOURCE G

Letter from Palmerston to Foreign Secretary Lord John Russell, 14 September 1862.

My dear Russell,

The detailed accounts given in the Observer *today of the battles of August 29 and 30 between the Confederates and the Federals show that the latter got a very complete smashing, and it seems not altogether unlikely that still greater disasters await them and that even Washington or Baltimore may fall into the hands of the Confederates. If this should happen would it not be time for us to consider whether in such a state of things England and France might not address the contending parties and recommend an arrangement upon the basis of separation?*

Commerce raiders

Although denied British recognition, the Confederacy received valuable aid from Britain. Confederate agents worked effectively to secure British military supplies. In particular, British shipbuilders built vessels for a variety of Confederate purposes. The majority were employed in running cargoes through the blockade. The Confederacy also purchased **commerce raiders**. In theory, British law forbade the construction of warships for a belligerent power. However, Confederate agents got round this by purchasing unarmed ships and then adding the guns elsewhere.

KEY TERM

Commerce raiders
Confederate warships that attacked Union merchant ships.

Confederate commerce raiders caused considerable damage to Union merchant shipping. The *Alabama*, for example, took 64 Union ships before finally being sunk off Brest. Altogether the North lost some 200 ships. While scarcely crippling trade, the raiders were a nuisance, driving Union shipping insurance rates to astonishing heights. Consequently, more and more Atlantic trade was transferred to neutral ships, which were not attacked by Confederate raiders. The main beneficiary was Britain.

The Laird rams

The last serious crisis between the Union and Britain came during the summer of 1863. Lincoln's government was aware that the Laird Brothers shipbuilders were building two ironclad ships for the Confederacy. These boats – the **Laird rams** – would be the strongest ships afloat. Charles Adams threatened war against Britain if the boats were sold to the Confederacy. The British government eventually bought the 'rams' itself and the crisis quickly fizzled out.

Conclusion

One of Palmerston's favourite sayings was: 'They who in quarrels interpose, will often get a bloody nose.' Given his cautious policy, it was always likely that Britain would remain neutral. While Seward, Lincoln and Adams deserve some credit, their diplomatic skill should not be overrated. Confederate diplomacy should not be castigated. Only if the Confederacy looked like winning would Britain recognise the Confederacy. Yet only if Britain recognised the Confederacy and went to war on its side was it likely that the Confederacy would win.

KEY TERM

Laird rams The distinguishing feature of these vessels was an iron ram that projected from the bow, enabling them to sink an enemy by smashing its hull.

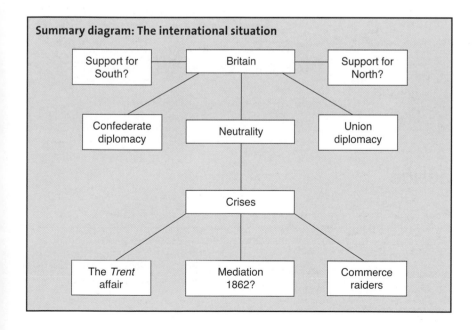

Summary diagram: The international situation

Chapter summary

The Confederacy, led by Jefferson Davis, and the Union, led by Abraham Lincoln, faced problems on the home front. Lincoln is usually seen as showing greater leadership qualities than Davis (although a case can be made for Davis being a reasonable leader). The Confederacy faced a number of problems: state rights, financial weakness and managing a war economy. Perceived failure on the home (and battle) front led to growing opposition to the war in the South. Nevertheless, most southerners supported the war until its end; most northerners were similarly committed to the war. Copperhead opposition in the West was never as strong as Republicans feared. The strength of the northern economy ensured that the Union was able to finance the war more successfully than the Confederacy. The war had less social impact in the North than in the South. The Union might well have lost the war if Britain had committed itself to the Confederacy, which provided most of its cotton. Despite some crises between 1861 and 1863, the British government remained committed to neutrality, which was a disaster for the Confederacy.

Refresher questions

Use these questions to remind yourself of the key material covered in this chapter.

1 How competent was Jefferson Davis?
2 How competent was Davis's cabinet?
3 How supportive was the Confederacy's Congress?
4 Did the Confederacy 'die of state rights'?
5 Did the Confederacy 'die of democracy'?
6 How successfully did the Confederacy finance the war?
7 How successful was the Confederate economy?
8 What impact did the war have on southern society?
9 Did internal opposition bring about Confederate defeat?
10 How competent was Abraham Lincoln?
11 How competent was Lincoln's cabinet?
12 How well did Congress cooperate with Lincoln?
13 How successfully did the Union finance the war?
14 What impact did the war have on the Union economy?
15 What impact did the war have on Union society?
16 How serious was internal opposition to the Union war effort?
17 Why did Britain not intervene in the war?

Question practice

ESSAY QUESTIONS

1 'The leadership of Jefferson Davis was the main cause of Confederate defeat.' Assess the validity of this view.
2 Assess the reasons for Britain's non-intervention in the American Civil War.
3 How serious was the internal opposition to Abraham Lincoln?
4 How successful was the Confederate war effort?

SOURCE ANALYSIS QUESTION

1 With reference to Sources 1, 2 and 3, and your understanding of the historical context, assess the value of these sources to a historian studying the internal situation in the Confederacy.

SOURCE 1

A letter from Joseph Brown, governor of Georgia to Confederate Vice-President Alexander H. Stephens, September 1862.

I have the pleasure to acknowledge the receipt of your letter of the 26th ult. and am gratified that you take the view which you have expressed about the action of Genl. Bragg in his declaration of martial law over Atlanta and his appoint[ment], as the newspapers say, of a civil governor with aids, etc.

I have viewed this proceeding as I have others of our military authorities of late with painful apprehensiveness for the future. It seems military men are assuming the whole powers of government to themselves and setting at defiance constitutions, laws, state rights, state sovereignty, and every other principle of civil liberty, and that our people engrossed in the struggle with the enemy are disposed to submit to these bold usurpations tending to military despotism without murmur, much less resistance. I should have called this proceeding into question before this time but I was hopeful from the indications which I had noted that Congress would take such action as would check these dangerous usurpations of power, and for the further reasons that I have already come almost into conflict with the Confederate authorities in vindication of what I have considered the rights of the State and people of Georgia, and I was fearful, as no other governor seems to raise these questions, that I might be considered by good and true men in and out of Congress too refractory for the times. I had therefore concluded to take no notice of this matter till the meeting of the legislature when I expect to ask the representatives of the people to define the bounds to which they desire the Governor to go in the defense of the rights and sovereignty of the state.

SOURCE 2

From the diary of Jones, a Confederate war clerk, writing of events in Richmond on 2 April 1863. For the sake of morale on the Confederate home front no newspaper reported it.

This morning early a few hundred women and boys met as by concert in the Capitol Square, saying they were hungry, and must have food. The number continued to swell until there were more than a thousand. But few men were among them … About nine a.m. the mob emerged from the western gates of the square, and proceeded down Ninth Street, passing the War Department, and crossing Main Street, increasing in magnitude at every step, but preserving silence and (so far) good order.

Not knowing the meaning of such a procession, I asked a pale boy where they were going. A young woman, seemingly emaciated, but yet with a smile, answered that they were going to find something to eat …

I did not follow, to see what they did; but I learned an hour after that they marched through Cary Street, and entered diverse stores of the speculators, which they proceeded to empty of their contents. They impressed all the carts and drays in the street, which were speedily laden with meal, flour, shoes etc. … an immense amount of provisions and other articles were borne by the mob which continued to increase in numbers …

About this time the President [Jefferson Davis] appeared, and ascending a dray, spoke to the people. He urged them to return to their homes, so that the bayonets there menacing them might be sent against the common enemy. He told them that such acts would bring famine upon them in the only form which could not be provided against, as it would deter people from bringing food to the city. He said he was willing to share his last loaf with the suffering people.

SOURCE 3

Jonathan Worth, an ex-Whig politician from North Carolina writing to his friend Jesse G. Henshaw in August 1863. Worth, the State Treasurer of North Carolina, had opposed secession but nevertheless gone with his state in 1861.

I hardly know whether I am in favor of the peace meetings or not. On the one hand, it is very certain that the President and his advisers will not make peace, if no forced into it by the masses and the privates in the army. Their cry echoed by almost every press is: 'Independence, or the last man and the last dollar.' The North will not make peace on the basis of Independence. The real question which nobody … will squarely present is, shall we fight on with certain desolation and impoverishment and probable ultimate defeat; or make peace on the basis of reconstruction? Nearly every public man – every journal, political and religious, and every politician, in the fervor of their patriotism, has vociferously declared in favor of 'the last man and the last dollar' cry. These classes cannot be consistent unless they still cry war. Many believe the masses in their saner hours never approved the war and would rather compromise on the basis of the Constitution of the U.S. with such additional securities against any future rupture as could be agreed on. If there be any sense in peace meetings they mean reconstruction. They may rather do mischief if they are not so imposing as to force the administration to reconstruction. They will be impotent and mischievous if the army is still for war to the last man and the last dollar. I do not know the sentiments of the rank and file of the army.

I am for peace on almost any terms and fear we shall never have it until the Yankees dictate it. Upon the whole I would not go into a peace meeting now or advise others to go into one, particularly in Randolph – but I have no repugnance to them in other places and see no other chance to get to an early end of this wicked war, but by the action of the masses who have the fighting to do.

CHAPTER 6

The war 1861–5

In the spring of 1861, thousands of men, egged on by family, friends and neighbours, rushed to volunteer, their main fear being that the war would be over before they could get a shot at the enemy. However, the war was to be different from their expectations. It was to drag on for four terrible years. Why did this happen? Why did the Union eventually win? This chapter will address these questions by examining the following themes:

★ Union and Confederate strengths and weaknesses

★ The nature of the war

★ The war in 1861–2

★ The war in 1863

★ Union victory 1864–5

The key debate on *page 173* of this chapter asks the question: Did the Confederacy defeat itself or was it defeated?

Key dates

1861	July	First Manassas	1864	March	Grant became general-in-chief
1862	April	Battle of Shiloh		May–June	Wilderness–Petersburg campaign
	June–July	Seven Day battles			
	Aug.	Second Manassas		Sept.	Fall of Atlanta
	Sept.	Battle of Antietam		Nov.	Lincoln re-elected president
	Dec.	Battle of Fredericksburg			
1863	May	Battle of Chancellorsville	1865	April	Fall of Petersburg and Richmond
	July	Battle of Gettysburg			
	July	Capture of Vicksburg		April	Lee surrendered at Appomattox
	Sept.	Battle of Chickamauga			

Union and Confederate strengths and weaknesses

▶ *What were the main Union and Confederate strengths and weaknesses?*

Napoleon Bonaparte thought most wars were won by the side with the 'big battalions'; that is, the side with most men and materials. The Union had the 'big battalions'; however, in 1861, most southerners, and many European observers, were confident that the Confederacy would triumph. Even after the war, many southerners were convinced that the Confederacy should have won. 'No people ever warred for independence', said General Beauregard, 'with more relative advantages than the Confederacy.'

Union advantages

- There were 22 million people in the North compared with only 9 million in the South (of whom only 5.5 million were white people).
- Four slave states, containing some 2 million people, remained loyal to the Union. These states would have added 80 per cent to the Confederacy's industrial capacity.
- The Union had a stronger pool of military experience. Most men in the US regular army remained loyal to the Union. Between 1820 and 1860, two-thirds of all the graduates at West Point, the USA's chief military academy, had been northerners.
- The Union enjoyed a huge naval supremacy (see pages 150–1).
- In 1860, the North had six times as many factories as the South, ten times its industrial productive capacity, and twice as many miles of railway track.
- The North produced more agriculturally.
- Not all the people within the Confederacy were committed to its cause. Pockets of Unionism existed, especially in the Appalachian Mountains. The Confederacy suffered a major setback when West Virginia seceded from Virginia.

Union slave states

The fact that four slave states remained loyal to the Union was of vital importance:

- There was never any likelihood that Delaware would secede. Less than two per cent of its population were slaves and its economic ties were with the North.
- In April 1861, Union soldiers passing through Baltimore, Maryland on their way to Washington, DC were attacked by pro-Confederate townspeople. Four soldiers and twelve civilians were killed – the first fatalities of the war. Helped

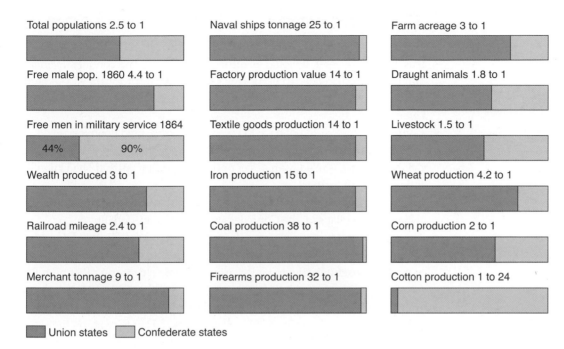

Figure 6.1 Comparative resources of Union and Confederate states.

by the pro-Union Maryland governor, Lincoln took strong action. Stretching the Constitution to its limits (and probably beyond), he sent in troops, suspended the writ of habeas corpus and allowed the arrest of suspected trouble-makers. Lincoln's tough measures helped to save Maryland for the Union. Elections in June were won by Unionist candidates and the state legislature voted against secession.

- Kentucky was deeply divided. Its governor leaned to the South but its legislature was opposed to secession. Attempting to remain neutral, Kentucky rejected calls for recruits from both sides and warned Lincoln and Davis to keep out of the state. Lincoln, aware that a false move on his part could drive Kentucky into the Confederacy, relied on patience and backstage manoeuvring rather than direct action. While paying (apparent) respect to Kentucky's integrity, his government supplied arms to Unionists within the state. Kentucky's neutrality was short lived. In September 1861, Confederate forces occupied Columbus. Union forces were quickly ordered into Kentucky and soon controlled most of the state.

- In 1861 it seemed likely that Missouri would join the Confederacy. In June its pro-Confederate governor called for 50,000 volunteers to defend the state against Union invasion. However, there was also considerable Unionist support, especially from the state's German population. Congressman Francis Blair and Captain Nathaniel Lyon helped to ensure that Unionists kept control of most of Missouri.

Confederate advantages

- The sheer size of the Confederacy – 2 million km² (750,000 square miles) – was its greatest asset. It would be difficult to blockade and conquer. Even if Union armies succeeded in occupying Confederate territory, they would have difficulty holding down a resentful population and maintaining their **supply lines**.
- Confederate forces did not have to invade the North, hold down occupied territory or capture Washington and New York to win. All they had to do was defend. Defence is usually an easier option in war than attack. The Union had little option but to attack.
- Southerners hoped that northern opinion might come to question high losses. If Union will collapsed, the Confederacy would win by default.
- The crucial theatre of the war was the land between Washington, DC and Richmond in North Virginia. Here a series of west to east running rivers were to provide a useful barrier to Union armies intent on capturing Richmond (see Figure 6.2 on page 156).
- Although slaves were a potential threat, slavery proved itself a real benefit to the Confederacy early in the war. Slaves could be left to work on the home front, enabling the South to raise more of its white manpower than the Union. Although the Confederacy did not allow slaves to fight, they nevertheless performed many invaluable military tasks, for example, building fortifications.
- Given that most of the war was fought in the South, southerners were defending their own land and homes, a fact that perhaps encouraged them to fight harder than northerners.
- Morale, commitment and enthusiasm were high in the South in 1861. Few southerners questioned the rightness of the Confederate cause. Southern Churches assured southerners that they had God on their side.
- Southerners were confident that they were better soldiers than northerners. The pre-war South had placed more emphasis on martial virtues than the North. In 1860 most of the USA's military colleges were in slave states. Southerners had usually dominated the senior posts in the US army. Most military experts assumed that farmers, who knew how to ride and shoot, were better soldiers than industrial workers.
- By using its road and rail systems, the Confederacy could move its forces quickly from one area to another. This meant that it should be able to concentrate its forces against dispersed Union forces.
- Although Maryland, Missouri and Kentucky did not secede, thousands of pro-Confederates in the three states fought for the South.
- Cotton was the Confederacy's great economic weapon. Cotton sales should enable it to buy military supplies from Europe. There was also the hope that Britain might break the Union naval blockade (see page 136) to ensure that cotton supplies got through to its textile mills. This would lead to war between Britain and the Union.

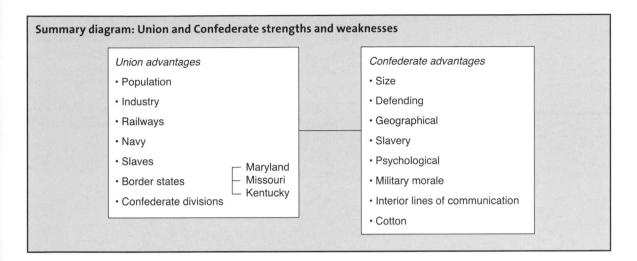

Summary diagram: Union and Confederate strengths and weaknesses

Union advantages
- Population
- Industry
- Railways
- Navy
- Slaves
- Border states — Maryland, Missouri, Kentucky
- Confederate divisions

Confederate advantages
- Size
- Defending
- Geographical
- Slavery
- Psychological
- Military morale
- Interior lines of communication
- Cotton

② The nature of the war

▶ *How prepared for war were both combatants in 1861?*

Neither side was prepared for war in 1861. The Union had only a 16,000-strong regular army, most of which was scattered out west. Lincoln had no military experience. Seventy-four-year-old General Winfield Scott, the leading Union general, had no general staff, no carefully prepared strategic plans and no programme for **mobilisation**. In April 1861, Lincoln appealed for 75,000 volunteers to serve for three months. It was soon obvious that this was insufficient. In July, Congress agreed to raise 500,000 men who would serve for three years.

The Confederacy had to start its military organisation from scratch. Davis at least had some military experience. The 300 or so officers who resigned from the regular army to fight for the Confederacy provided a useful pool of talent. Southern state militias, were, on balance, better prepared for war than those in the North. In February 1861, the Confederate Congress agreed to raise 100,000 volunteers for up to a year's service. In May, it authorised an additional 400,000 troops for three years' service. Given its limited manufacturing capacity, the South's main problem was equipping the volunteers.

KEY TERM

Mobilisation Preparing for war, especially by raising troops.

'Armed mobs'?

Helmuth von Moltke, the Prussian chief of staff in the 1860s and 1870s, characterised the military operations of the Civil War as merely, 'Two armed mobs chasing each other around the country, from which nothing could be learned.' There was some justification for this view in 1861. Compared with European armies, both the Union and Confederate armies were amateurish, from the top down:

- Neither side had a recognisable high command structure.
- Taking whatever advice seemed appropriate, both Lincoln and Davis had the job of appointing the chief officers. Political criteria, not just military concerns, played a role in these appointments. While some 'political' generals became first-rate soldiers, many were incompetent.
- Only a few junior officers had any military qualifications. Many were elected by the men under their command or were appointed by state governors, usually because of their social standing or political influence.
- Most ordinary soldiers, unused to military discipline, had little time for army spit and polish. There was thus widespread insubordination.

Mass armies

From Lincoln's and Davis's points of view, the main requirement in 1861 was to raise men quickly. Accepting locally and privately raised volunteer units met those needs much more rapidly and at less expense than recruiting regular troops. In 1861 the problem was not for authorities to obtain men but to hold volunteers to manageable numbers.

By early 1862, the flood of recruits had become a trickle. In March 1862, Davis decided he had no option but to introduce conscription. Every white male, aged 18–35 (soon raised to 45), was liable for military service. The length of service of those already in the army was extended to the duration of the war.

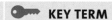

KEY TERM

Militia draft Conscription of men in the state militias.

In the North, most states adopted a carrot and stick approach. The carrot was bounties – large sums of money offered to men who enlisted. The stick, initially, was the Militia Law (July 1862). This empowered Lincoln to call state militias into Union service. Most states managed to enrol enough men but some had to introduce a **militia draft** to fill their quotas. In March 1863 the Union introduced conscription for all able-bodied men aged 20–45. As in the South, this was criticised, not least because it was possible to avoid the draft by hiring a substitute.

Under one-tenth of the men who fought in the Civil War were conscripted. But this statistic does not reflect the full effect of the conscription laws. The fact that conscripts were treated with contempt by veteran soldiers and had no choice in which regiment they would serve encouraged men to volunteer. Both sides raised massive armies. By 1865 some 900,000 men had fought for the Confederacy; the Union enlisted about 2.1 million men.

The impact of the rifle-musket

Improvements in military technology were to change the nature of warfare. In previous wars the smoothbore musket, which had an effective range of less than 100 metres, had been the main infantry weapon. Given the range of the smoothbore musket, infantry charges could often overwhelm an enemy position, as US troops had shown in the Mexican War (pages 00–000). However, by 1861 the smoothbore had been supplanted by the rifle-musket.

SOURCE A

Photograph of Confederate soldiers posing outside their tent in 1861.

What does Source A suggest about the nature of the Confederate army?

Rifling itself was not new, but loading rifled weapons prior to 1855 was a slow process. With the adoption of the **minié ball**, the rifle-musket could be fired as quickly as the smoothbore. Rifle-muskets were still **muzzle-loading** and single-shot (skilled men could fire three shots a minute) but the vital fact was that they were accurate at up to 600 metres. This was to have a huge impact on the battlefield.

In 1861–2, Union ordnance chief Ripley opposed the introduction of repeating rifles on the grounds that soldiers might waste ammunition, which was in short supply. In 1864–5 repeating rifles, used mainly by cavalry units, gave Union armies an important advantage. If Ripley had contracted for repeating rifles in 1861–2, the war might have ended sooner.

Communications

Strategy and tactics were affected by improvements in communication:

- Both sides made use of railways to move masses of men and to keep them supplied. The Confederacy found it hard to maintain its railway system and thus maximise its lines of interior communication.
- On the Mississippi and its tributaries, steamboats played a vital supply role.
- The telegraph enabled commanders to communicate directly with units on widely separated fronts, thus ensuring co-ordinated movement.

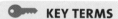 **KEY TERMS**

Minié ball A lead ball that expanded into the rifling of the rifle-musket's barrel.

Muzzle-loading Loaded down the barrel.

The war's main theatres

- The Confederate capital, Richmond in Virginia, the principal target of Union forces, was only about 170 km from Washington, DC. The area north of Richmond was to be the scene of bitter fighting. In north Virginia flat coastal strip gave way to rolling hills and then to the Appalachian Mountains. Geographical factors – dense forests, swampy areas and half a dozen major rivers running west to east – favoured the defender. So did the fertile Shenandoah Valley. This ran from north to east (near Washington, DC) to southwest (away from Richmond).
- Between the Appalachians and the Mississippi lay a vast region of plains and hills, extending from Kentucky and Tennessee in the north to the Gulf coast in the south. The sheer size of the West, its lack of natural lines of defence, and the fact that the main rivers flowed into the heart of the Confederacy meant that the West was the **rebels'** 'soft underbelly'.
- West of the Mississippi was a huge but thinly populated area. The fighting here was small scale; none of the campaigns had a major effect on the war's outcome.

Guerrilla war

There was a guerrilla dimension to the war, especially in Missouri, Kentucky, Arkansas and Tennessee. Confederate guerrilla units gathered when the call went out, engaged in an operation (for example, attacking Union outposts) and then returned to homes and hideouts until needed again.

The naval war

In April 1861, the Union, on paper, had a fleet of 90 ships but few were ready for action. There were only 8800 men in the navy. However, the Union did have a large **merchant marine**, from which it could draw vessels and men. The Confederacy had no navy at all in 1861. Although some 300 naval officers joined the Confederacy, the likelihood of their finding ships to command seemed minimal. Nearly all US shipbuilding capacity was in the North.

As soon as the war began, the North bought scores of merchant ships, armed them and sent them to do blockade duty. By December 1861 the Union had over 260 warships on duty and 100 more were under construction. Much of this expansion was due to the dynamism of Navy Secretary Gideon Welles and Assistant Secretary Gustavus Fox.

Blockading the South was crucial. If the Confederacy could sell its cotton in Europe and purchase weapons and manufactured goods in return, the war might continue indefinitely. Given the 5500 km of southern coastline, the blockade was easier to declare than to enforce. But as the months went by the blockade grew tighter, hindering the Confederacy's war effort. The Union was also able to use its naval supremacy to transport its troops and to strike

KEY TERMS

Rebels Confederates were called rebels or 'rebs' by Union forces.

Merchant marine Ships involved in trade, not war.

at Confederate coastal targets. In April 1862 New Orleans, the Confederacy's largest town, was captured by Admiral Farragut. Loss of many of its coastal towns weakened the Confederacy and depressed southern morale.

The secretary of the Confederate navy, Stephen Mallory, had the unenviable job of creating a navy from scratch. Appreciating that the Confederacy could never out-build the Union, he realised that its only hope was the bold adoption of new weapons. Aware of British and French experiments with **ironclad warships**, Mallory believed that the best chance to break the Union blockade was for the Confederacy to build several of these revolutionary vessels. In the summer of 1861 he ordered the conversion of the *Merrimack* (a scuttled Union frigate which the Confederacy had managed to raise) into an ironclad.

The Confederacy's greatest moment in the naval war came on 8 March 1862 when the *Merrimack* (now renamed the *Virginia* and with its sides sheathed with iron plate) sank two blockading ships. For one day the Confederate navy ruled the waves. Unfortunately for Mallory, by March 1862 the Union had its own ironclad, the *Monitor*. On 9 March, the first ironclad encounter in history occurred. Neither the *Virginia* nor the *Monitor* was able to sink the other, but the *Virginia* was so damaged that it was forced to return to port and was later abandoned. The Confederacy could scarcely retain a monopoly of new naval weapons. It had to stretch its resources to build one ironclad, whereas the Union was able to mass produce them.

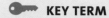

KEY TERM

Ironclad warship Ship made of iron or protected by iron plates.

The 'inland sea'

Confederate craft were no match for the heavily armed and armoured Union squadrons operating on the western rivers. Gunboats played a crucial role in helping Union troops to capture a number of key Confederate fortresses. By August 1862, Union forces controlled all the Mississippi except a 250-km stretch from Vicksburg to Port Hudson.

Commerce raiders

The Confederacy purchased a number of fast raiders such as the *Alabama* and the *Florida* from Britain. These raiders sank or captured some 200 Union merchant ships. Although never seriously threatening Union commerce, the raiders' exploits helped southern morale. Unable to find safe ports for refitting, most were eventually hunted down and sunk.

A 'total' war?

Historian Mark Neely Jr (2007) has claimed that the war was not total. He stresses that the Union government never tried to control the North's economy or to mobilise all its resources. Moreover, there was little of the ruthlessness and cruelty that characterised twentieth-century wars. On the whole, civilians were safe. Women were rarely raped. The 'hard war' policies adopted by the Union in 1864 (see page 170) were designed to damage property, not kill. However, as historian James McPherson has pointed out, 'The Civil War mobilised human resources on a scale unmatched by any other event in American history except, perhaps, World War II.' In fact, far more American men (proportionately) were mustered than in the Second World War. The war was more total in the South than in the North. A quarter of white men of military age in the Confederacy lost their lives. Moreover, the Union eventually did all it could to destroy the South's economic resources as well as the morale of its civilians.

The first modern war?

Given railways, the telegraph, the rifle-musket and iron, steam-driven ships, many historians see the Civil War as more akin to the First World War (1914–18) than the French Revolutionary and Napoleonic Wars (1792–1815). However, there was no battle in the entire war with more than 100,000 men on each side. The strategy and tactics of the armies would have been familiar to Napoleon and British Admiral Nelson would have felt at home in most of the ships. Horse-drawn transport remained the norm. Experiments with machine guns, submarines and underwater mines were rudimentary and made little impact on the war's outcome. Given the state of communications, Civil War generals could barely command, still less control, their men on battlefields.

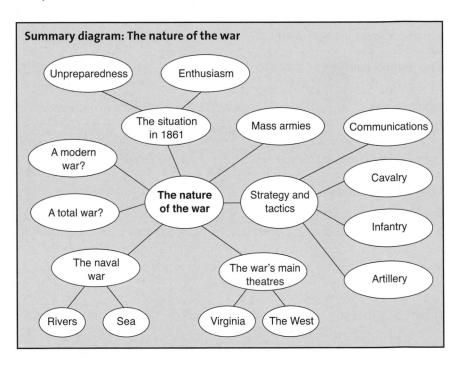

Summary diagram: The nature of the war

3 The war in 1861–2

▶ *Why did the war not end in 1861 or 1862?*

Winfield Scott, Union general-in-chief, thought it would take many months to train and equip the armies needed to crush the insurrection. He supported the Anaconda Plan, the aim of which was slowly to squeeze life out of the Confederacy by naval blockade and by winning control of the Mississippi River. But Lincoln looked for a quick, decisive blow. He accepted that Union troops were untrained but as he wrote to General McDowell, who commanded Union forces around Washington, DC: 'You are green, it is true, but they are green; you are all green alike.' Lincoln thus urged McDowell to march on Richmond.

Meanwhile, Jefferson Davis pledged himself to defend every part of the Confederacy. He realised that lost territory would result in a depletion of resources and a decline in morale.

First Manassas

The main Confederate army of 22,000 men, led by General Beauregard, was positioned in north Virginia, south of the Bull Run River at Manassas. General Joe Johnston commanded another army of 11,000 men in the Shenandoah Valley. On 16 July, Union General McDowell marched south with some 30,000 men. His attack on 21 July came near to winning a decisive victory. However, Confederate forces fought bravely, especially Thomas Jackson's brigade which stood 'like a stonewall' (hereafter Jackson became known as 'Stonewall') and were saved by the arrival of Johnston's troops, many of whom travelled by train from the Shenandoah. Union troops panicked and fled. The Confederacy had won the first major battle. The South suffered 2000 **casualties**; the Union suffered 3000 casualties. Southerners, who usually named battles after the nearest settlement, called the battle Manassas. Northerners, who usually named battles after the nearest geographical feature, called it Bull Run.

The Confederacy made no attempt to follow up its victory by marching on Washington, DC. Some see this as a missed opportunity to win the war. But the southern army was as disorganised as the routed Union army. Desperately short of supplies, it was in no condition to attack Washington's defences. Even if the Confederates had captured Washington, it is unlikely that this would have ended the war.

Victory in the war's first major battle was a mixed blessing. It may have made some southerners overconfident and complacent. Defeat, on the other hand, spurred the North on to more determined efforts. But victory did give the Confederates in Virginia a confidence boost, reinforced by a further victory at Ball's Bluff in October. Over the winter Johnston maintained the Confederate line along the Potomac River.

> **KEY TERM**
>
> **Casualties** The number of soldiers dead, wounded, taken prisoner and missing.

General McClellan

After Manassas, McDowell was replaced by 34-year-old General George McClellan. Credited with some minor victories in West Virginia, he exuded an air of optimism and soon replaced Scott as general-in-chief. McClellan remains one of the most controversial figures of the war. An able administrator, he restored the morale of the main Union army, now called the Army of the Potomac. He was popular with the soldiers, who referred to him affectionately as 'Little Mac'. McClellan's supporters claim he was a man of strategic vision who was betrayed by Republican political intrigue (McClellan was a Democrat) and by poor intelligence. Anxious not to create scars that might take a generation to heal, his hope of winning the war by manoeuvre and bringing it to an end without too much gore made – humane – sense.

Even McClellan's supporters concede, however, that he was an arrogant egotist. He failed to work collaboratively with his political masters, whom he constantly derided. The main charge levied against McClellan is that, having built a fine army, he was too reluctant to use it. Overcautious and indecisive, he had a chronic disposition to exaggerate the odds against him. This was apparent over the winter of 1861–2. Although his army was twice the size of the rebel force facing him, he believed he was outnumbered. Lincoln and the northern public grew increasingly impatient as McClellan refused to move.

The west 1861–2

The Confederates won the first major battle in the West, at Wilson's Creek in Missouri in August 1861. Lacking resources, they were unable to follow up their victory. In Missouri, and across the West as a whole, Confederate forces were greatly outnumbered by Union troops. In 1861, Lincoln divided the Union's western forces: General Halleck was to concentrate on winning control of the Mississippi while General Buell was to drive Confederate forces from Kentucky and Tennessee. Lincoln hoped for a joint offensive. However, neither Halleck nor Buell was prepared to risk failure by attacking too soon. General Albert Sidney Johnston commanded the Confederate forces between the Appalachian and Ozark Mountains. He scattered his 40,000 troops along the southern borders of Kentucky and Missouri, hoping that a number of forts built at strategic points on the important rivers would hold up any Union advance.

Grant's success

In February, Halleck sent 15,000 men under General Ulysses S. Grant (see page 167), accompanied by a flotilla of gunboats commanded by Andrew Foote, to capture the key river forts. Foote's ships forced Fort Henry to surrender. A few days later Fort Donelson, defended by 16,000 men, surrendered to Grant. Union forces now controlled the Tennessee and Cumberland rivers, vital arteries into the South. Johnston retreated to Corinth, leaving Kentucky and most of

Tennessee under Union control. Halleck now ordered Grant and Buell to push into southwest Tennessee.

Shiloh

In early April Grant, with over 40,000 men, encamped on the west bank of the Tennessee River at Shiloh, waiting for Buell's army. On 6 April, Johnston launched a surprise attack. Many Union troops panicked and fled but enough regiments held out to ensure that the rebels did not win a total victory. The Confederate cause was not helped by the death of Johnston in the midst of battle. Beauregard took over. As the first day of battle ended, he telegraphed to Davis that he had won a 'complete victory'.

That night, 25,000 men from Buell's army arrived to reinforce Grant's army. The next day the Confederate army was forced to retreat. At Shiloh the rebels suffered 10,600 and the Union 13,000 casualties. While Shiloh was certainly not Grant's best fought battle, its outcome was of great importance. The Union had turned back the rebel bid to regain the initiative. Halleck now assumed full command and advanced – or rather crawled – towards Corinth. (It took him nearly a month to cover 35 km.) Davis, displeased by Beauregard's evacuation of Corinth, replaced him with General Bragg. On the Union side, Halleck was appointed general-in-chief. Lincoln hoped he would become a vigorous commander, co-ordinating Union strategy. Instead, he became something of a pen-pusher who neither laid down nor enforced a comprehensive strategy for the war as a whole.

The peninsula campaign

Anxious to avoid a frontal attack, McClellan planned to attack Richmond up the peninsula between the York and James Rivers. Thus, in April 1862 the Army of Potomac, 121,000 strong, was transported to Fortress Monroe, 112 km from Richmond. Instead of attacking, McClellan settled down to besiege Yorktown, giving Davis time to send more men to the peninsula. Just as he was ready to attack Yorktown, the Confederates withdrew. McClellan advanced cautiously, not reaching the outskirts of Richmond until late May. His forces greatly outnumbered the Confederates opposing him, but McClellan, convinced he was outnumbered, awaited reinforcements.

The Shenandoah Valley

McClellan never got his reinforcements, largely because of Stonewall Jackson's Shenandoah Valley campaign. Jackson, with 18,000 men, was sent into the valley to ensure that (far larger) Union forces did not move south to Richmond. Jackson, a religious fanatic who saw himself as God's instrument, proved himself a brilliant soldier. From March to June 1862 he fought six battles, inflicted 7000 casualties on the enemy, diverted 60,000 Union troops from other tasks, and inspired the South. Lincoln, worried at the threat that Jackson posed

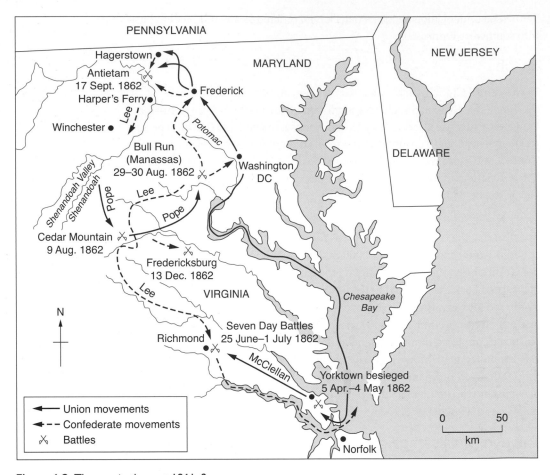

Figure 6.2 The war in the east 1861–2.

to Washington, DC, did not send men to help McClellan. Instead, it was Jackson who marched south to fight McClellan.

Confederate problems

Despite Jackson's success, the Confederacy seemed to be on the verge of defeat in May. Confederate forces had suffered severe setbacks, including the loss of New Orleans (see page 151). Most of the Mississippi Valley was now in Union hands and McClellan seemed certain to capture Richmond.

Robert E. Lee

On 31 May, General Johnston attacked McClellan's forces outside Richmond. The result was a costly draw: the South lost 6000 casualties and the North 5000. The most important outcome was the fact that Johnston was wounded and replaced by 55-year-old Virginian Robert E. Lee. Considered by many to be America's finest soldier in 1861, Lincoln had offered him high command in the

Robert E(dward) Lee

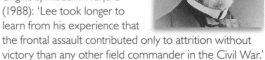

1807	Born in Virginia
1829	Graduated from West Point
1831	Married Mary Custis, daughter of George Washington's adopted son: he inherited her father's mansion at Arlington, along with 63 slaves
1846–8	Won renown in the Mexican War
1848–61	Served as an engineer in the West and superintendent at West Point
1862	Appointed commander of the Army of Northern Virginia
1862–3	Won a series of major battles
1863	Defeated at Gettysburg
1865	Surrendered to Grant at Appomattox Court House
1870	Died

Historians disagree about Lee. Some think he was the Confederacy's greatest hero. Others think that he was the reason the Confederacy lost.

Edward Hagerman, *The American Civil War and the Origins of Modern Warfare* (1988): 'Lee took longer to learn from his experience that the frontal assault contributed only to attrition without victory than any other field commander in the Civil War.'

James McPherson, *Drawn with the Sword* (1996): '… the Confederacy had a chance to win the war – not by conquering the North or destroying its armies, but by sapping the Northern will and capacity to conquer the South and destroy Confederate armies. On three occasions the Confederacy came close to winning on these terms. Each time it was Lee who almost pulled it off. His victories at the Seven Days and second Manassas battles and the invasion of Maryland in the summer of 1862; his triumph at Chancellorsville and the invasion of Pennsylvania in 1863; and the casualties his army inflicted on Grant's forces in the Wilderness–Petersburg campaign in the spring and summer of 1864 … these three campaigns each came close to sapping the Northern will to continue the war … Of all Confederate commanders, Lee was the only one whose victories had some potential for winning the war. The notion that a more gradual strategy would have done better is speculative at best.'

Union army but Lee had remained loyal to his state. The early part of the war had not gone well for him: after setbacks in West Virginia and the Carolinas, he became Davis's military adviser.

Lee now had the opportunity to display his prowess. Renaming his army the Army of Northern Virginia, he determined to seize the initiative by joining up with Jackson and attacking McClellan. Although some historians have been critical of Lee's so-called 'offensive–defensive' strategy (which he was to use time and again in 1862–3), it is hard to imagine a better one. A war fought purely on the defensive was unlikely to be successful. By going on the offensive, Lee hoped to win a major victory which would seriously damage northern morale.

The Seven Days

Lee attacked at the end of June. The week of battles that followed is known as the 'Seven Days'. The Seven Days cost the Confederacy 20,614 men; Union losses were only 15,849. Overcomplicated battle-plans and defects in command structure led to Lee making a number of disjointed attacks. He was also let down by Jackson, who was strangely lethargic. Nevertheless, Lee's offensive had saved Richmond, forcing a demoralised McClellan to retreat back down the peninsula.

Second Manassas

Lincoln now appointed General Pope to command the Union forces around Washington, DC. McClellan was ordered to evacuate the peninsula and join Pope. With a united army, Pope would then advance on Richmond. Determined to strike first, Lee headed north in mid-August with some 55,000 men. Dividing his army, he sent Jackson on a long sweep west and north of Pope, who was still awaiting McClellan's slow arrival. On 26–27 August, Jackson's 25,000 troops captured Pope's main supply depot at Manassas. Pope, strengthened at last by advanced units of McClellan's army, attacked Jackson's outnumbered force. Second Manassas, fought on 29–30 August, was a Union disaster. Failing to appreciate that the rest of Lee's army was marching to Jackson's aid, Pope was defeated when General Longstreet attacked his left flank. Lee came close to winning the decisive victory that he was seeking. However, most Union troops escaped and retreated towards Washington, DC. The Union lost 16,000 men, the Confederacy 9000. Reluctantly, Lincoln reappointed McClellan as commander-in-chief.

Antietam

In September, Lee sent Jackson to capture Harper's Ferry while he himself invaded Maryland with 40,000 men. He aimed to:

- protect Virginia's harvest
- gain Maryland volunteers
- win a decisive victory
- demoralise the North
- persuade Britain to recognise the Confederacy.

However, Lee's invasion did not go to plan. He lost more soldiers by straggling and desertion than he gained from Maryland. He also lost a copy of his operational orders, which mysteriously fell into McClellan's hands. Aware that Lee's army was divided, McClellan was in a tremendous position to defeat him. Although he frittered away much of his advantage, he did force Lee back toward the Potomac River. Instead of retreating into Virginia, Lee took up a position behind Antietam Creek.

Given that he was hopelessly outnumbered, that both his flanks were vulnerable and that he had the Potomac behind him, Lee's decision to offer battle seems incredible. If McClellan had attacked on 15 or 16 September, Lee must surely have been defeated. Fortunately for Lee's reputation, McClellan did not attack. On 16 September Jackson's corps rejoined Lee's army, which reduced the odds. Even so, McClellan still had a two-to-one advantage when he finally attacked on 17 September.

Antietam, partly because it was so badly handled by McClellan, was really three separate battles. All three Union attacks were partially successful but none was followed through to complete success and Lee managed to hang on. Antietam was the bloodiest single-day battle of the war. Lee lost 11,000 men, McClellan 12,000.

McClellan was able to claim victory because on 18 September Lee retreated into Virginia. Indeed, Antietam can be seen as the turning point of the war. Within days of the battle Lincoln issued his famous Emancipation Proclamation (page 187). Lee's failure to win a decisive victory meant there was now little likelihood of British intervention. But McClellan failed to follow up his 'victory'. Exasperated with his excuses for inactivity, Lincoln relieved him of command in November, replacing him with General Burnside.

SOURCE B

Photograph of Confederate soldiers killed during the battle of Antietam.

Look at Source B. When and why do you think this photograph was taken?

Fredericksburg

Burnside, with 100,000 men, marched south. Lee's army, 75,000-strong, took up a strong position behind Fredericksburg. On 13 December, Burnside launched a series of suicidal attacks. Union forces lost 11,000 men. Lee lost fewer than 5000. Burnside pulled back across the Rappahannock. Union morale was not helped when Burnside's attempt to turn Lee's flank in January 1863 got bogged down in mud.

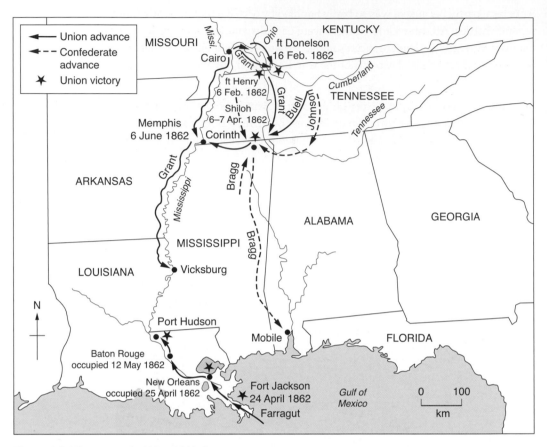

Figure 6.3 The war in the West 1861–2.

The war in the West in 1862–3

In the late summer Bragg advanced into Kentucky. Blundering into a Union army at Perryville in October, Bragg won a tactical victory but, facing serious supply problems, had to retreat into Tennessee. In December 1862, General Rosecrans tried to drive Bragg out of Tennessee. On 31 December, the two armies severely mauled each other at Murfreesboro (or Stones River). Bragg renewed the battle two days later but his attack was beaten back and he had to withdraw.

Over the winter of 1862–3, Union forces under Grant tried to take Vicksburg. The fortified town prevented Union control of the Mississippi. In Jefferson Davis's view, Vicksburg was vital to the Confederate cause: it was 'the nail-head that held the South's two halves together'. The town was probably not as important as Davis thought. By this stage there was actually little Confederate traffic across the Mississippi. Nevertheless, Vicksburg did have a symbolic importance. Its capture would demoralise the South and bolster the North.

As the Union threat to Vicksburg grew, Davis appointed Joseph Johnston to oversee Confederate operations in the West. His hope that Johnston would bring a unified vision to the West was not realised. Nevertheless, Vicksburg's natural defences made it difficult to capture.

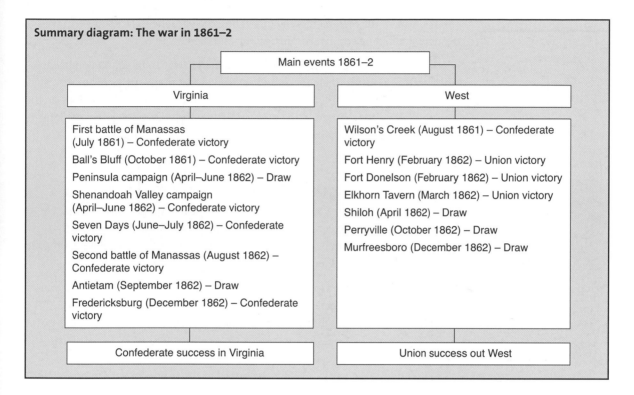

Summary diagram: The war in 1861–2

Main events 1861–2

Virginia	West
First battle of Manassas (July 1861) – Confederate victory	Wilson's Creek (August 1861) – Confederate victory
Ball's Bluff (October 1861) – Confederate victory	Fort Henry (February 1862) – Union victory
Peninsula campaign (April–June 1862) – Draw	Fort Donelson (February 1862) – Union victory
Shenandoah Valley campaign (April–June 1862) – Confederate victory	Elkhorn Tavern (March 1862) – Union victory
Seven Days (June–July 1862) – Confederate victory	Shiloh (April 1862) – Draw
Second battle of Manassas (August 1862) – Confederate victory	Perryville (October 1862) – Draw
Antietam (September 1862) – Draw	Murfreesboro (December 1862) – Draw
Fredericksburg (December 1862) – Confederate victory	
Confederate success in Virginia	Union success out West

④ The war in 1863

▶ *Which was the most important battle in 1863?*

In January 1863, Lincoln replaced Burnside with 'Fighting' Joe Hooker. Hooker was known to be an intriguer. There were even rumours that he intended to set himself up as military dictator. Lincoln was prepared to risk the dictatorship. What he wanted more than anything else was military success.

Chancellorsville

By April Hooker, with 130,000 men – twice as many as Lee – was ready to move. While General Sedgewick threatened Lee at Fredericksburg, the bulk of Hooker's army crossed the Rappahannock upstream, threatening Lee's left flank. By 30 April the main Union army had reached Chancellorsville in the heart of an area of undergrowth known as the Wilderness.

Lee now showed himself at his most brilliant. Leaving General Early with 10,000 men to hold Sedgewick, Lee led 50,000 Confederates to meet Hooker. On 2 May, he further divided his army by sending Jackson with 28,000 men to attack Hooker's right flank. Jackson attacked just before dusk, driving Union troops back in confusion. Nightfall brought an end to the fighting – and to Jackson, shot in the arm by his own men while inspecting the battlefield. Jackson's arm was amputated but he contracted pneumonia and died on 10 May.

Jackson's efforts at least ensured a Confederate victory. Injured and bemused by events, Hooker retreated. Lee had achieved what many see as his most impressive victory. With far fewer men, Lee had inflicted 17,000 casualties on the enemy, losing 13,000 men in the process. Although Jackson's death cast a long shadow, Confederate morale was sky high.

Gettysburg

Convinced that only victories on northern soil would force Lincoln to accept southern independence, Lee now insisted on an invasion of Pennsylvania. He got his way and in mid-June began his advance northwards. Hooker tried to follow Lee but with little real idea of where he was heading. On 28 June, Lincoln replaced Hooker with General Meade.

On 1 July, rebel soldiers stumbled across Union troops at Gettysburg. Lee and Meade ordered their forces to converge on the small town. Thus began the greatest battle ever fought on the American continent.

The battle

The first day of the battle – 1 July – belonged to the Confederacy. Union troops retreated on to Culp's Hill and Cemetery Hill. If the rebels had pushed home their attack they might have triumphed. Lee considered his options. Meade's army of 85,000 men was strongly positioned on hills south and east of Gettysburg. Rather than attack, General Longstreet favoured swinging around the Union left flank and finding a strong position in Meade's rear, forcing Meade to attack. Lee, aware of his army's supply problems, would have none of this. 'I am going to whip them here' he declared, 'or they are going to whip me.'

On 2 July, Longstreet attacked the Union left. The Confederates had some success against Union troops who had unwisely advanced into the Peach Orchard. They also nearly captured the strategically important Little Round Top on the extreme left of the Union position. The fighting on Little Round Top was symbolic of rebel fortunes on 2 July. Lee's men came close, but not close enough, to victory. The day ended in stalemate.

On 3 July, Lee launched his main attack on the Union centre; 15,000 men, led by General Pickett, advanced up Cemetery Ridge. The charge was a disaster. In less than one hour the Confederates suffered 6500 casualties. Lee had been beaten.

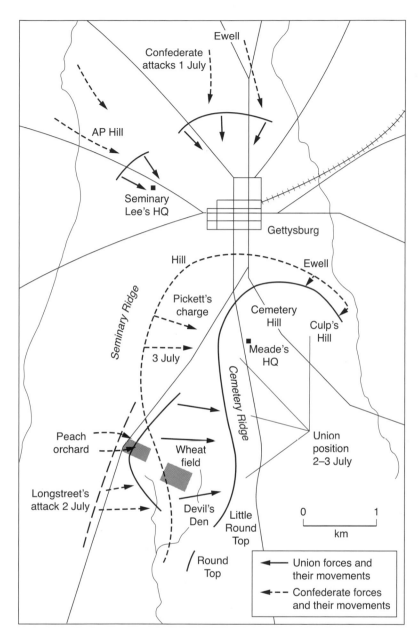

Figure 6.4 The battle of Gettysburg, 1–3 July 1863.

In three days he had lost 28,000 men – one-third of his command. (The Union army lost 23,000.) Lee retreated back to Virginia. He accepted full responsibility for Gettysburg: 'The army did all it could. I fear I required of it impossibilities.' He offered his resignation. Davis refused to accept it.

Why, according to Source C, did Davis refuse to accept Lee's resignation?

SOURCE C

Part of Jefferson Davis's reply to Lee's letter of resignation, August 1863.

To ask me to substitute you by someone in my judgment more fit to command, or who would possess more of the confidence of the army, or of the reflecting men of the country, is to demand an impossibility. It only remains for me to hope that you will take all possible care of yourself, that your health and strength may be entirely restored, and that the Lord will preserve you for the important duties devolved upon you in the struggle of our suffering country for the independence which we have engaged in war to maintain.

The results of Gettysburg

Gettysburg was a serious defeat for the Confederacy. The myth of Lee's invincibility had been broken and this in itself was a huge morale booster for the Union. After Gettysburg Lee was never again strong enough to launch a major invasion of the North. But Gettysburg was probably not the main turning point of the war.

- If Lee had won, he could not have held a single northern city for any length of time and would ultimately have had to retreat.
- Given events in the West (see below), it seems unlikely that Union morale would have collapsed.
- Gettysburg did not make Confederate defeat inevitable. The battle was not decisive because Meade was unable to follow up his victory. For the rest of 1863 there were few major engagements in Virginia.

The capture of Vicksburg

In April 1863, Grant, still seeking a way of capturing Vicksburg, determined to gamble. Marching his army down the west side of the Mississippi, he relied on Admiral Porter's ironclad fleet sailing past Vicksburg. This was achieved on the night of 16–17 April. Two weeks later Grant's army was ferried across the Mississippi.

The ensuing campaign was brilliant. Largely ignoring his line of communications, Grant cut inland. In three weeks he won several battles and was finally able to besiege Vicksburg. On 4 July, 30,000 Confederate troops in Vicksburg surrendered. The capture of Port Hudson five days later meant that the Confederacy was cut in two.

Chattanooga

Lincoln, anxious to press the Confederacy on all fronts, demanded more decisive action from General Rosecrans in Tennessee. Threatened with dismissal, Rosecrans advanced against Bragg. Reinforced by 12,000 men from the Army of Northern Virginia, Bragg gave battle at Chickamauga (19–20 September). Bragg, with more troops than Rosecrans, came close to winning a decisive victory.

Only a brave rear-guard action by Thomas enabled the Union army to retreat to Chattanooga. The battle of Chickamauga cost the Confederates 18,500 casualties compared to the Union's 16,500. Bragg now besieged Chattanooga. The Union defenders were so short of food it seemed they might be forced to surrender. Grant, placed in command of all the Union's western forces, acted swiftly, first ensuring that Chattanooga was supplied and then storming Lookout Mountain (24 November). The next day Grant's men seized Missionary Ridge. Rebel forces retreated in disarray. The Union victory confirmed that Grant was the Union's greatest general.

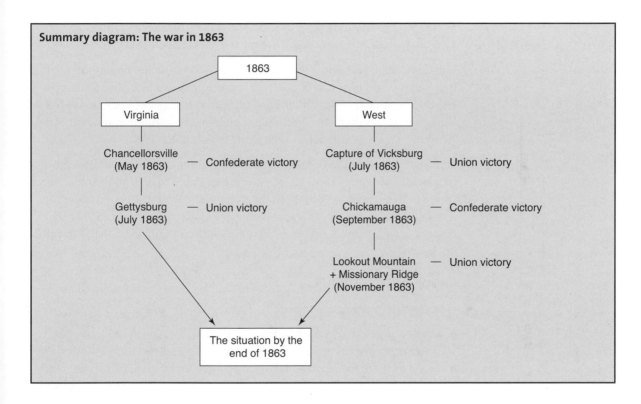

Summary diagram: The war in 1863

5 Union victory 1864–5

▶ *Why were Union armies successful in 1864–5?*

The defeats at Gettysburg, Vicksburg and Chattanooga were severe blows to southern morale. By December 1863, large areas of Arkansas, Tennessee and Louisiana were under Union control and Union forces were preparing to invade Georgia. Nevertheless, the South was far from beaten. Out west the Union faced the problem of long supply lines. In the east the Confederacy still had Lee and the Army of Northern Virginia.

In March 1864, Lincoln appointed Ulysses S. Grant general-in-chief of all the Union armies. He immediately came east to supervise the effort to destroy Lee. Sherman took over command in the West. Determined to make use of the Union's greater manpower, Grant planned for a 'simultaneous movement all along the line':

- The 115,000-strong Army of the Potomac would attack Lee.
- Sherman would capture Atlanta and then 'get into the interior of the enemy's country … inflicting all the damage you can'.
- 30,000 men in Louisiana, led by General Nathaniel Banks, were to capture Mobile.
- Butler's 30,000-strong army at Yorktown was to threaten Richmond.
- Sigel, with 26,000 men, was to occupy the Shenandoah Valley.

The Confederacy, desperate for manpower, passed legislation making all men between the ages of 17 and 50 liable for conscription. Even so, rebel forces were less than half those of the Union. Nevertheless, the morale of the Army of North Virginia remained high and General Joseph Johnston, again in command of the Army of Tennessee, improved Confederate morale in the West.

Although they would be outnumbered in the coming campaigns, at least most rebel soldiers were veterans. Many experienced Union troops, on the other hand, were due to go home in 1864 when the three-year enlistment period ended. Rather than force the veterans to re-enlist, the Union offered them $400 and 30 days' leave. Some 136,000 men, scenting victory, re-enlisted; 100,000 decided not to do so.

Grant's plan unfolds

Grant's strategy did not go to plan:

- Banks was defeated in the Red River area.
- Butler failed to exert pressure on Richmond.
- Union forces in the Shenandoah were defeated. In July a 10,000-strong rebel force pushed up the valley and reached the suburbs of Washington, forcing Grant to send reinforcements to defend the capital.

The Army of the Potomac had mixed success. With a two-to-one superiority in manpower, Grant hoped to manoeuvre Lee into an open-field combat. Lee's strategy was straightforward: keep Grant from Richmond, force him to attack fortified positions, and make the cost of trying to defeat the Confederacy so high that northerners would refuse to pay the price and vote out Lincoln in November.

In May, Grant threatened to slip round Lee's flank. On 5–6 May, Union and rebel forces met again in the same Wilderness area that had foiled Hooker one year earlier (see pages 161–2). The Union army suffered 18,000 casualties in confused, ferocious fighting – twice the losses sustained by Lee. But Grant

Ulysses S. Grant

1822	Born Hiram Ulysses Grant
1839	Entered West Point: as a result of an error, he was called Ulysses S. Grant
1846–8	Served in the Mexican War
1854–61	Failed in a number of civilian trades; finally worked in his father's shop in Galena, Illinois
1861	Promoted to general thanks to political influence
1862	Won battle of Shiloh
1863	April–July, captured Vicksburg
	November, saved Chattanooga
1864	March, appointed general-in-chief
	May–June, Wilderness–Petersburg campaign
1865	Received Lee's surrender at Appomattox
1868	Won presidential election
1872	Re-elected president
1885	Died

Contemporaries at the time and historians since have debated what made Grant such a good general.

President Lincoln: 'The great thing about Grant … is his perfect coolness and persistency of purpose. I judge he is not easily excited – which is a great element in an officer.'

General Sherman: 'I am a damn sight smarter than Grant. I know a great deal more about war, military history, strategy, and administration, and about everything else than he does. But I tell you where he beats me, and where he beats the world. He don't care a damn for what the enemy does out of his sight, but he scares me like hell.'

Grant had his own views: 'The art of war is simple enough. Find out where your enemy is. Get at him as soon as you can. Strike at him as hard as you can and as often as you can, and keep moving on.'

(unlike Hooker in 1863) did not retreat. Instead, he edged southwards, trying to get between Lee and Richmond.

For the next month the opposing armies were never out of contact. Grant's probings were foiled by Lee's skilful defence. On 3 June at Cold Harbor Grant lost 7000 men in just over one hour; Lee lost 1500. In the first 30 days of his offensive, Grant lost 50,000 men; twice as many as Lee. But the slogging match had just as great an impact on the Army of Northern Virginia. By June, Lee was desperately short of men and had lost many of his best officers.

The siege of Petersburg

On 12 June, Union forces crossed the James River, threatening Richmond from the south and almost capturing Petersburg, a crucial railway junction. Luck and inspired resistance from a small force led by Beauregard saved the day for the Confederacy. Lee, aware that the loss of Petersburg would result in the loss of Richmond, was forced to defend the town. Both sides dug trenches and the siege of Petersburg began. On 30 July, the Union army tried to blast a way through southern defences, exploding tons of gunpowder below the rebel lines. In the fighting that followed, Union forces got bogged down in the crater created by the explosion and suffered 4500 casualties. The Confederates hung on.

Although Grant had not yet defeated Lee, he had at least forced him on to the defensive and ensured that he was no longer able to fight the type of war at which he excelled: a war of manoeuvre. Both Grant and Lee knew that a **war of attrition** favoured the Union.

The Shenandoah Valley

In the autumn of 1864 the Confederacy suffered serious setbacks in the Shenandoah Valley. Sheridan, the new Union commander, chased the Confederates up the valley, winning battles at Winchester and at Cedar Creek.

The Atlanta Campaign

In May 1864, Sherman, with 100,000 men, left Chattanooga and headed towards Atlanta, state capital of Georgia and an important industrial and rail centre. His Confederate opponent, General Johnston, who commanded some 70,000 men, retreated rather than fight. By July, Union forces had reached the outskirts of Atlanta. Davis now replaced Johnston with 33-year-old John Bell Hood. Hood, who had lost an arm at Gettysburg and a leg at Chickamauga, was a brave fighter but had little skill as a commander. 'All lion, none of the fox',

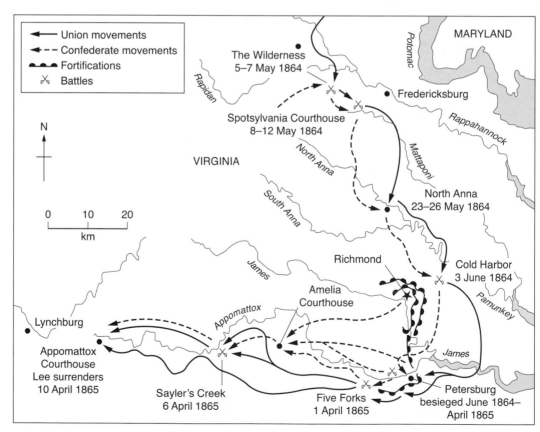

Figure 6.5 The Virginian campaign 1864–5.

SOURCE D

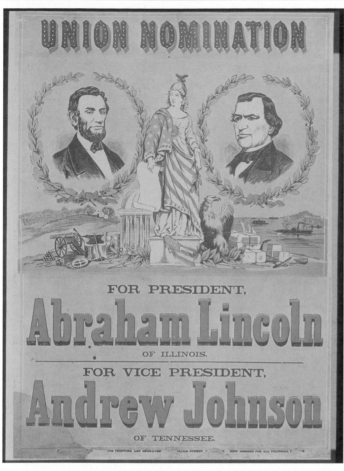

Union Poster 1864. (The Republicans called themselves the National Union Party in 1864, hoping to encourage Democrats to vote for Lincoln.)

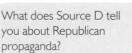

What does Source D tell you about Republican propaganda?

was Lee's view, a view that Hood soon confirmed. A series of attacks on Union lines resulted in the loss of 20,000 Confederates. At the end of August, Hood was forced to abandon Atlanta. Its capture was an important boost to northern morale.

The 1864 election

The Confederacy's last (and best) hope was that Lincoln would be defeated in the 1864 election. This hope was a realistic one. In August, with the war going badly, Lincoln said, 'I am going to be beaten and unless some great change takes place, badly beaten.' The Democrat convention, hoping to capitalise on northern war weariness, called for a negotiated peace, condemned Lincoln's arbitrary measures and pledged to preserve states' rights. However, General McClellan, the Democrat presidential candidate, would not agree to the peace platform. This meant that his party was in something of a muddle.

Lincoln was not popular with all Republicans. Many wanted to nominate General Grant as presidential candidate but he made it clear that he would not stand. John C. Frémont, the 1856 Republican candidate, created his own political party (the Radical Democrats) and threatened to split the Republican vote.

Lincoln was renominated at the Republican convention in June. Andrew Johnson of Tennessee was chosen as his running mate. The fact that Johnson was both a southerner and a War Democrat seemed to strengthen the Republican ticket. The Republican platform endorsed a policy of unconditional surrender and called for a constitutional amendment which would end slavery. In August, wide cracks appeared between the president and his party over reconstruction policy (see pages 195–6). But with the election only a few weeks away, Republicans rallied round Lincoln.

In September the war turned in Lincoln's favour:

- Admiral Farragut won an important naval victory at Mobile.
- Atlanta fell.
- Sheridan was successful in the Shenandoah.

Frémont now withdrew from the race and the election became a straight contest between Lincoln and McClellan. Republicans ridiculed McClellan's military record and did their best to depict the Democrats as at best unpatriotic defeatists and at worst traitors.

The election results

In November, Lincoln won 2,213,645 popular votes (55 per cent of the total) and 212 electoral college votes to McClellan's 1,802,237 votes (45 per cent) and 21 electoral votes. The Republicans increased their majorities in both houses of Congress. Native-born, Protestant Americans remained loyal to Lincoln. Particularly remarkable was the backing Lincoln received from Union troops. Most states enacted provision for soldiers to vote in the field. Those states which blocked this measure failed to stop the soldiers from voting. The War Department allowed whole regiments to return home to vote. Lincoln received 78 per cent of the soldier vote. The election was really a referendum on whether the North should continue fighting. Lincoln's success was the death knell of the Confederacy.

Marching through Georgia

In the autumn of 1864 Sherman divided his army. Leaving Thomas to watch Hood, Sherman set off from Atlanta in mid-November with 62,000 men on a march through Georgia to Savannah on the coast. Cutting adrift from supply lines, Sherman's aim was to demoralise the South, destroying both its capacity

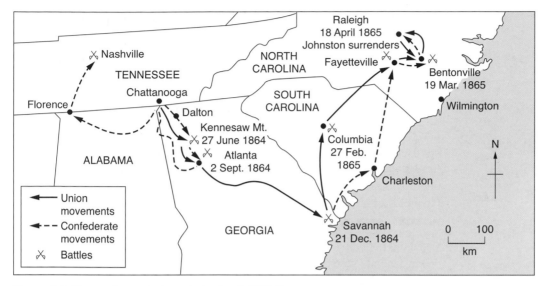

Figure 6.6 Sherman's march through the South 1864–5.

and its will to fight. Convinced that his men could live off the land, he was aware that the Confederacy was not in a position to mount effective opposition. His march – intended to make Georgia 'howl' – went much to plan. Leaving a swathe of destruction some 100 km wide, Union forces captured Savannah in mid-December. The 450-km march inflicted some $100 million damage on Georgia, crippled much of the state's railway network, and gave a lie to the Confederate government's promise of protection for its people.

Franklin and Nashville

Instead of trying to stop Sherman, Hood invaded Tennessee. His scheme – to defeat Thomas, reconquer Kentucky and then march to help Lee – came to nothing. On 30 November, Hood ordered a suicidal assault on Union forces at Franklin. His losses were three times those of the North. The Union army now pulled back to Nashville, which Hood 'besieged' for two weeks. Given that Hood had 23,000 men and Thomas 50,000, it was hard to know who was besieging whom. On 15–16 December, Thomas, one of the Union's unsung heroes, struck, winning the most complete victory of the war. The battle of Nashville effectively destroyed Hood's Army of Tennessee.

The end of the Confederacy

In his December 1864 address to Congress Lincoln spoke confidently of victory. Union resources, he said, were unexhausted and inexhaustible; its military and naval forces were larger than ever, and its economy was prospering. The Confederacy's situation, by contrast, was desperate. Its western armies were in tatters and Lee's Army of Northern Virginia suffered from mass desertions as troops received despairing letters from home.

In early February, Confederate Vice-President Stephens (with Davis's approval) met Lincoln to see if it was possible to arrange peace. The talks were unproductive. Lincoln was not prepared to compromise on either slavery or disunion and Davis was not prepared to surrender.

Lee, now given overall command of all that was left of the Confederate armies, faced a desperate situation. In January 1865 Wilmington, the last major Confederate port, was closed with the Union capture of Fort Fisher. In February, Sherman headed north. South Carolina suffered worse deprivation than Georgia. Lee gave Johnston the thankless task of trying to resist Sherman's remorseless march towards Richmond.

Grant did not really need Sherman's army. By March, rebel trench lines extended 56 km around Petersburg and Lee had fewer than 50,000 half-starved troops to man them. Grant had 125,000 men, not counting Sheridan approaching from the north and Sherman approaching from the south. On 1 April, Sheridan won a decisive victory at Five Forks. The following day Grant ordered a full-scale assault and the Union army broke through Lee's lines. Lee had to abandon both Petersburg and Richmond. Davis fled.

Confederate surrender

Lee headed westwards, hoping to join up with Johnston's forces. Instead, he found himself surrounded by Union forces. On 6 April, he fought his last battle at Sayler's Creek, losing 8000 men. On 9 April, he realised, 'There is nothing left for me to do but to go and see General Grant and I would rather die a thousand deaths.'

Lee and Grant met at Appomattox Court House on 10 April. Lee surrendered and Grant was generous in victory: Confederate troops could keep their side-arms and horses, and Grant gave the hungry rebels Union army rations. Lee, meeting his troops for the last time, said, 'Boys, I have done the best I could for you. Go home now, and if you make as good citizens as you have soldiers, you will do well, and I shall always be proud of you.'

Lee's surrender was the effective end of the war. Davis, fleeing southwards, exhorted the Confederacy to fight on. But most southerners showed no interest in a guerrilla war. On 16 April, Johnston surrendered to Sherman. Davis was captured on 10 May.

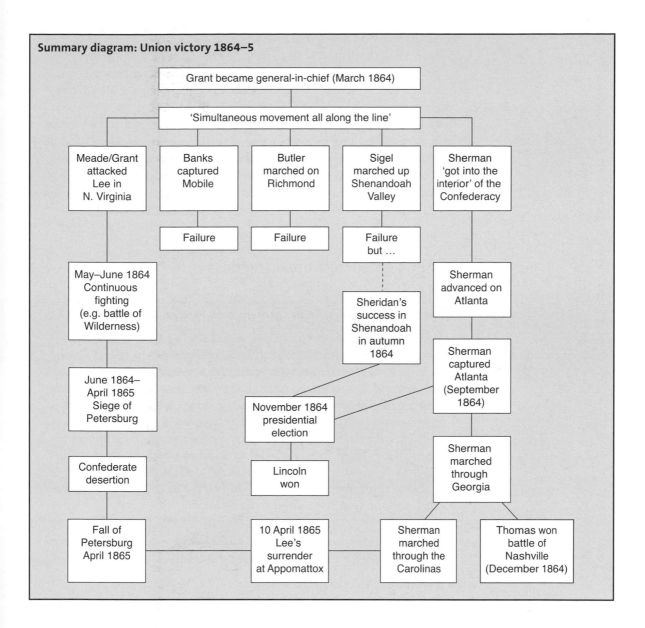

Summary diagram: Union victory 1864–5

Grant became general-in-chief (March 1864)

'Simultaneous movement all along the line'

| Meade/Grant attacked Lee in N. Virginia | Banks captured Mobile | Butler marched on Richmond | Sigel marched up Shenandoah Valley | Sherman 'got into the interior' of the Confederacy |

Failure — Failure — Failure but …

May–June 1864 Continuous fighting (e.g. battle of Wilderness)

Sherman advanced on Atlanta

Sheridan's success in Shenandoah in autumn 1864

June 1864– April 1865 Siege of Petersburg

Sherman captured Atlanta (September 1864)

November 1864 presidential election

Confederate desertion

Lincoln won

Sherman marched through Georgia

| Fall of Petersburg April 1865 | 10 April 1865 Lee's surrender at Appomattox | Sherman marched through the Carolinas | Thomas won battle of Nashville (December 1864) |

⑥ Key debate

▶ *Did the Confederacy defeat itself or was it defeated?*

On 10 April 1865, Robert E. Lee wrote a farewell address to his soldiers: 'After four years' arduous service, marked by unsurpassed courage and fortitude, the Army of Northern Virginia has been compelled to yield to overwhelming numbers and resources.' According to Lee, the Confederacy lost the war not because it fought badly but simply because the enemy had more men and guns.

Historian Richard Current (1960), reviewing the statistics of Union strength – two and a half times the South's population, three times its railway capacity, nine times its industrial production, overwhelming naval supremacy – concluded that: '… surely in view of the disparity of resources, it would have taken a miracle … to enable the South to win. As usual, God was on the side of the heaviest battalions.' Yet not all historians would accept that the Union's superior resources were the prime cause of Confederate defeat. Many insist that Confederate defeat was due to Confederate mistakes and/or problems within the Confederacy which had little to do with resources. Historians R.E. Beringer, H. Hattaway, A. Jones and W.N. Still, for example, write: 'We contend that lack of will constituted the decisive deficiency in the Confederate arsenal.'

So did the Confederacy defeat itself or was it defeated?

Missed Confederate opportunities

EXTRACT 1

? Which of Extracts 1 and 2 provides a more convincing interpretation of Confederate defeat?

From James McPherson, *Battle Cry of Freedom*, Penguin Books, 1990, p. 858.

Of all the explanations for Confederate defeat, the loss of will thesis suffers most from its own particular fallacy of reversibility – that of putting the cart before the horse. Defeat causes demoralization and loss of will; victory pumps up morale and the will to win. Nothing illustrates this better than the radical transformation of northern will from defeatism in August 1864 to a 'depth of determination … to fight to the last' that 'astonished' a British journalist a month later. The southern loss of will was a mirror image of this northern determination. These changes of mood were caused mainly by events on the battlefield. Northern victory and southern defeat in the war cannot be understood apart from the contingency that hung over every campaign, every battle, every election, every decision during the war.

At many stages events on the battlefield might have gone differently and if they had, the course of the war might have been different:

- Confederate forces might have done more after First Manassas (see page 153).
- Had Stonewall Jackson been up to par in June–July 1862 Lee might have triumphed in the Seven Days battles (see pages 157–8).
- Who knows what would have happened had Lee's battle orders not fallen into Union hands in Maryland in September 1862 (see page 158) or Jackson had not been killed at Chancellorsville (see pages 161–2).
- Better Confederate leadership in 1863 might have prevented the loss of Vicksburg and brought victory at Gettysburg (see pages 162–4).

In short, the Confederate cause was not inevitably a 'lost cause'.

Political leadership

Historian Potter claimed that 'If the Union and Confederacy had exchanged presidents with one another, the Confederacy might have won its independence.' Lincoln is generally seen as more eloquent in expressing war aims, more successful in communicating with the people, more skilful in keeping political factions working together, and better able to endure criticism and work with his critics. He is lauded for appointing the winning military team, for picking able administrative subordinates, and for knowing how to delegate.

Lincoln's superiority to Davis might seem self-evident. Nevertheless, Lee could think of no one in the South who could have done a better job than Davis. Davis's government is often charged with failing to manage the country's economy and finances efficiently. The main criticism is that it printed too much money. This fuelled inflation, which ravaged the economy and damaged southern morale. However, given the Union blockade, inflation was inevitable. Despite its economic problems, the Confederacy maintained over three per cent of its population under arms – a higher figure than the North. In terms of the management of military supply, the Confederacy could boast some organisational successes. Ordnance Chief Josiah Gorgas, for example, built an arms industry virtually from scratch. The main problem was the shortage, not the management, of supplies.

Military leadership

The key aspect of leadership in the Civil War, as in any war, was military leadership.

Was the Confederacy too attack-minded?

Many historians claim that Davis and Lee pursued a flawed military strategy. They chose to pursue what has been labelled an 'offensive–defensive' strategy. This consisted of placing conventional armies in an essentially defensive posture to protect as much territory as possible and launching offensive movements when circumstances seemed promising. Lee emphasised the 'offensive' in 'offensive–defensive', seeking to gain and hold the initiative.

Lee's penchant for attack has been criticised. Arguably, a more defensive strategy would have conserved manpower, thereby enabling the Confederacy to prolong the war and perhaps exhaust Union will. Historians Grade McWhiney and Perry Jamieson argue that the Confederacy literally bled itself to death in the first three years of the war by making costly attacks and losing its bravest men. Lee is seen as a main culprit. His battles in 1862–3 were certainly costly: from Seven Days to Chancellorsville his army suffered 65,000 casualties.

Would a purely defensive strategy have been more successful? General Joseph Johnston was the Confederate exponent of defensive warfare. Rather than stand and fight, he surrendered huge chunks of land virtually without a struggle in

North Virginia in 1862 and in Georgia in 1864. This did not enhance southern morale. Moreover, Confederate retreats often led to disastrous sieges and surrenders, for example Fort Donelson (1862), Vicksburg (1863) and Atlanta (1864).

In Lee's view, an 'offensive–defensive' strategy was the best hope of winning a decisive, overwhelming military victory. On several occasions he came tantalisingly close to success. When finally forced on the defensive in 1864–5 and deprived of the opportunity to manoeuvre, his defeat was inevitable.

Despite being outnumbered in every major campaign, Lee won victories which depressed Union and bolstered Confederate morale. Without Lee's generalship the Confederacy would have crumbled earlier. If other Confederate generals had fought as well, the war might have had a different outcome.

Should the Confederacy have relied more on guerrilla warfare?

The Confederate leadership has been taken to task for attempting to fight a conventional rather than a guerrilla war. However, a purely guerrilla-style war strategy in 1861 was inconceivable:

- It would have meant the loss of territory (and thus of slaves). This would have seriously damaged Confederate morale.
- Davis hoped to win British and French recognition. Neither country would have recognised a fledgling Confederacy that relied on guerrilla units rather than on a formal army.

During the war there was considerable Confederate guerrilla activity in Florida, Tennessee, Virginia and Missouri (where it was particularly nasty).

Did the Confederacy focus too much on Virginia?

Some historians think that Lee's strategic vision was limited to Virginia, where his influence concentrated Confederate resources at the expense of the West. The result was that the Confederacy lost the West, and thus lost the war. Such criticism is unfounded. Lee was commander of the Army of Northern Virginia; Virginia was thus his rightful priority. If anyone was to blame for a Virginia-focused strategy it was Davis. In fairness to Davis, it seems highly unlikely that the Confederacy could have won the war by concentrating most of its forces in the West, where military conditions, especially control of the major rivers, favoured the Union. Virginia, the South's most important industrial state, had to be defended. In Virginia geographical conditions favoured the defender. It thus made sense to give most resources to the best army (the Army of Northern Virginia) and the best general (Lee).

Indeed, Davis might be criticised not so much for his preoccupation with Virginia, but instead for dividing scarce resources more or less equally between East and West. However, Davis knew that the Confederacy could not survive

CHAPTER 7

Reconstruction

In 1861 Frederick Douglass predicted, 'The American people and the government of Washington may refuse to recognize it for a time but the inexorable logic of events will force it upon them in the end; that the war now being waged in this land is a war for and against slavery.' Douglass's prediction proved correct. By 1865 American slaves had been freed. The impact of emancipation was one of the problems of Reconstruction – the process of restoring the Confederate states to the Union. How successful was Reconstruction? What impact did Reconstruction, and indeed the Civil War, have on the USA as a whole? In examining these issues, this chapter will focus on:

★ The emancipation of the slaves

★ The African American war effort

★ The problem of Reconstruction

★ Reconstruction in the South 1867–77

★ The results of Reconstruction

★ The impact of the Civil War

Key dates

1861		First Confiscation Act
1862	July	Second Confiscation Act
	Sept.	Emancipation Proclamation
1863	Jan.	Emancipation Proclamation came into effect
	Dec.	Lincoln's Ten Percent Plan
1864		Wade–Davis bill
1865	April	Lincoln assassinated. Andrew Johnson became president
1865	Dec.	Thirteenth Amendment added to the Constitution
1866		Civil Rights Act
1867		Military Reconstruction Act
1868		Fourteenth Amendment added to the Constitution
1870		Fifteenth Amendment added to the Constitution
1877		Rutherford Hayes inaugurated president

The emancipation of the slaves

▶ *Why was the slavery issue so difficult for Lincoln in 1861–2?*

Lincoln was determined to maintain northern unity. An avowed policy of **emancipation** of the slaves would alienate not only northern Democrats, but also the four Union slave states (Kentucky, Maryland, Missouri and Delaware), which together had about 400,000 slaves. It would also spur southerners to an even greater effort and leave no possibility of a compromise peace.

In April 1861, Lincoln declared, 'I have no purpose, directly or indirectly, to interfere with the institution of slavery in the states where it exists. I believe I have no lawful right to do so, and I have no inclination to do so.' Congress supported this stance. In July, the Crittenden Resolution, which disclaimed any intention of meddling with 'the rights or established institutions' of the South, won overwhelming approval in Congress.

'Contraband'

A set of forces placed pressure on the federal government to take some action with regard to emancipation. One problem was what to do with refugee slaves who came to the camps of Union armies occupying parts of the South. By the letter of the Fugitive Slave Act (see page 51), they should have been returned to their owners. Some Union soldiers did just that. Others, on both humane and pragmatic grounds – the slaves would be punished and could also help the rebel war effort – opposed such action.

In May 1861, General Benjamin Butler declared that slaves who came to his camp were to be confiscated as **contraband of war**, thus ensuring that they were not returned to their Confederate owners. This neatly avoided the question of whether or not the fugitives were free and turned the southerners' argument that slaves were property against them. Butler's action was supported by the terms of the Confiscation Act (August 1861), which threatened any property used 'for insurrectionary purposes' with confiscation. It left unsettled the issue of whether or not 'confiscated' slaves became free.

Radical Republicans

As it became clear that there was little likelihood of the Confederate states being enticed back into the Union, radical Republicans began to make their influence felt. To most radicals it seemed that to fight slaveholders without fighting slavery was (in Frederick Douglass's words) 'a half-hearted business'. Radicals wanted to abolish slavery and create a new order in the South. They had a variety of motives:

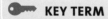 **KEY TERM**

Contraband of war Goods which can be confiscated from the enemy.

- Some, but not all, were genuinely concerned for black Americans.
- Most, if not all, had a loathing of slaveholders, who they blamed for causing the war.
- All were concerned that if the Union was restored without slavery being abolished, nothing would have been solved.
- If emancipation became a Union war aim there was little chance that Britain would support the Confederacy (see pages 135–7).

By December 1861 most Republicans supported a tougher stand against slavery. The House of Representatives now refused to reaffirm Crittenden's resolution. To one Congressman it seemed that a powerful faction was already forming whose watchword was 'Emancipation – the utter extinction of slavery.'

Lincoln's views in 1861

In August 1861, General Frémont, the 1856 Republican presidential candidate and now Union commander in Missouri, issued a proclamation freeing the slaves of all Confederate supporters in Missouri. In Lincoln's view this was a step too far and he ordered that Frémont rescind his order. When Frémont refused, Lincoln removed him from his command.

Radicals implored Lincoln to declare his support for emancipation. He remained hesitant. While he shared the radical conviction that slavery was a moral evil, he still had no wish to alienate northern Democrats or the Union slave states, and feared that if emancipation became a Union war aim, the conflict would degenerate into a 'violent and remorseless struggle'. 'We didn't go to war to put down slavery – but to put the flag back', declared Lincoln in December 1861: '… the thunderbolt will keep.'

SOURCE A

A family of former slaves outside their ramshackle house in Virginia in 1862.

Examine Source A. Why do you think the photograph was taken? (Remember that taking photographs in the 1860s was an expensive business.)

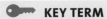
Congressional measures in 1862

In the spring of 1862 Congress began to take action against slavery. In April, slavery in Washington was abolished: provision was made to compensate slave owners and to support the **colonisation** of ex-slaves to Liberia or Haiti. In June, Congress abolished slavery in all federal territories. In July, a second and much more sweeping Confiscation Act was enacted. This allowed the seizure of all enemy 'property': slaves in such cases were to be set 'forever free'. Lincoln also received authority to employ 'persons of African descent' in any capacity deemed necessary for the suppression of the rebellion. As a sweetener to Lincoln, Congress again set aside $500,000 for colonisation expenses.

The Confiscation Act met with considerable resistance in Congress. Some thought it went too far. Others thought it did not go far enough and were disappointed that the measure proposed to do nothing about slavery in the Union slave states. Lincoln had doubts about the bill, but in the end signed it. In fact, the second Confiscation Act was not as radical as it seemed. The only way that a slave could actually gain freedom was on a case-by-case basis before a federal court, and this court had to find that the slave owner was, in fact, a rebel.

Lincoln's views, spring/summer 1862

In July 1862, abolitionist William Lloyd Garrison described Lincoln's handling of the slavery issue as, 'stumbling, halting, prevaricating, irresolute, weak, besotted'. At best Lincoln had followed northern opinion; others – Congressmen and army officers – had led it. However, by mid-1862, Lincoln, certain that it was his responsibility to make the final decision on the emancipation issue, was convinced that a bold step was necessary.

Even before the summer of 1862 Lincoln had begun to take action. In March 1862 he sent Congress a request that compensation be given to any state which adopted the principle of gradual abolition of slavery. Owners would be given $400 for every slave freed. He hoped that the Union slave states would adopt their own emancipation laws and that some of the rebel states might then follow suit. Abolitionists denounced Lincoln's measure, arguing that justice would be better served by compensating the slaves for their long years in bondage rather than by indemnifying slaveholders. Nevertheless, Congress approved the scheme for gradual compensated emancipation. However, to Lincoln's chagrin, the Union slave states refused to implement emancipation on any terms.

Thwarted in the North, Lincoln determined to act in the South. The situation had changed since 1861. The allegiance of Kentucky, Maryland and Missouri was now secure. He was aware of the pressure from radical Republicans and reluctant to alienate them. Lincoln was also concerned that if the Union won, and the southern states re-entered the Union with slavery untouched, it would remain a source of future strife. His main belief, however, was that a bold statement on emancipation would weaken the Confederacy.

In July 1862 Lincoln presented his Emancipation Proclamation to his cabinet. Many of its members greeted the news with astonishment. 'The measure goes beyond anything I have recommended', said Stanton. All except Postmaster Montgomery Blair – who feared that the Proclamation would harm Republican chances in the autumn mid-term elections – approved. However, William Seward recommended that it should only be issued after a military success; otherwise it would seem like an act of desperation born of weakness. Lincoln accepted the logic of this and waited patiently.

When **Horace Greeley** wrote a bitter editorial criticising him for not doing more on the slavery front, Lincoln still did not reveal his intentions. He responded to Greeley by saying, 'If I could save the Union without freeing any slave I would do so and if I could save it by freeing all the slaves I would do it; and if I could save it by freeing some and leaving others alone I would also do that.'

KEY FIGURE

Horace Greeley (1811–72)

A newspaper editor, politician and outspoken opponent of slavery. The *New York Times*, which he founded and edited, was the USA's most influential newspaper from the 1840s to the 1870s.

SOURCE B

Lincoln, in discussion with some Chicago Christian ministers, in early September 1862, quoted in Mark E. Neely, Jr, *The Last Best Hope of Earth*, Harvard University Press, 1993, p. 112.

There are about fifty thousand bayonets in the Union armies from the border slave states. It would be a serious matter if, in consequence of a proclamation such as you desire, they should go over to the rebels. I do not think they all would – not so many indeed as a year ago, or as six months ago – not so many today as yesterday … Let me say one thing more. I think you should admit that we already have an important principle to rally and unite the people in the fact that constitutional government is at stake. This is a fundamental idea, going down about as deep as anything.

Why was it strange that Lincoln spoke as he did in Source B?

The Emancipation Proclamation

The proclamation was issued on 22 September 1862 after the battle of Antietam (see page 158). Justified by Lincoln as 'a fit and necessary war measure', it seemed, on the surface, to be cautious:

- Slavery was to be left untouched in states that returned to the Union before 1 January 1863.
- Thereafter all slaves in enemy territory conquered by Union armies would be 'forever free'.

Thus, the Proclamation had no effect whatsoever in the Union slave states. It did not even affect slavery in those areas that had already been brought back under Union control.

Reaction to the proclamation

The *Spectator*, published in London, said that the principle behind the proclamation seemed to be, 'not that a human being cannot justly own another, but that he cannot own him unless he is loyal to the United States'. Nevertheless, most American abolitionists were delighted. 'God bless Abraham Lincoln', wrote Greeley. 'Thank God, the skies are brighter and the air is purer, now that slavery has been handed over to judgment', said Sumner. Radical Republicans appreciated that Lincoln had gone as far as his powers allowed in making the war a war to end slavery. (Many British commentators misunderstood Lincoln's constitutional powers and the fact that he had no power to act against slavery in areas loyal to the USA unless this could be seen as essential to the Union war effort.) As Union forces advanced, slavery in the Confederacy would end, and once it ended there it could not survive in the border states. According to historian Roger Ransom (1989), 'with the stroke of a pen, the president had turned the war into a revolution'.

The mid-term elections

Northern Democrats, convinced that the proclamation would make it impossible to bring the Confederate states back into the Union, denounced the measure. Aware of the fear of a migration of ex-slaves northwards, Democrats made emancipation a central issue in the mid-term elections in autumn 1862. Historians once claimed that these elections were a triumph for the Democrats, and thus proof that most northerners were opposed to emancipation. The Republicans lost control of several states, and also lost 35 Congressional seats. Lincoln acknowledged that his proclamation contributed to the setbacks. However, on closer analysis, the election results suggest that emancipation had less impact than Lincoln believed. Overall the Republicans retained control of most states and easily kept control of Congress. Democrat majorities in Pennsylvania, Ohio, New York and Indiana were very small and could be explained by the inability of Republican-supporting soldiers to vote. The Republicans actually suffered the smallest net loss of a party in power for twenty years.

The impact of the Emancipation Proclamation

On 1 January 1863, Lincoln proclaimed that the freedom of all slaves in rebellious regions was now a Union war aim: 'an act of justice' as well as 'military necessity'. Not wishing to be held responsible for a bloody slave revolt, he urged slaves 'to abstain from all violence, unless in necessary self-defence'. At the same time, he called on Union forces to protect the rights of those they made free.

Davis condemned the proclamation as 'the most execrable measure recorded in the history of guilty man'. In the short term it may well have helped to stiffen Confederate resistance. However, in the long term it weakened the Confederacy, who now stood little chance of winning British support. By encouraging slaves to flee to Union lines the proclamation worsened the South's manpower shortage. As Lincoln said: 'Freedom has given us the control of 200,000 able-bodied men … It will give us more yet. Just so much has it subtracted from the strength of our enemies.'

The Thirteenth Amendment

The Emancipation Proclamation was a war measure that would have questionable force once the war ended. Consequently, the Republicans determined to pass a constitutional amendment prohibiting slavery. The Senate passed the amendment in 1864 but it failed to get the necessary two-thirds support in the House.

In June 1864, the Republican national convention, urged on by Lincoln, agreed to endorse the constitutional amendment to end slavery. Interpreting Republican election success in November (see page 170) as public support for the amendment, Lincoln redoubled his efforts to secure Congressional approval, applying patronage pressure to several Democrats in the House, and to good effect. On 31 January 1865, the House approved (with three votes to spare) the Thirteenth Amendment for ratification by the states.

Lincoln was delighted. It was, he said, 'a king's cure for all the evils. It winds the whole thing up.' It hardly did that, but it was a major step forward.

The Great Emancipator?

From January 1863 Union soldiers fought for the revolutionary goal of a new Union without slavery. Many – but by no means all – northerners came to accept this. Most would not have accepted it in 1861. During the war opinion changed. Lincoln's policies reflected and influenced that change. He moved cautiously, his actions based more on pragmatism than on morality. From start to finish his main aim was to preserve the Union, not free the slaves. But by mid-1862 Lincoln believed that the two issues had become nearly one and the same. By freeing the slaves he could help to preserve the Union.

Some scholars have claimed that Lincoln did his best to evade the whole question of black freedom and that it was escaping slaves who forced him to embrace emancipation. However, the argument that the slaves freed themselves has been pushed too far. Only Union victory brought slavery to an end. Ultimately, slaves were freed by the Union army. Lincoln was commander-in-chief of that army. The fact that he was also committed to freeing the slaves was crucial.

By 1865, many abolitionists were prepared to give credit where credit was due. In 1865, Garrison (who had castigated Lincoln for being a 'wet rag' in 1862) commended him for having done a 'mighty work for the freedom of millions … I have the utmost faith in the benevolence of your heart, the purity of your motives and the integrity of your spirit.' Frederick Douglass commented: 'Viewed from the genuine abolition ground, Mr Lincoln seemed tardy, cold, dull and indifferent; but measuring him by the sentiment of his country, a sentiment he was bound as a statesman to consult, he was swift, zealous, radical and determined.'

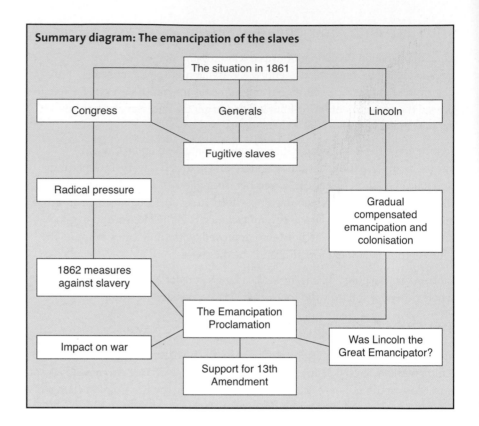

Summary diagram: The emancipation of the slaves

The situation in 1861

Congress

Generals

Lincoln

Fugitive slaves

Radical pressure

Gradual compensated emancipation and colonisation

1862 measures against slavery

The Emancipation Proclamation

Impact on war

Was Lincoln the Great Emancipator?

Support for 13th Amendment

2 The African American war effort

▶ *How significant was the black contribution to the war?*

From the start of the war, Lincoln had faced conflicting pressure on the question of whether to enlist black soldiers into the Union army. Initially, most northerners, hating the notion of blacks fighting against whites, opposed black recruitment. Black leaders and abolitionists, however, were anxious that black men should fight in a war that was likely to destroy slavery. Pointing out that black sailors were serving in the Union navy, they pushed for similar enlistment of black soldiers. 'This is no time to fight with one hand, when both are needed', declared Douglass: 'this is no time to fight with your white hand and allow your black hand to remain tied'.

Recruitment of black soldiers

Lincoln, anxious to preserve northern unity, initially stood firm against black recruitment. This did not prevent some attempts to recruit black soldiers. General Hunter, for example, raised a regiment of black volunteers on the Sea Islands off the coast of South Carolina in early 1862. Receiving no financial support from the War Department, Hunter was forced to disband his regiment. The July 1862 Confiscation Act gave Lincoln the power to use ex-slaves as a military force but he interpreted this narrowly, insisting that black people should simply be employed as army labourers, not front-line troops.

In August 1862, Secretary of War Stanton authorised the creation of a regiment of 5000 black troops to be recruited in Union-occupied areas of Louisiana. Lincoln did not object, and in September the first official regiment of black soldiers was mustered into Union service. After the Emancipation Proclamation, Lincoln's resistance abated and there was a large influx of black men into the Union army. As in so many respects, Lincoln was in tune with northern opinion. Given the mounting casualty lists there was far more support for black soldiers than there had been in 1861.

Of the 46,000 free black men of military age in the North, 33,000 joined the Union armies. Most black troops, however, were ex-slaves. Some 100,000 were recruited from the Confederacy. Another 42,000 slaves from Kentucky, Delaware, Maryland and Missouri also enlisted. (This was the swiftest way for border state slaves to get their freedom.) In June 1863, black troops acquitted themselves well at Milliken's Bend, Louisiana. Many black regiments took part in the 1864–5 fighting around Petersburg. They fought as well as white regiments.

The significance of black participation

The fact that black soldiers had fought for freedom bolstered black confidence and pride. Military service also carried with it an assumption of US citizenship. Douglass commented: 'Once let the black man get upon his person the brass letters US, let him get an eagle on his buttons and musket on his shoulder … and there is no power on earth which can deny that he has earned the right to citizenship in the USA.'

The impact of black soldiers on the outcome of the war should not be exaggerated. Of the 37,000 black soldiers who died, only 3000 were killed in combat; the rest died of disease. Nevertheless, black troops aided the Union war effort at a critical time when northern whites were increasingly reluctant to fight. By 1865 there were nearly as many black soldiers in arms against the Confederacy as there were white soldiers defending it.

SOURCE C

Lincoln writing in September 1864.

Any different policy in regard to the colored man [than black recruitment] deprives us of his help and this is more than we can bear … This is not a question of sentiment or taste, but one of physical force which can be measured and estimated as [can] horse power and steam power … Keep it up and you can save the Union. Throw it away and the Union goes with it.

Why, according to Source C, did Lincoln change his views on black participation in the war? **?**

Slavery in the Union-occupied South

As the war progressed, the Union army occupied large parts of the South. Some land was confiscated, but far more came into federal hands because southerners had not paid their taxes or had simply abandoned their property. What to do with this land, coupled with the organisation of its black labour, was a major problem. There was little agreement on the critical issue: would confiscated and abandoned land be sold or distributed to freedmen?

Given no firm presidential or Congressional guidance, the situation in the reoccupied areas of the Confederacy was chaotic, varying from place to place and from time to time. Federal agents in the South, especially army officers, instituted their own remedies. The most famous 'rehearsal for Reconstruction' occurred on the Sea Islands, occupied by Union forces in 1861. Black people, who pooled their meagre resources, were allowed to buy plots of land. This well-publicised (albeit small-scale) development was not typical. In most occupied areas plantations were administered by 'superintendents of Negro affairs' or leased to northern investors whose main purpose was monetary profit. Some plantations were still controlled by former slaveholders who were prepared to take an oath of allegiance to the Union.

In these circumstances life for most ex-slaves did not change very much (except they were no longer whipped). They continued to work on the same plantations, closely supervised by white managers. While they were now paid wages, most of the money earned was withheld to pay for food and clothing, and they were forbidden to leave the land on which they worked.

Colonisation schemes

Fearing that blacks and whites could not live peacefully together, Lincoln supported the idea of colonising ex-slaves in the Caribbean or Latin America. Several attempts were made to put colonisation schemes into effect. All foundered, largely because few black people agreed to participate.

The situation in 1865

- In January 1865, General Sherman declared that freed slaves should receive 40 acres (16 hectares) of land and a surplus mule. Sherman was far from a humanitarian reformer: his main concern was to relieve the pressure caused by the large number of impoverished black people following his army (see pages 170–2). He stressed that Congress would have to agree to his plan. Nevertheless, his actions raised black hopes and expectations.
- By 1865, most Republican Congressmen favoured confiscating plantation land and redistributing it among freedmen and loyal whites. Such action would reward the deserving and punish the guilty. However, unable to agree on a precise measure, Congress failed to pass a redistribution bill.
- While some northerners were anxious to help the ex-slaves, many had a real antipathy to blacks and feared an exodus of ex-slaves to the North.

- Most border state whites had no wish to give blacks equal rights. Although Missouri and Maryland freed their slaves in 1864, Kentucky still had 65,000 slaves in bondage in April 1865. Slavery survived in the state until December 1865.
- In 1865, only five free states allowed blacks to vote on equal terms with whites.
- In March 1865, Congress set up the Freedmen Bureau. Its aim was to help relieve the suffering of southern blacks (and poor whites) by providing food, clothes and medical care. Although envisaged as a temporary measure, its creation symbolised the widespread Republican belief that the federal government should shoulder some responsibility for the freedmen's well-being.

The situation in the South

Most black people remained slaves throughout the war. Given that they comprised more than a third of the Confederacy's population, they made a significant contribution to its war effort:

- They worked in factories and mines, maintained the railways and helped to grow and harvest crops.
- Many southern states passed laws enabling them to conscript slaves for military labour. In 1863 the Confederate Congress passed a general impressment law. Slaves played an important military role, erecting fortifications and helping behind the lines.

The war had a major impact on slave–master relations. As the conflict intensified, there were fewer white men left to supervise the slaves. Supervision, therefore, fell to women and young and old men. Most proved less effective taskmasters than their pre-war predecessors. Slaves took advantage of the situation, working less diligently. Slave owners on the coast or in the path of invading Union armies often sent their slaves to safer areas of the Confederacy. Such dislocations undermined traditional authority patterns.

For many slaves the war was a time of great privation:

- General shortages of goods resulted in planters cutting back on the food and clothing given to slaves.
- For impressed slaves labour was often harder than on the plantation.

Despite southern whites' fears, there was no major slave rebellion. Aware that freedom was coming, most slaves bided their time. Few showed much loyalty to their owners. Whenever an opportunity came to escape most took it. In the course of the war some 500,000 slaves fled.

Confederate recruitment of slaves

By 1864 some influential southerners were arguing in favour of arming slaves to fight for the Confederacy. Most southerners opposed the idea. 'Whenever we establish the fact that they are a military race, we destroy our whole theory that they are unfit to be free', said Governor Brown of Georgia. However, in February 1865 Robert E. Lee, desperately short of men, supported arming slaves and in March the Confederate Congress passed a law providing for the arming of 300,000 slaves. The measure came too late. A few black companies were raised but not in time to see action. Whether slaves would have fought loyally for the rebel cause – even if they had been offered their freedom – must remain in doubt.

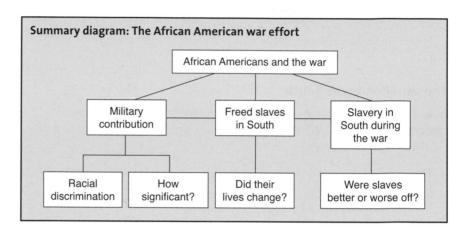

Summary diagram: The African American war effort

The problem of Reconstruction

3

> ▶ Why was Reconstruction a problem for Presidents Lincoln and
> Johnson?

In 1865 the triumphant federal government faced the problem of restoring the Confederate states to the Union. This process is known as Reconstruction. The period from 1865 to 1877 is often called the 'age of Reconstruction'. However, Reconstruction was not something that began in 1865: it was an issue from 1861 onwards and it was really what the war was all about. Nor did the process of Reconstruction end in 1877: in most southern states it ended much earlier. The debate over timescale is by no means the only debate about Reconstruction. Virtually every aspect of the topic has been the subject of controversy.

If reconstructing Reconstruction is hard for historians, the reality was even harder for US politicians at the time. There were no precedents and the Constitution provided little guidance. There were also fundamental disagreements about the basic issue of bringing the seceded states back into the Union. Ironically, the ex-Confederate states now claimed that they had never legally been out of it. Equally ironically, many Republicans, who had insisted that the Confederate states could not secede, now claimed that they had in fact seceded, thereby reverting to territorial status.

There were other important matters to be resolved:

- A feeling of loyalty to the Union had to be restored among white southerners.
- The war-torn economy of the South had to be rebuilt.
- Newly freed slaves had to be given the opportunity to enjoy their freedom.

From 1861, as Union troops pushed remorselessly into the South, Lincoln's administration faced the problem of how to restore loyal governments in the rebel states. In fact, there was a series of interrelated problems:

- On what terms should the states be reunited to the Union?
- How should white southerners be treated?
- Should Congress or the president decide Reconstruction policy?

Northern opinion was divided on all these matters. As well as differences between Republicans and Democrats, there were differences within the Republican Party.

Lincoln and Reconstruction

Lincoln was convinced that Reconstruction was a presidential concern. The Constitution gave him the power of pardon and he was also commander-in-chief. He realised, however, that once the war ended, his powers would be considerably reduced. If he was to control Reconstruction he needed to establish firm principles during the war.

Lincoln's strategic aim was consistent throughout the war: he wanted to restore the Union as quickly as possible. His usual policy was to install military governors in those areas that had been partially reconquered. The governors were expected to work with whatever popular support they could find. Lincoln hoped that military government would last only until enough loyal citizens could form a new state government.

The Ten Percent Plan

Lincoln spelt out his Reconstruction ideas in December 1863. He offered pardon to white southerners who would take an oath of allegiance to the Union. When ten per cent of the 1860 electorate had taken this oath, a new state government could be established. Provided the state then accepted the abolition of slavery, Lincoln agreed to recognise its government. In early 1864 Tennessee, Louisiana and Arkansas used this Ten Percent Plan to set up new governments.

Radical Republican opposition

Radical Republicans disagreed with Lincoln's actions. Their leaders included:

- **Thaddeus Stevens**, a Pennsylvanian industrialist
- Charles Sumner, the senator beaten in 1856 (see page 70)
- Benjamin Wade, a politician from Ohio.

 **KEY FIGURE**

Thaddeus Stevens (1792–1868)

One of the leaders of the radical Republicans in Congress. A fierce opponent of slavery and discrimination, he sought to secure African American rights during Reconstruction.

Many had sat in Congress for many years. This enhanced their influence, ensuring that they were well represented on key committees. Most had good abolitionist credentials and some had long supported equal rights for black Americans. Although the radicals did not work in close and constant harmony, most held similar views with regard to Reconstruction:

- They wanted to impose a harsh settlement on the South, punishing the main rebels by confiscating their land.
- They believed that ex-slaves should have the same rights as white Americans.

Political motivation?

It has been claimed that radical concern for black rights, particularly black suffrage, was triggered by shabby political motives rather than idealism. Certainly radicals feared that once the southern states were back within the Union, the Democrat Party would again be a major threat. There seemed two ways to prevent this: first, to ensure that ex-slaves could vote (they would surely vote Republican); and second, to disfranchise large numbers of rebels. Many radicals did not separate idealism and political pragmatism; they believed that black Americans should be entitled to vote and were not ashamed to assert that such a policy would ensure Republican ascendancy.

Whatever their motives, most radicals were convinced that the southern states, by seceding, had reverted to the condition of territories and should be subject to Congress's authority. Congress, not the president, should thus control the Reconstruction process.

The Wade–Davis bill

Radical dissatisfaction with Lincoln's Ten Percent Plan was soon apparent. In April 1864 a Louisiana convention had drawn up a constitution banning slavery, but not giving black people (47 per cent of the state's population) the vote. Over ten per cent of Louisiana's electorate voted in favour of the constitution. Lincoln immediately recognised the new Louisiana government and treated the state as if it had been restored to the Union. However, Congress rejected Louisiana's constitution and refused admission to its two senators.

Henry Davis and Benjamin Wade now introduced a bill requiring not ten but 50 per cent of the people of the Confederate states to take an 'ironclad oath' – an oath that they had never voluntarily supported the rebellion – before the states could return into the Union. Moreover, anyone who had held political office during the Confederacy or had voluntarily borne arms against the Union was to be excluded from the political process.

The Wade–Davis bill was not a fully fledged radical measure; it did not, for example, guarantee blacks equal political rights. Its main purpose was to postpone Reconstruction until the war was over, when Congress would have more control. The bill easily passed both houses of Congress. Lincoln, aware of the political storm that would (and did) follow, vetoed the bill. His hopes of formulating a definitive method by which former Confederate states would be allowed back into the Union had failed.

Lincoln's views in 1865

Precisely where Lincoln stood on many Reconstruction issues by 1865 is a matter of debate. He seems to have been moving cautiously towards supporting the view that black people should have equality before the law and talked in terms of giving some, especially those who had fought for the Union, the vote. On such matters as confiscation of property (slaves apart) and punishment of Confederate leaders, he was prepared to be generous. In his second inauguration speech in March 1865 he talked of 'malice towards none' and the need for a 'just and lasting peace'. But it was clear that he faced problems. His executive power had not enabled him to bring a single rebel state back into the Union. His party, even his own cabinet, was divided on a host of Reconstruction matters.

Lincoln's assassination

Just what Lincoln would have done will remain forever a mystery. On 14 April 1865 he was shot by the actor John Wilkes Booth in the Ford Theatre in Washington and died the following morning. Booth escaped, but within days had been tracked down and killed by Union troops. Four others – three men and a woman – who were involved in the assassination were tried, found guilty and hanged. While most northerners assumed that Confederate leaders had instigated the murder, it seems likely that the plot arose in the fevered mind of Booth alone. He had long wanted to strike a blow for the southern cause. The murder of Lincoln did little to help that cause.

Andrew Johnson and Reconstruction

After Lincoln's assassination Vice-President Andrew Johnson, an ex-Democrat and ex-slave owner from Tennessee, became president. A self-made man who had risen from tailor's apprentice to prosperous landowner, he had been the only senator from any of the Confederate states to stay loyal to the Union. In 1864, in an effort to balance the Republican/Unionist ticket, Johnson was nominated vice-president.

SOURCE D

Radical Republican G.W. Julian of Indiana, April 1865.

I spent most of the afternoon in a political caucus, held for the purpose of considering the necessity for a new Cabinet and a line of policy less conciliatory than that of Mr Lincoln: and while everybody was shocked at his murder, the feeling was nearly universal that the accession of Johnson to the presidency would prove a godsend to the country. Aside from Mr Lincoln's known policy of tenderness to the Rebels … his views of the subject of reconstruction were as distasteful as possible to radical Republicans.

Look at Source D. Why were some radical Republicans privately pleased at Johnson becoming president?

Andrew Johnson

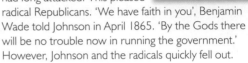

1808	Born, in extreme poverty, in North Carolina
1826	Moved to Tennessee
1827	Married Eliza McCardle, who taught him to read and write
1853	Elected governor of Tennessee
1857	Became a Senator
1862	Appointed military governor of Tennessee
1864	Nominated as Lincoln's vice-president
1865	Became president
1868	Faced impeachment trial
1875	Died

Throughout his political career, Johnson stressed his working-class origins and claimed a special identification with ordinary Americans. In 1865 it seemed likely that he would take a tough stand against the Confederate leaders, especially the great plantation owners whom he had long attacked. This pleased radical Republicans. 'We have faith in you', Benjamin Wade told Johnson in April 1865. 'By the Gods there will be no trouble now in running the government.' However, Johnson and the radicals quickly fell out.

Historians have generally given Johnson a poor press. He has been criticised for sharing the racial views of most white southerners and being unconcerned about the plight of ex-slaves. He has also been attacked for stubbornly ignoring the northern political mood. However, some recent biographers have been more sympathetic, arguing that Johnson's Reconstruction policies were essentially right, his main failure being his inability to carry them out.

A few radicals were (privately) pleased that Johnson had replaced Lincoln, even if they disliked the circumstances. They hoped he would take a tougher stance against the rebel leaders. 'Traitors', Johnson had declared in 1864, 'must be punished and impoverished'. This was the kind of talk that radicals liked to hear. However, the Johnson–radical honeymoon was short-lived. Differences over Reconstruction policies were soon to lead to bitter separation.

The situation in the South

The war was effectively over by May 1865. Confederate soldiers returned home and there was no major guerrilla resistance. This meant that Johnson's administration could quickly demobilise Union armed forces. By late 1866 the Union army was only 38,000 strong. However, there were serious problems in the South:

- A quarter of all white southern men of military age had died in the war. Another quarter had been seriously wounded. (Mississippi spent a fifth of its revenue in 1865 on purchasing artificial limbs for Confederate veterans.)
- The southern economy was in tatters. Union armies had caused widespread devastation.
- The southern banking system was in chaos.
- Large numbers of black and white southerners were dependent on federal aid for subsistence.
- The emancipation of the slaves meant that the South had lost over $2 billion of capital.

Black expectations

In 1865 most black people relished the opportunity to flaunt their liberty and enjoy its material benefits. Many walked off the plantations to test their freedom, to search for loved ones who had been sold, or to seek their fortunes. In the summer of 1865 black leaders organised mass meetings and petitions demanding civil equality. Such demands were supported by thousands of black soldiers who had served in the Union army. Ex-soldiers, often literate thanks to army schools, frequently became the leaders of black political movements post-1865.

The fact that many blacks had great expectations (which might be difficult to realise) was one problem. The attitude of southern whites was another. The vast majority did not consider blacks to be their equals. Resentful and fearful of emancipated slaves, many were appalled at what they saw as black insubordination, and a wave of violence raged almost unchecked in many parts of the South. Black people were assaulted and sometimes murdered for trying to leave plantations.

Johnson's aims

Johnson, who kept Lincoln's cabinet, claimed that his intention was to continue Lincoln's policy. Viewing Reconstruction as an executive not a legislative function, he hoped to restore the southern states to the Union before Congress met in December 1865. Keen that the USA should return to its normal functioning as soon as possible, Johnson saw no alternative but to work with ex-Confederates. He thus favoured leniency. Committed to state rights, he believed it was not the federal government's responsibility to decide suffrage issues or to involve itself in economic and social matters. Nor had he any wish to promote the position of ex-slaves. Shaped by a lifetime in Tennessee, he did not consider blacks to be equal to whites and opposed black suffrage.

Presidential Reconstruction

In May 1865, Johnson extended recognition to the southern governments created under Lincoln's administration (none of which had enfranchised black Americans). The same month he issued a general amnesty to southerners who were willing to swear an oath of allegiance and support emancipation. While major Confederate office holders were exempted, they could apply for a presidential pardon. Over the summer Johnson granted thousands of pardons. Johnson also ordered that confiscated land be returned to pardoned southerners. This necessitated the army evicting thousands of freedmen across the South.

Why Johnson so quickly abandoned the idea of punishing the southern élite is something of a mystery. There were rumours at the time that some southerners used bribery – or the charms of their wives and daughters – to win pardons. In fact, Johnson viewed cooperation with southerners as indispensable to two interrelated goals: the maintenance of white supremacy in the South; and his re-election as president in 1868. To achieve the latter, he needed to retain the support of northern Republicans, win over moderate northern Democrats and build up a following in the South.

Johnson made the process by which southern states would return to the Union easy. He appointed provisional state governors who did their best to cooperate with white southerners. Their main task was to hold elections (in which only whites could vote) for state conventions. The conventions were to draw up new constitutions that accepted that slavery was illegal. Once this was done the states would be readmitted to the Union.

Johnson's scheme was approved by his cabinet and seemed (in 1865) to have the support of most northerners. While many Republicans favoured black suffrage, few – the radicals apart – saw it as a reason to repudiate the president. Moderate Republicans, anxious to keep their party united, realised that black rights was a potentially divisive issue in the North.

'Reconstruction Confederate style'

White southerners set about implementing Johnson's terms. State conventions acknowledged the end of slavery. Southern states then proceeded to elect legislatures, governors and members of Congress. Thereafter, the new southern governments searched for means of keeping the freedmen under control. No state enfranchised black people. All introduced 'Black Codes', designed to ensure that black people remained second-class citizens:

- Most states required black people to possess contracts which provided evidence of employment. Those who were unemployed or who broke the contracts could be forcibly set to work.
- Black children could be taken as 'apprentices' and put to work on plantations.
- Some codes prevented black people from renting or buying land, marrying white people, serving on juries, and receiving poor relief or education.

The codes were enforced by a white legal system that made little pretence of meting out justice fairly. Texas courts, for example, indicted some 500 white men for the murder of black people in 1865–6, but not one was convicted.

The aim of 'Reconstruction Confederate style' was to resurrect as near as possible the old order. Johnson did not approve of all the developments in the South and expressed some concern for the freedmen. But given his state rights' ideology, he believed he had no alternative but to accept what had occurred. In December 1865 he announced that the work of 'restoration' was complete. He followed this up by granting (on Christmas Day 1865) an unconditional pardon to all Civil War participants, except high-ranking military and civil officials.

Congress versus the South

By the time Congress met in December 1865 there were misgivings about Johnson's leniency. After four years of war northerners still had a profound distrust of the South. The fact that the southern Congressmen who turned up in Washington, DC included Stephens (the Confederate vice-president), four Confederate generals and 58 Confederate Congress members did not reassure northerners of the South's good intent. Nor did the Black Codes. Unless the federal government took action, black people would not have equal opportunity. Moreover, there seemed every likelihood that southerners, with their northern Democrat allies, would soon dominate the political scene. In 1865 northern Democrats held only a quarter of the seats in Congress. The return of the southern states would bring in 22 senators and 63 members of the House, the majority of whom would be Democrat.

Most Republican Congressmen were moderates, not radicals. Many were not enthusiastic about black suffrage; nor did they wish to greatly expand federal authority. But most thought that Confederate leaders should be barred from holding office and that the basic rights of ex-slaves should be protected. Thus, Congress refused to admit the southern Congressmen or to recognise the new regimes in the South. In an effort to control developments, a Committee on Reconstruction was formed to recommend a new policy. This committee had the support of most Republicans and was not dominated by radicals. The moderate Republican majority still hoped to work out a compromise that would guarantee basic rights to southern black people and be acceptable to Johnson.

Congress versus Johnson

Instead of working with the moderate Republicans, Johnson chose to side with the Democrats. When Congress tried to enlarge the powers of the Freedmen's Bureau he vetoed it, claiming that it was an unwarranted continuation of war power. Moderate Republicans were horrified. Despite huge problems the bureau had operated effectively, providing basic welfare provision for ex-slaves. Johnson's veto helped to convince many Republicans that they could no longer work with the president.

The 1866 Civil Rights Act

Moderate and radical Republicans now joined forces to introduce a Civil Rights Act which aimed to guarantee minimal rights to black people. Defining all people born in the USA (except untaxed Native Americans) as national citizens, the measure asserted the right of the federal government to intervene in state affairs where and when necessary to protect the rights of US citizens. The bill received almost unanimous support from Congressional Republicans.

Johnson stuck to his guns. Arguing that civil rights were a state matter, he vetoed the measure. Congress struck back. In April 1866, a two-thirds majority ensured that Johnson's veto was overridden and the Civil Rights Act became law. A few weeks later Congress passed a second Freedmen Bureau Act over Johnson's veto.

The Fourteenth Amendment

To ensure that civil rights could not be changed in future, both Houses of Congress now adopted the Fourteenth Amendment (which embodied the Civil Rights Act). This guaranteed all citizens equality before the law. If individual states tried to abridge the rights of US citizens, the federal government could intervene. It also banned from office Confederates who before the war had taken an oath of allegiance to the Union, required of officials ranging from the president down to postmasters. This made virtually the entire political leadership of the South ineligible for office. Rejected by all the ex-Confederate states (except Tennessee), it failed to get the approval of 75 per cent of the states that was necessary for it to become law.

Race riots

In the summer of 1866 there were serious race riots in the South, first in Memphis (May) and then in New Orleans (July). Gangs of whites attacked black 'agitators', resulting in 80–90 black deaths. Most northerners were appalled. They were similarly appalled by the rise of secret paramilitary organisations such as the Knights of the White Camelia and the Ku Klux Klan (see pages 209–10), which aimed to terrorise blacks and those whites who sympathised with them.

The 1866 mid-term elections

The 1866 mid-term elections seemed to provide Johnson with an opportunity to strengthen his position. Hoping to unite Democrats and conservative Republicans he supported the National Union convention, which met in Philadelphia in July. The convention called for the election of Congressmen who would support Johnson's policies. Johnson threw himself into the election campaign, speaking in many of the USA's largest cities. His efforts backfired:

- Confronted by hecklers, Johnson often lost his temper and in so doing surrendered his presidential dignity.
- His hopes of establishing a new party did not materialise. The National Union movement soon became little more than the Democrats in a new guise.
- The Republicans had no difficulty campaigning against both Johnson and the Democrats. Republican leaders harked back to the war, insisting that the fruits of victory would be lost if northerners voted Democrat/National Union.

The election results were a disaster for Johnson and a triumph for the Republicans, who won all but three states. In the new Congress, the Republicans would have a comfortable two-thirds majority in both Houses, ensuring that that they could override any presidential veto.

Radical (or Congressional) Reconstruction

The Republican-dominated Congress, which met between December 1866 and March 1867, now took over the Reconstruction process. In the spring of 1867 Congress passed a Military Reconstruction Act. This stated that:

- No legal government existed in any ex-Confederate state (except Tennessee).
- The ten southern states were to be divided into five military districts, each placed under a federal commander.
- To get back into the Union, southern states had to elect constitutional conventions which would accept black suffrage and ratify the Fourteenth Amendment.

The bill, which appalled Johnson, was passed despite his veto. Congress then moved to weaken Johnson's power:

- A Command of the Army Act, recognising the importance of the army in the Reconstruction process, reduced Johnson's military powers.
- The Tenure of Office Act barred him from removing a host of office-holders, including members of his own cabinet.

The Tenure of Office Act was designed to protect Secretary of War Stanton, a fierce critic of Johnson, who had still not resigned from his cabinet. Johnson did not accept this muzzling without a fight and proceeded first to suspend and then to dismiss Stanton.

Johnson impeached

Republicans in the House of Representatives, convinced that Johnson had broken the law, determined in February 1868 (by 126 votes to 47) to **impeach** him for 'high crimes and misdemeanours'. The impeachment proceedings took place in the Senate in the spring of 1868. Johnson faced a mixed bag of charges but essentially they narrowed down to the removal of Stanton from office and not cooperating with Congress. Underpinning these 'crimes' was the fact that many Republicans were out for revenge and anxious to get rid of Johnson, whom they believed was impeding the implementation of Congress's Reconstruction policy. After a two-month trial, 35 Senators voted against Johnson and nineteen for him. This was one vote short of the two-thirds majority needed to impeach him. Although he had survived, for the rest of his term he was very much a 'lame duck' president.

President Grant

In 1868 the Republicans chose General Grant as their presidential candidate. Grant, who had shown little interest in party politics and voted Democrat before the Civil War, was ambitious, felt honoured to be nominated, and thought it was his duty to stand. Without ever being a fully fledged radical, he was prepared to support radical Reconstruction. His Democrat opponent, Horatio Seymour, campaigned against black equality. Although Grant easily won the electoral college vote (by 214 votes to 80), he won only 52 per cent of the popular vote. His popular majority was the result of southern black support.

 **KEY TERM**

Impeach To charge a public official with an offence committed while serving in office.

The Fifteenth Amendment

Given the 1868 election result, Republicans had even better cause to support black suffrage. In 1869 the Fifteenth Amendment was introduced. (It was ratified in 1870.) This stated that, 'The right to vote should not be denied … on account of race, color or previous conditions of servitude.' To Democrats, this seemed a revolutionary measure: the crowning act of a Republican plot to promote black equality. Although some feminists were critical of the amendment because it said nothing about giving women the vote, most northern reformers hailed the amendment as the triumphant conclusion to the decades of struggle on behalf of black Americans. A few years earlier such an Amendment would have been inconceivable. As late as 1868 only eight northern states allowed blacks to vote. With civil and political equality seemingly assured, most Republicans believed that black people no longer possessed a claim on the federal government. Their status in society would now depend on themselves.

Summary diagram: The problem of Reconstruction

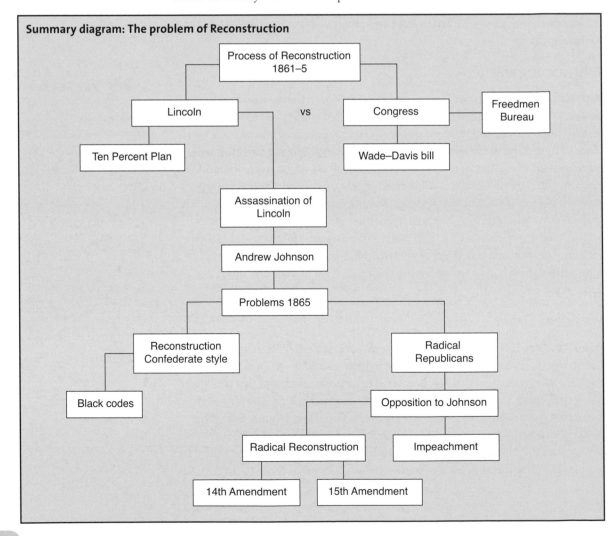

Reconstruction in the South 1867–77

▶ *To what extent did white southerners suffer from Reconstruction?*

Following the Military Reconstruction Act, all the ex-Confederate states, except Tennessee, were under military rule before being eventually readmitted to the Union. The extent to which the South was under the heel of a 'military despotism' should not be exaggerated. There were never more than 20,000 troops in the whole of the South. Moreover, military rule was short lived.

From the autumn of 1867 onwards, southern Republicans produced the necessary constitutions and in every state, except Virginia, took over the first restored state governments. By June 1868 Republican governments in Alabama, Arkansas, Florida, Georgia, Louisiana, North Carolina and South Carolina had ratified the Fourteenth Amendment and been received back into the Union. Texas, Virginia, Georgia and Mississippi were readmitted in 1870.

Republican rule in the South

Republican government in the South frequently depended on the support of federal troops. However, southern Republicans in 1867–8 did have a reasonable, indeed often considerable, amount of popular support and thus a democratic mandate to rule (particularly as many white southerners were disqualified from participating in the electoral process). Nevertheless, the Republicans faced fierce opposition from Democrats who sought to **redeem** their states.

Black Reconstruction?

Historian William Dunning in the early twentieth century referred to the period of Republican rule as 'Black Reconstruction'. He thought the new governments represented the worst elements in southern society – illiterate blacks, self-seeking **carpetbaggers** and treacherous **scalawags** – given power by a vengeance-seeking Republican Congress. Dunning depicted 'Black Reconstruction' as essentially undemocratic, with the Republicans ruling against the will of a disfranchised white majority. However, most of Dunning's views have been challenged, including the very term 'Black Reconstruction', which implies that blacks dominated the Reconstruction process. This was at best a half-truth.

Black power?

Black southerners certainly wielded some political power. Having been given the vote, most black Americans were determined to use it and large numbers flocked to join the Union League, which became an important arm of the Republican Party in the South. In South Carolina and Mississippi, black voters constituted

 KEY TERMS

Redeem To restore to white rule.

Carpetbaggers Northern whites who settled in the South. (A carpetbag was the suitcase of the time.)

Scalawags Southern whites who supported the Republican Party.

a real majority of the electorate. In three other states (by September 1867) black voters outnumbered white voters because so many rebels were disenfranchised. The result was that in the two decades after 1867, southern black Americans were elected to national, state and local office. Two black Senators and fifteen black Representatives were elected to Congress before 1877. At state level, black Americans had even more power. In 1873, South Carolina's House of Representatives had 123 members. Only 23 of them were white men.

While this was a revolutionary break with the past, black political influence never reflected black numbers. Few of the top positions in state governments went to black people. The majority of black office-holders were local officials, for example justices of the peace. But even at this level black people did not hold a proportionate share of offices. Black leaders increasingly balked at the fact that they were merely junior partners in white-dominated Republican coalitions.

Why was black power limited?

The lack of black experience, education and organisation, and divisions within the black community, particularly between free-born blacks and ex-slaves, help to explain why black office-holders did not equate with black voters. But perhaps the main reason was the fact that black people were a minority in most states. If Republican governments were to be elected, the Republicans needed to win white support. Assured of black votes, the Republican Party often put forward white candidates for office hoping to attract white voters. Moreover, many white Republicans privately shared the Democrat view that black men were not competent to govern.

How well did black politicians perform?

The excesses of the Reconstruction governments were invariably blamed on black members, even though power in southern states remained largely in white control. In reality, those black politicians who came to office performed as well – and as badly – as white ones. Most were moderates who displayed little vindictiveness towards white politicians. Few showed much enthusiasm for disfranchising ex-Confederates and banning them from state politics. Nor did most display any determination to confiscate plantation land and redistribute it to freedmen. They were aware that such a policy would alienate white southerners who Republicans were seeking to attract.

Carpetbaggers

If the notion that Reconstruction was imposed on the South by black people is wrong, so also is the notion that it was controlled by northern carpetbaggers who sought to profit at the South's expense. Relatively few northerners actually settled in the South; in no state did they constitute more than two per cent of the total population. Nor were they set on fleecing the South economically. Many were teachers, clergy, officers of the Freedmen Bureau or agents of the various benevolent societies engaged in aiding ex-slaves. Some were army veterans who had served in the South, liked what they saw and determined to remain there. Others were talented lawyers, businessmen and newspaper editors who headed to the South (often taking considerable capital with them) hoping for personal advancement. Most supported the Republican Party because they believed that Republican policies were best for both the country and the South.

Scalawags

Without winning some support from southern-born white voters, few Republican governments would have been elected. The scalawags are difficult to categorise: they came from diverse backgrounds and voted Republican for a variety of reasons. Some were rich planters, merchants and industrialists who had once been Whigs. Others were self-sufficient farmers, usually from upland areas, many of whom had opposed the Confederacy. Most scalawags did not support full racial equality. Alliance with black voters was a marriage of convenience. They realised that if they were to have any chance of maintaining political control, they must retain the black vote.

Corruption and inefficiency

Southern Democrats bitterly attacked Republican rule in the South for corruption and inefficiency on a grand scale. Historians have found plenty of evidence to corroborate this charge:

- Many Republican politicians used their powers of patronage to benefit both themselves and their supporters.
- Bribery, especially by railway companies, was commonplace.
- Southern state debts multiplied and taxes sharply increased.
- The Freedmen Bureau, seen as a Republican-sponsored organisation, was similarly indicted (then and since) for being corrupt and inefficient and for encouraging a dependency culture.

However, the late 1860s and 1870s saw corruption and inefficiency everywhere in the USA. Corruption in the South did not begin to compare with that in the city of New York. Moreover, there had been massive corruption in southern state governments pre-1861 and similar corruption after the states had been 'redeemed'. Southern Republican governments had little option but to raise and spend large sums of money:

- Most inherited empty treasuries and large public debts.
- Much of the southern transportation system had been destroyed during the war.
- Public buildings needed to be repaired.
- Schools, hospitals, orphanages and asylums had to be built for black people as well as for white.

The fact that new schools, hospitals, prisons and railways were built indicates that the money spent was not always wasted. Historians have also come to the defence of the Freedmen Bureau, which seems to have had a good record in terms of providing poor black and white people with basic health care, education and jobs.

Economic Reconstruction

From 1867 to 1873 the South benefited from general prosperity and from high cotton prices. Railways were rebuilt and there was an increase in textile and other manufacturing. But promising as this was, it did not keep pace with industrial progress elsewhere. Short of cash and credit, the South remained essentially agricultural, heavily dependent on cotton. In many parts of the South the old plantations remained, sometimes with new owners, sometimes not. Black people continued to do most of the hard labour.

During the 1870s most black people became sharecroppers. White landowners provided the land, seed and tools; black tenants supplied the labour. Whatever crop was produced was divided in a fixed ratio, often half to the landowner and half to the tenant. Sharecropping provided black farmers with freedom from

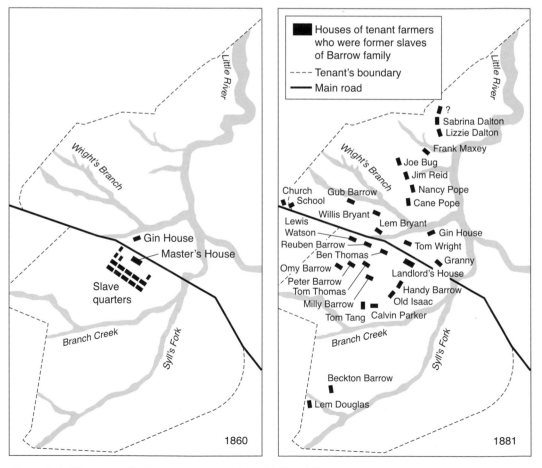

Figure 7.1 Changes on the Barrow plantation from 1860 to 1881.

day-to-day white supervision and some incentive to work hard. But neither the freedom nor the incentive should be exaggerated.

In the early 1870s, a worldwide glut of cotton led to a disastrous fall in prices, which resulted in most sharecroppers being in a perpetual state of indebtedness to landowners and local storekeepers. In turn, landowners and storekeepers were often in debt to southern merchants and bankers, who themselves were in debt to northern banks. These piled-up debts ensured that the South remained mainly a one-crop economy because everyone pressed the people below to produce crops – chiefly cotton – that had a ready market value. The South did remarkably well in terms of total cotton output. In 1860 it had produced about 4.5 million bales of cotton. By 1880 it produced over 6.3 million bales. But the increased production simply added to the cotton glut; consequently, prices continued to tumble. And the only way for farmers to make ends meet was to try and produce more.

The result was that the South became the poorest section in the USA. In 1860, the southern states produced 30 per cent of the nation's wealth. In 1870 they produced only twelve per cent. In 1860 the average white southerner's income was similar to that of the average northerner. By 1870 southern income had fallen to less than two-fifths that of northerners. The Republican governments in the South were victims rather than perpetrators of this situation, which continued long after the states had been redeemed.

The Ku Klux Klan

Republican rule sparked a vigorous backlash as southern whites determined to recover political ascendancy. In 1866 paramilitary groups formed in most southern states to fight for white rights. The most notorious was the Ku Klux Klan. Established in Tennessee and led for a time by war hero Nathan Bedford Forrest, the Klan spread rapidly in the years 1868–71: by 1870 Forrest claimed that there were over 500,000 Klansmen in the South. Clad in white robes and hoods, Klansmen sought to destroy Republican political organisations by intimidation and physical force. The Klan drew support from all sections of the white community and was often encouraged in its violent actions by 'respectable' southern Democrat leaders.

In the early twentieth century, historians saw the Klan as a natural reaction to 'Black Republican' rule. Indeed, it was lavished with praise in Thomas Dixon's novel *The Clansman* (subsequently adapted for the cinema in D.W. Griffith's 1915 epic, *The Birth of a Nation*). Recent historians have been far more critical of its terrorist activities, which reached their peak in the years 1869–71. Black people who held public office were particular targets. So were black schools and churches.

Southern Republican governments tried to proscribe the Klan's activities by introducing laws which banned people from joining organisations that disturbed the peace. But most states found it hard to enforce the laws effectively. Nor could they easily deal with Klan violence. When Klan suspects were arrested, witnesses were reluctant to testify and Klansmen were ready to perjure themselves to provide one another with alibis. If there was a Klansman on a jury it was impossible to convict.

Force Acts

Some state governors appealed to Congress for help. Thus, in 1870–1 Congress passed three Force Acts, authorising President Grant to use the army to break up the Klan. Heavy penalties were imposed on those who used force, bribery or intimidation to hinder or prevent anyone from voting. Grant showed he meant business, imposing martial law in several parts of the South. Hundreds of suspected Klansmen were imprisoned. While this reduced Klan terrorism, violence and intimidation continued after 1872, especially in Louisiana, Mississippi and South Carolina – states still under Republican control. Detachments of ex-Confederate soldiers often accompanied Democrat speakers to political rallies and paraded through black areas. These shows of strength, coupled with sporadic attacks on opponents, made it difficult for Republicans to campaign and vote in some southern states.

SOURCE E

? Examine Source E. What do you think was the purpose of the drawing?

The White League and the Klan. The drawing from 1874 shows members of these organisations joining hands over a black family.

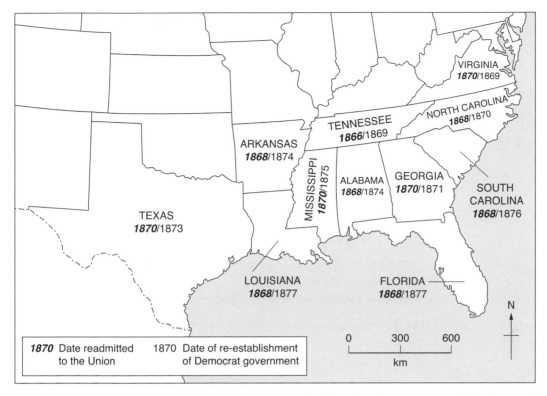

VIRGINIA
1870/1869

NORTH CAROLINA
1868/1870

TENNESSEE
1866/1869

ARKANSAS
1868/1874

MISSISSIPPI
1870/1875

ALABAMA
1868/1874

GEORGIA
1870/1871

SOUTH
CAROLINA
1868/1876

TEXAS
1870/1873

LOUISIANA
1868/1877

FLORIDA
1868/1877

N

1870 Date readmitted to the Union	1870 Date of re-establishment of Democrat government

0   300   600

km

Figure 7.2 The southern states redeemed. The map shows the date when the states rejoined the Union and when Democrat governments were elected.

The South 'redeemed'

Radical Reconstruction was a limited process. In many southern states it was over almost before it began. Tennessee was under Democrat control by 1869; Virginia and North Carolina were redeemed in 1870, Georgia in 1871, Texas in 1873, Arkansas and Alabama in 1874, and Mississippi in 1875. By 1876 only Louisiana, Florida and South Carolina were still, theoretically, under Republican control. The Democrat regimes, which replaced the Republican governments, shared a commitment to reducing:

- the political, social and economic power of blacks
- the scope and expense of government
- taxes.

The reasons for southern Republican defeat

Several factors played a part in Republican defeat. While most historians have emphasised the importance of white intimidation, others have stressed the destructive effect of factionalism within Republican parties at state and local level. Bitter internal feuds, which often centred on the spoils of office rather than actual policy, were a luxury the Republicans could scarcely afford. While black and white Republicans quarrelled, there was also inter-black and inter-white rivalry.

Historian John Hope Franklin suggested that a Republican coalition might have survived had the party been able to unite over economic and social policy. He argued that the Republican Party's best chance of success was to present itself as the poor man's party, championing policies that appealed to poverty-stricken white and black voters. While some favoured this strategy, most Republican leaders had no wish to embark on radical policies which were likely to prevent outside capital being attracted to the South and which would end all hope of winning 'respectable' white support.

As it was, Republican fiscal policies at state level did not assist the party's cause. Heavy taxation helped to drive white farmers from the party. Nor were the Republicans helped by the economic depression which started in 1873:

- Cotton prices fell by nearly 50 per cent.
- Most railway building ceased.
- Many long-established southern industries were forced into bankruptcy.

Those Republican regimes still in power were usually blamed for people's misfortunes.

Arguably, southern Republicans were betrayed by the northern wing of the party. After 1867 radical influence within the party declined as radical leaders died or retired. Most northern Republicans, who had never been radicals, did not want to see federal power used aggressively to overrule states' rights. Like most Americans at the time, they believed that liberty meant freedom from government intervention, not the use of government power to help minority groups. By the early 1870s many Republicans felt the time had come to leave the South to sort out its own problems.

President Grant

Grant's administration has often been blamed for lacking commitment, vision and clear aims with regard to Reconstruction. This is not altogether fair. Grant took tough action against the Ku Klux Klan. However, he was anxious to end federal government involvement in the South and ready to build bridges to white southerners. Two actions in 1872 symbolised this desire for accommodation:

- An Amnesty Act resulted in 150,000 ex-Confederates having their rights returned.
- The Freedmen's Bureau collapsed.

In 1872 Grant easily defeated the **Liberal Republican** candidate Horace Greeley (who was reluctantly supported by the Democrats, who realised they had no chance of defeating Grant with a candidate of their own) in the presidential election. Unfortunately, Grant's second term was dominated by two issues: the

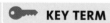 **KEY TERM**

Liberal Republican Party
A new party that came into existence in 1872, largely because of dissatisfaction with Grant. While some major Republican figures joined the party, it had little support from Republican rank and file. The party quickly disappeared after 1872.

economic depression and a number of serious political scandals involving some of Grant's close associates, which damaged his standing.

The congressional situation

In the 1874 mid-term elections the Democrats won control of the House of Representatives. Thereafter, there was little that the Republican Party or Grant could do in terms of embarking on new initiatives to help southern Republicans.

The 1875 Civil Rights Act

The last measure that aimed to help southern black people was the 1875 Civil Rights Act. Supposedly designed to prevent discrimination by hotels, theatres and railways, it was little more than a broad assertion of principle and had little impact.

The situation by the mid-1870s

Although other factors played a part, the end of radical Reconstruction was almost inevitable given that whites were the majority in most southern states. The two main political parties had distinct racial identities. The Democrat Party was the white party; the Republican Party the black party. The notion that a strong Republican Party might have been founded on policies that appealed to poor white and black voters is probably a delusion. The reality was that (for racist reasons) few poor white people identified with poor black people.

Given that race was the dominant issue, many of the election campaigns in the South in the 1870s were ugly and few elections were conducted fairly. White southerners organised new paramilitary groups – Rifle Clubs, Red Shirts, White Leagues – the ostensible aim of which was to maintain public order. Their real mission, however, was to overthrow the southern Republican governments and banish blacks from public life. Unlike the Klan, these groups drilled and paraded openly. On election days, armed whites did their best to turn blacks away from the polls. Republican leaders, by contrast, tried to ensure that blacks did vote – often several times!

The situation in Louisiana and Mississippi

Events in Louisiana were typical of events throughout the Deep South. Every election in the state between 1868 and 1876 was marred by violence and fraud. After 1872 two governments claimed legitimacy in the state:

- A Republican regime, elected by black voters and protected by the federal army and black militia units, was the legitimate government.
- A Democrat government, elected by white voters and aided by the White League, controlled much of the countryside.

Violence was common. Thirty people died in September 1874 in a battle between the White League and the state militia. In 1874 the Republicans stayed in power by throwing out the results from many Democrat areas. Grant reluctantly sent troops to prop up Louisiana's corrupt Republican regime.

Strangely, Grant did nothing to help the Republican government in Mississippi, where there was similar violence. Mississippi Democrats intimidated any white man not enrolled in a Democrat club. The result was that Mississippi was redeemed in 1875. Historian Eric Foner thinks that Grant's failure to intervene in Mississippi was a 'milestone in the retreat from Reconstruction'.

The 1876 presidential election

Even though most states had been redeemed well before, the 1876 presidential election is often seen as the end of Reconstruction. The Republican candidate was **Rutherford Hayes**. The Democrats chose Samuel Tilden. In November 1876 it was clear that Tilden, helped by the effects of the depression, had won the popular vote, gaining 4,284,000 votes to Hayes's 4,037,000. But US presidential elections are determined by the electoral college, not by the popular vote. Tilden had 184 electoral college votes to Hayes's 165. However, the voting returns from Oregon, South Carolina, Louisiana and Florida – with twenty electoral college votes between them – were contested. If just one state went to Tilden, he would become president.

There was never much doubt that Oregon's votes would go to Hayes. The real problem lay in the South. Democrats justifiably claimed that Republicans had manipulated the vote and that many blacks had voted umpteen times. Republicans claimed, with equal justification, that blacks had been intimidated from voting. It was – and is – impossible to know how far Democrat intimidation offset Republican fraud. The dispute lingered on over the winter. Some southerners talked of fighting a new civil war to ensure that Tilden became president. But behind the scenes powerful forces worked for a settlement. Eventually, Congress established a Commission to review the election returns. Eight commissioners were Republicans; seven were Democrats. By votes of eight to seven the Commission awarded every one of the disputed elections to Hayes.

The Compromise?

The 1877 Compromise ended the crisis. While nothing was agreed in writing, the Compromise seems to have been as follows. The Democrats would accept Hayes as president. Hayes, in return, agreed to withdraw all troops from the South, recognise Democrat governments in the three disputed states, appoint a southerner to his cabinet and look kindly on southern railway interests. Hayes claimed that he had made no concessions to the South. Whatever had – or had not – been agreed, he did withdraw troops from the South, with the result that South Carolina, Louisiana and Florida immediately fell under Democrat control. Thus, by 1877 all the ex-Confederate states had returned to white rule. Hayes continued his policy of conciliation, appointing a white southerner to his cabinet and visiting the South on a goodwill tour. While Hayes's presidency is usually

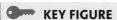

KEY FIGURE

Rutherford Hayes (1822–93)

A successful lawyer, he led a company of volunteers in the Civil War, becoming a general. After the war he entered politics, serving in Congress and as governor as Ohio. He became president in 1877.

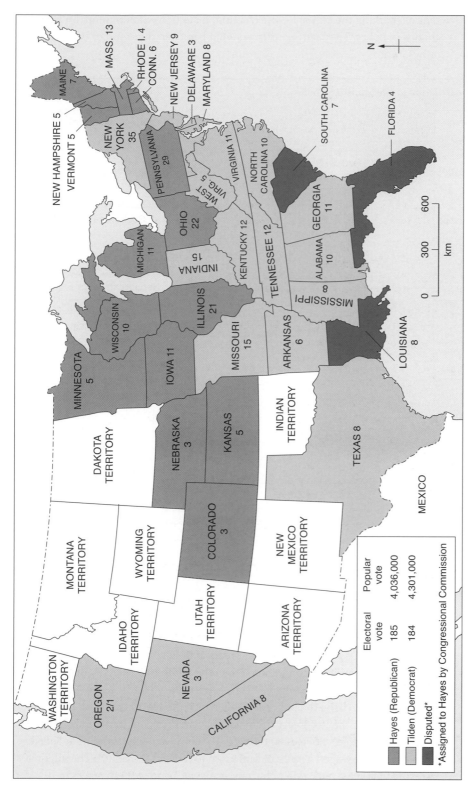

Figure 7.3 US election results of 1876.

Electoral vote | Popular vote
Hayes (Republican) | 185 | 4,036,000
Tilden (Democrat) | 184 | 4,301,000
Disputed*

* Assigned to Hayes by Congressional Commission

seen as marking the end of Reconstruction, his actions did not mark an abrupt change in policy. They only confirmed what had been done earlier by Congress or by Grant.

Summary diagram: Reconstruction in the South 1867–77

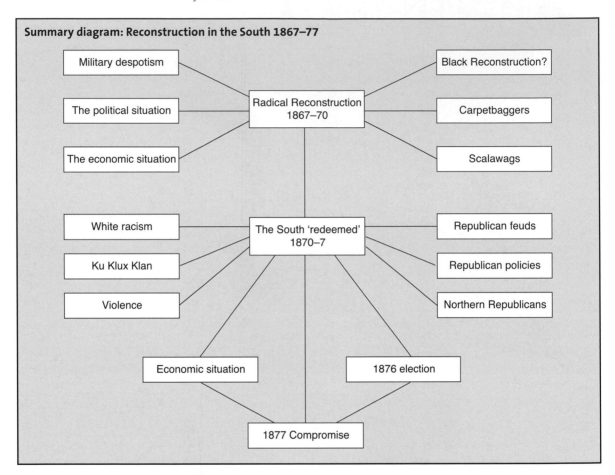

5 The results of Reconstruction

▶ *Was Reconstruction a tragic failure for African Americans?*

In the early twentieth century, white southern historians, such as Dunning, saw Reconstruction as the 'Tragic Era' – a dreadful time when southerners suffered the indignity of military occupation, when the South was ruled by incompetent, corrupt governments, and when ex-slaves, unprepared for freedom, proved incapable of exercising the political rights which the North thrust on them. In Dunning's view, the Reconstruction heroes were President Johnson, who tried to continue Lincoln's policies, and white southern Democrats and their Ku Klux Klan allies, who waged a forceful campaign to redeem the South. The villains were the vindictive radical Republicans, scalawags and carpetbaggers.

In the 1950s and 1960s historians such as Kenneth Stampp and John Hope Franklin depicted Reconstruction very differently. 'Rarely in history', said Stampp, 'have participants in an unsuccessful rebellion endured so mild penalties as those Congress imposed upon the people of the South and particularly upon their leaders.' In Stampp's opinion, the villains were Johnson, white Democrats and the Klan. The heroes were the radical Republicans and black freedmen who fought nobly (but ultimately unsuccessfully) for the rights of ex-slaves. In this view, black, not white, southerners were the real losers of Reconstruction.

Currently, the vast majority of historians agree with the Stampp–Franklin view. However, more recently, Eric Foner has stressed that a great deal was achieved for – and by – African Americans in the Reconstruction process.

The treatment of southern whites

Given the scale of the Civil War, the North was remarkably generous to southern whites. Most southerners, even those who had held high office under the Confederacy, were quickly pardoned. Jefferson Davis spent two years in prison but was then freed. Slavery apart, there was no major confiscation of property. For decades to come the Democrat Party, the political agency of white supremacy, controlled the South. However, white southerners had not escaped scot-free. Control had been wrested away from them for at least a few years. Moreover, the years after 1865 saw a major reduction of southern political influence.

The treatment of ex-slaves

The main debate about Reconstruction has been its impact on the ex-slaves. W.E.B. Dubois, writing in the 1930s, said: 'The slave went free; stood a brief moment in the sun; then moved back again towards slavery.' Was Reconstruction a tragic failure for black Americans?

Economic failure?

Critics claim that black people came out of slavery with little or no land. By the 1870s most black Americans eked out a living as sharecroppers. Perpetually in debt, they had little economic independence. Those who moved to cities found themselves restricted to the more menial and less well-paid occupations. Nevertheless, the notion that African Americans were hardly better off than they had been under slavery is probably mistaken:

- There was a major improvement in black living standards in the four decades after 1865 and a corresponding reduction in black mortality rates.
- Sharecropping was a significant improvement over slavery.
- Black land-ownership steadily increased. By 1900, nearly a fifth of black farmers owned their land.

- Black business grew, particularly those catering for black customers. This was one of the few advantages of segregation.
- The number of black professional people grew.
- With the end of slavery, black people also had mobility. While most remained in the South, some moved to northern cities or out west.

SOURCE F

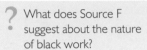
What does Source F suggest about the nature of black work?

Black sharecroppers harvesting cotton in the fields of Georgia in the 1880s.

Civil Rights failure?

A second major criticism of Reconstruction is that it failed to guarantee black civil rights. By the first decade of the twentieth century, black people were regarded and treated by most white people as second-class citizens in the South. The principle of segregation was systematically extended by state and local law to every area of southern life: schools, churches, transport, sport, restaurants, hospitals, even cemeteries. Black facilities were generally markedly inferior to white. While a rigid legalised segregation system did not exist in most states until the 1890s, the so-called **Jim Crow laws** did not represent a shift in the actual degree of segregation. These laws simply confirmed segregation, which had been a fact of southern life since 1865.

Black people were more likely to be illiterate, more likely to live in wretched housing and more likely to suffer from malnutrition. They were also taught

KEY TERM

Jim Crow laws Segregation laws, passed in most southern states in the 1890s. (It remains something of a mystery why they were called Jim Crow laws.)

to know their place. There was massive intimidation: physical, psychological and economic. 'Uppity' black people were likely to receive brutal treatment. Lynchings of suspected and convicted murderers and rapists were a common aspect of southern life in the late nineteenth and early twentieth centuries.

The situation was rather more complex than historians have sometimes inferred. Southern blacks were not just victims or objects to be manipulated, they were also important participants in the Reconstruction process. Segregation was not something which was simply imposed on black people by the white South. Quite naturally, given their experiences under slavery, many black Americans had no wish to mix socially with white people. As a result, segregation was often simply a statement of black community identity. After 1865, for example, there was an almost total black withdrawal from white churches as black people tried to achieve self-determination. Churches – the first and most important social institutions to be fully controlled by black people – became a focal point of black life. Black Americans also established their own welfare institutions, trade associations, political organisations and benevolent societies. The fact that there were black institutions, paralleling those of the white people, meant there were opportunities for black people to lead and manage.

Some black leaders, most notably Booker T. Washington, accepted that black people were second-class citizens. Washington believed that black people must seek to better themselves through education and hard work. Only by so doing could they prove their worth to white Americans. His faith in education was shared by many black people. After 1865, many black communities made great financial sacrifices, raising money to build their own schools and to pay teachers' salaries. At first, most teachers were white; many were northern women, young and idealistic. But black people wanted to control their own education and after 1870 most teachers in black schools and colleges were themselves black. Black education was one of the successes of Reconstruction.

Political failure?

By 1900, southern state governments had introduced a variety of measures – poll tax tests, literacy tests and residence requirements – to ensure that black Americans were unable to vote. However, disfranchisement of black voters did not occur on a major scale until the 1890s. For most of the 1870s and 1880s, black people voted in large numbers and continued to be appointed to public office. Historian Eric Foner claims that black participation in southern political life after 1867 was 'a massive experiment in interracial democracy without precedent in the history of this or any other country that abolished slavery in the nineteenth century'.

Conclusion

Reconstruction was far from a total failure. The essential fact was that black people were no longer slaves. Most left slavery with a rather more realistic opinion of what was achievable than many later historians. If Reconstruction did not create an integrated society, it did establish the concept of equal citizenship. If black Americans did not emerge from Reconstruction as equal citizens, at least the Fourteenth and Fifteenth Amendments were enshrined in the Constitution and could be invoked by later generations of civil rights' activists.

6 The impact of the Civil War

▶ *Was the Civil War the USA's second revolution?*

In March 1865, Lincoln talked of the 'fundamental and astounding' changes which had occurred as a result of the war. Many contemporaries agreed. Historians continue to debate whether the Civil War was the USA's second revolution. (The War of Independence is seen as the first.)

SOURCE G

US historian George Ticknor, writing in 1869, quoted in George S. Hillard, editor, *Life, Letters and Journals of George Ticknor*, 1876.

The late conflict has riven a great gulf between what happened before in our century and what has happened since or what is likely to happen hereafter. It does not seem to me as if I were living in the country in which I was born.

? Does Source G prove that a revolution had occurred?

The emancipation of the slaves

The Civil War resulted in the emancipation of 4 million slaves. Given the southern commitment to slavery, it seems unlikely that it would have withered and died in the final decades of the nineteenth century. The confiscation of the principal form of property in one-third of the country was without parallel in US history. Emancipation had a major impact on both slaveholder and slave. By the early 1870s black people were elevated (in theory) to civil equality with white people. However, emancipation had little practical impact on most – northern – Americans. Moreover, black people remained the poorest ethnic group in the USA and by the start of the twentieth century had lost most of their civil and political rights (see pages 218–19).

The balance of government

Arguably, the war changed the whole emphasis of the constitution, shifting the balance of the federal system in a national direction at the expense of state rights. During the war, the federal government asserted its power in ways unimaginable in 1861:

- It mobilised hundreds of thousands of men.
- It levied new sources of revenue.
- It set up a national bank and issued a paper currency.

The changes wrought by the war, it is often implied, were not undone, largely because the war resulted in a major change in ideology. This claim can (apparently) be substantiated by examination of changes to the Constitution. The first ten constitutional amendments had set out to limit national authority. But after 1865 six of the next seven amendments empowered the federal government to act. Congress now had the power to end slavery (Thirteenth Amendment), protect civil rights (Fourteenth Amendment) and end racial discrimination in voting (Fifteenth Amendment). However, many would argue that the war years were an aberration:

- It was inevitable that during the conflict federal power would increase.
- After the war there was a rapid return to normalcy and for the rest of the nineteenth century the federal government had a minimal impact on the lives of Americans.
- Belief in state rights remained an article of faith of most Americans, not just southerners.
- Given that successive federal governments lacked the will to enforce the principles contained in the Fourteenth and Fifteenth Amendments, state power was not effectively reduced.

The economic effects

Historian Charles Beard saw the war as the triumph of the forces of industrialism over plantation agriculture. The war, in Beard's view, was 'a social cataclysm … making vast changes in the arrangements of classes, in the distribution of wealth, in the course of industrial development.' While most historians today regard such views as far too sweeping, some think the war did nourish the growth of business enterprise, ensuring that the USA became the world's greatest economic force. During the war the Republicans passed a broad spectrum of laws which underpinned the country's future economic growth: higher tariffs, a national banking system and government loans to build the first transcontinental railway. Republican policies, as well as the demands of the war itself, may also have encouraged the growth of big business. Many of the great industrialists of the late nineteenth century were set on the path to wealth by the war. Nor did they forget the lessons it taught, especially the advantage of large-scale enterprise.

There are many counterarguments to the notion that the war resulted in major economic change:

- The USA was already a great economic power, second only to Britain, in 1861.
- The crucial innovations in transport, agriculture and manufacturing had begun well before 1861.
- It is possible that the war retarded the country's economic expansion. The 1860s show up poorly in statistical terms when measured against earlier and later decades.

- To argue that the war transferred economic and political power into the hands of industrial capitalists is simplistic. If the big manufacturers proved to be the chief economic beneficiaries of the war (and this is debatable), their victory was an incidental rather than a planned result of the conflict.

The social effects

The emancipation of slaves apart, the war produced no major upheaval in the social order. If it had opened up doors of opportunity for women, those doors were quickly closed. Nor did the loss of 620,000 men have much effect. Natural increase and high immigration ensured that by 1870 the American population far exceeded that of 1860.

The political effects

The main political result of the war was the effect it had on the sectional balance of power. Between 1789 and 1861, a southern slaveholder had been president of the USA for 49 years, 23 of the 36 speakers of the House of Representatives had been southerners, and the Supreme Court had always had a southern majority. After the war 100 years passed before a resident of an ex-Confederate state was elected president, for 50 years none of the House speakers came from the South, and only five of the 26 Supreme Court justices appointed during the next 50 years were southerners. However, whether this change merits the label of revolution is debatable. Arguably, northern dominance would have happened anyway.

Conclusion

Had the Confederacy won, the Civil War would have been one of the great turning points in modern history. Indeed, the long-term implications of a Confederate victory for both the USA and the world are so far-reaching as to be incalculable. Union victory meant in effect that the *status quo* was preserved, which is hardly revolutionary! Indeed, in many respects the war scarcely affected the deeper currents of US economic, social and political development.

Yet many of those who lived through the war shared a sense of having lived through events that had radically changed their world. US writer Mark Twain, for example, wrote that the war had 'uprooted institutions that were centuries old … and transformed the social life of half the country'. Twain was surely correct to stress that the war had a massive impact on 'half' the country. While it is easier to see continuity than revolution in the North, the war had a dramatic impact on the South. By 1865 slavery was gone and the South had lost much of its economic and political power.

Southern whites salvaged what they could from the wreck of defeat and their counter-revolution had some success. By 1877 all the southern states had white-controlled governments. Notwithstanding the Fourteenth and Fifteenth

Amendments, southern black Americans did not have equal civil rights until the second half of the twentieth century. Nevertheless, the ending of slavery and the passing of the Fourteenth and Fifteenth Amendments were extraordinary developments in terms of what might have been anticipated in 1861. In that sense, the changes wrought by the war were revolutionary.

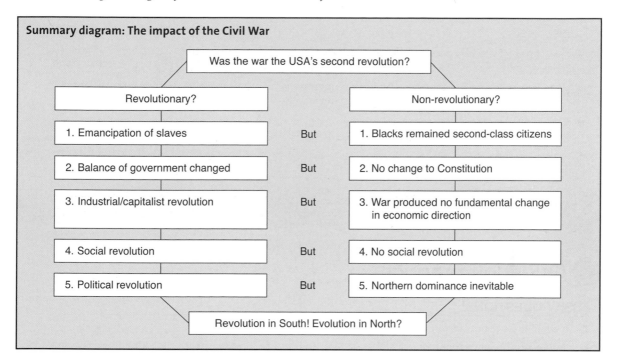

Summary diagram: The impact of the Civil War

Was the war the USA's second revolution?

Revolutionary?		Non-revolutionary?
1. Emancipation of slaves	But	1. Blacks remained second-class citizens
2. Balance of government changed	But	2. No change to Constitution
3. Industrial/capitalist revolution	But	3. War produced no fundamental change in economic direction
4. Social revolution	But	4. No social revolution
5. Political revolution	But	5. Northern dominance inevitable

Revolution in South! Evolution in North?

Chapter summary

The role of African Americans in the Civil War and in the South post-1865 is complex. African Americans had more control over their destiny than historians once imagined. They played an important role in the Civil War itself, helping the Union to triumph. Their actions encouraged Lincoln to support emancipation and Republicans to support civil rights for African Americans. However, Lincoln's determination to grant emancipation and his skilful (if sometimes pragmatic) actions were crucially important.

Although African American expectations and aspirations in 1865 were not attained, especially economically, there were some achievements on the political and social fronts. Unfortunately, these achievements did not survive the end of Reconstruction in the 1870s. Much of what had been gained was lost in the 1880s and 1890s when most African Americans became second-class citizens.

Refresher questions

Use these questions to remind yourself of the key material covered in this chapter.

1 Why was the slavery issue so difficult for Lincoln in 1861–2?

2 How significant was the Emancipation Proclamation?

3 Does Lincoln deserve the accolade of being the 'Great Emancipator'?

4 How significant was the black contribution to the war?

5 How much had been done to help black people by 1865?

6 What were Lincoln's aims with regard to Reconstruction?

7 What were the aims of the radical Republicans?

8 Did Andrew Johnson continue Lincoln's Reconstruction policies?

9 Why did Congress take over the Reconstruction process?

10 To what extent did the South suffer from military despotism?

11 To what extent did black Americans control 'Black Reconstruction'?

12 How successful was economic Reconstruction?

13 Why were southern whites able to re-establish control in the South?

14 Was Reconstruction a tragic failure?

15 Was the Civil War the USA's second revolution?

 Question practice

ESSAY QUESTIONS

1 To what extent does Lincoln deserve the title 'The Great Emancipator'?

2 How far do you agree that the Civil Rights Acts of 1866 and 1875 were effective in extending civil rights to freed slaves?

3 To what extent did the position of African Americans improve in the years 1865–77?

4 'The principles for which the Civil War was fought were sacrificed after 1865.' Assess the validity of this view.

SOURCE ANALYSIS QUESTION

1 With reference to Sources 1, 2 and 3, and your understanding of the historical context, assess the value of these sources to a historian studying slavery emancipation.

SOURCE 1

The Preliminary Emancipation Proclamation, issued by President Lincoln on 22 September 1862.

And by virtue of the power, and for the purpose aforesaid, I do order and declare that all persons held as slaves within said designated States, and parts of States, are, and henceforward shall be free; and that the Executive government of the United States, including the military and naval authorities thereof, will recognize and maintain the freedom of said persons.

And I hereby enjoin upon the people so declared to be free, to abstain from all violence, unless in necessary self-defence; and I recommend to them that, in all cases when allowed, they labour faithfully for reasonable wages.

And I further declare and make known, that such persons of suitable condition, will be received into the armed service of the United States to garrison forts, positions, stations, and other places, and to man vessels of all sorts in said service.

And upon this act, sincerely believed to be an act of justice, warranted by the Constitution upon military necessity, I invoke the considerate judgment of mankind, and the gracious favour of Almighty God.

SOURCE 2

Adapted from 'The Proclamation in Secessia', an article in a weekly political magazine, *Harper's Weekly*, 18 October 1862, describing southern reaction to the Preliminary Emancipation Proclamation.

The Southerners call Mr. Lincoln an 'ape', a 'fiend', a 'beast', a 'savage', a 'highwayman'. Their Congress is resolved into a dozen committees, each trying to devise some new form of retaliation to be inflicted upon United States' citizens and soldiers, if we dare to carry the proclamation into effect, and tamper, to use the words of the Richmond Enquirer, *with 'four thousand millions' worth of property!' They are going to hoist the black flag. They are going to put to death not only soldiers on the battlefield, but every Northerner found on Southern soil. No one has yet suggested torture before execution but that will probably come. It will be nothing new in parts of the South. As to Negro insurrections, when this war first broke out it was commonly supposed that the Negroes would rise in the South. This expectation has not been fulfilled. There have been Negro insurrections. But they have been so promptly and so thoroughly suppressed that they have exercised no appreciable influence on the war.*

SOURCE 3

Adapted from a letter from General Robert E. Lee to Andrew Hunter of the Virginia State Legislature, 11 January 1865. Hunter had previously asked Lee his opinion about enlisting black troops.

The employment of Negro troops would, in my opinion, greatly increase our military strength and enable us to relieve our white population to some extent. I think we could dispense with the reserve forces except in cases of necessity. It would disappoint the hopes which our enemies base upon our exhaustion, deprive them in a great measure of the aid they now derive from black troops, and thus throw the burden of the war upon their own people. In addition to the great political advantages that would result to our cause from the adoption of a system of emancipation, it would exercise a salutary influence upon our whole Negro population, by rendering more secure the fidelity of those who become soldiers, and diminishing the inducements to the rest to abscond.

I can only say in conclusion that whatever measures are to be adopted should be adopted at once. Every day's delay increases the difficulty. Much time will be required to organize and discipline the men, and action may be deferred until it is too late.

CHAPTER 8

The winning of the West 1865–c.1900

Western expansion in the mid-nineteenth century had been a major factor in bringing about civil war. That expansion did not end with, or even during, the war. Indeed, after 1865 it picked up speed, so much so that by 1890 the Superintendent of the Census, in his annual report, declared that there was no longer a western frontier in the USA. In little more than a generation, a tide of settlement had swept over the West. The power of the Plains Indian tribes was broken and their hunting grounds became the domain of miners, cattlemen and farmers. To explain how and why this happened, this chapter will focus on the following:

★ The situation in 1865

★ The Indian Wars of the 1860s/1870s

★ The mining frontier

★ The impact of the railways

★ Farmers, cowboys and shepherds

★ The romance of the West

Key dates

1858–9		Pikes Peak gold rush	1864	Sand Creek massacre
1859		Comstock Lode discovered	1869	Transcontinental railway completed
1862	May	Homestead Act		
	July	Pacific Railroad Act	1876	Battle of the Little Bighorn
	Sept.	Sioux War broke out in Minnesota	1887	Dawes Act
			1890	Battle of Wounded Knee

The situation in 1865

▶ *How 'wild' was the West in 1865?*

By 1860, the USA's western frontier lay a little beyond the Mississippi, running (albeit irregularly) from mid-Minnesota in the north to mid-Texas in the south. Americans had also leapfrogged across the continent, establishing important settlements on the Pacific coast in California and Oregon (see the map on page 45).

The Wild West

Between the USA's eastern and western frontiers lay 2500 km of wilderness, comprising nearly half of the present USA – 500 million hectares of land. This area – the Wild West – was made up of three distinct geographical regions:

- the Great Plains stretching from the Mississippi to the Rockies and from Canada to Texas
- the Rocky Mountains and the Sierra Nevada Mountains
- the Great Basin, a region of high grassy plateaux and deserts between the Plains and the mountains.

These great expanses were the home of some 300,000 Native Americans. Apart from a Mormon settlement in Utah (see page 50), the only white people in the region were traders, **prospectors** and trappers, people almost as far removed from the ways of US civilisation as the Native Americans. Many white Americans had once believed that the arid and timberless Plains were unsuitable for agriculture and thus uninhabitable. The fact that Native Americans were prepared to fight savagely to defend their homelands was a further disincentive for white settlers. Nevertheless, in the two decades before the Civil War, white farmers had begun to settle on the fertile prairies of Iowa, Minnesota, Kansas and Nebraska, and prospectors had begun to mine gold in both the Rockies and the Sierras.

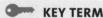 **KEY TERM**

Prospectors People who searched for precious metals, especially gold.

The impact of the Civil War on western development

The Civil War did little to slow down the settlement of the West. Given that regular troops were needed in the east, western militia units defended settlers from Indian attack. While farmers continued to move westwards, miners moved eastwards from California. In 1858, gold had been discovered in the Colorado Rockies near Pike's Peak. Within a year 50,000 'fifty-niners' had made their way to the diggings. The boom soon collapsed: there was simply not enough gold. But the discovery of the Comstock Lode, the greatest single deposit of gold and silver ever found in the USA, resulted in prospectors pouring into western Nevada. In 1861, Nevada became a territory and in 1864 a state. Western gold and silver greatly assisted the Union's ability to fund its war effort.

Three important acts, which affected western development, were passed in 1862:

- the Homestead Act (see pages 247–8)
- the Morrill Land Grant Act (see page 250)
- the Pacific Railroad Act (see page 243).

Given that all three measures had previously been blocked by southern Congressmen, it may be that the Civil War actually encouraged western settlement.

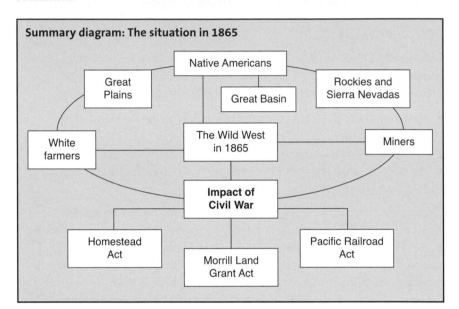

Summary diagram: The situation in 1865

2 The Indian Wars of the 1860s/1870s

▶ *How and why were the Plains Indians defeated?*

Native Americans had long been forced from their land and driven westwards by advancing white settlers (see pages 36–9). Nevertheless, in 1865 Native Americans were still free to roam over half the total area that is today the USA. In 1865 there were four main Native American groups:

- Plains Indians
- survivors of the Five Civilised Tribes, driven from their homelands in the South and forced to settle in the area known as Indian Territory (present-day Oklahoma)
- a few small tribes, like the Nez Perce (in the north) and the Apache (in the south), who inhabited the area between the Rockies and the Sierra Nevadas
- peaceful farmers (like the Navaho) in the southwest.

In the two decades after the Civil War, most Native Americans were driven from their last strongholds. The Plains Indians offered the most implacable resistance to the white settlers' advance.

The Plains Indians

In 1860 there were some 250,000 Plains Indians. From the Sioux of Minnesota and the Dakotas, to the Cheyenne of Colorado and Wyoming, and the Comanches, Pawnees, Kiowas and Arapahos of the central and southern Plains, these tribes possessed a similar culture. All lived by hunting the buffalo (or bison) which ranged over the Plains by the millions, providing most of the Indians' needs, especially food, clothing and shelter. But there was considerable physical, linguistic and cultural diversity among the tribes. While some were traditional allies, others were bitter enemies, the enmity arising from cultural differences, old feuds or disputes over hunting grounds. Such divisions prevented the Plains Indians from presenting a united front against the common foe. Moreover, most lived in groups (or bands) of several hundred people. These bands were largely autonomous and usually had little to do with each other. It was quite common for some bands to be at war while other bands of the same tribe were at peace.

Although divided, Plains Indians were a dangerous foe for white settlers:

- Their nomadic way of life made them singularly elusive.
- Their hunting and riding abilities enhanced their military skills.
- War absorbed a great part of male energies.

Indian youth were taught that war was the noblest of all activities: a test of manhood and honour. To die fighting in battle was the highest fulfilment since it ensured a happy afterlife, a notion which derived its sanction from the Plains Indians' religious beliefs. So did the cruel practices which characterised the Plains Indian concept of war. Torture was the means whereby a captive might show himself worthy of divine protection. The scalping and mutilation of slain enemies was justified as a safeguard against their becoming threats in the spirit world.

As thousands of emigrants crossed the Plains to reach California, Oregon and Utah, there were occasional conflicts between whites and Native Americans. Consequently, the federal government tried to reach some accommodation with the tribes. In 1851, at a meeting at Horse Creek near Fort Laramie (see the map on page 232), most Plains' tribes agreed to accept definite limits to their hunting grounds. The Sioux were to keep north of the Platte River, while the Cheyenne and Arapaho were to confine themselves to the Colorado foothills. In return, the tribes were promised gifts and annual payments. This policy was designed to cut down on intertribal warfare and, more importantly, to enable the government to negotiate separately with each tribe. Relations between the Plains Indians and Americans did not greatly improve after 1851:

- The US government showed little interest in honouring Indian treaties. Once the Kansas–Nebraska Bill became law (see page 59), tribes like the Omaha and Pawnee were pressured to make further concessions of territory. By 1860 much of Kansas and Nebraska had been cleared of Indians.
- The gold rush into Colorado in 1859 (see page 240) resulted in thousands of prospectors entering land guaranteed to the Cheyenne and Arapaho.
- Nineteenth-century Americans displayed a lack of talent for administration in Native American affairs. The **Bureau of Indian Affairs** had charge of tribal affairs. Unfortunately, many of its agents were corrupt, systematically cheating the Native Americans. Congress aggravated the situation by its meanness in granting funds.

KEY TERM

Bureau of Indian Affairs
Created within the War Department in 1824 and charged with handling all matters relating to Native Americans. In 1849 the Bureau was shifted from the War Department to the Department of the Interior.

The impact of the Civil War

In 1861–2 regular troops were pulled out of the West for service in the east. This seemed a good opportunity for the Plains Indians to drive out white intruders. However, western militia units, mainly from California, quickly replaced the regular troops; by 1865 there were some 20,000 soldiers in the West, almost double the 1860 figure. The fact that so many troops were committed to the West in the Civil War indicates the importance that President Lincoln's administration attached to western gold for the prosecution of the war. Lincoln, it should be said, left Native American affairs almost entirely to Congress and the Bureau of Indian Affairs. While many easterners had some sympathy for Native Americans, most western Congressmen favoured military measures aimed at destroying the Plains Indians.

The Sioux War in Minnesota

The most serious trouble developed in Minnesota in 1862 when federal authorities failed to give the Dakota Sioux their yearly supplies. Angered by broken promises, Sioux tribesmen wrought havoc, killing or capturing some 1000 white Americans. Militia units soon defeated the Dakota and over 300 tribesmen were sentenced to death by a military commission. Lincoln pardoned the majority of the condemned men but 38 were hanged from a single scaffold in December 1862. The Dakota lost their lands in Minnesota and were exiled to poor-quality land further west.

The Sand Creek massacre

When Cheyenne and Arapaho chiefs in Colorado accepted a treaty banishing them westward, protesting tribesmen raided the trails and mining camps. In 1864 the territorial governor persuaded most of the renegades to gather at Fort Lyon on Sand Creek, where they were promised protection. Despite this promise, militia forces led by Colonel John Chivington attacked the camp in November 1864. 'Kill and scalp all, big and little', shouted Chivington, a former Methodist minister. Some 450 Indians were killed. Pregnant Indian women were disembowelled; Indian children were clubbed to death. Many eastern

Americans were appalled at the massacre. But Chivington and his men were acclaimed as heroes by most western whites. (Chivington successfully exhibited his personal collection of 100 Indian scalps in Denver.) In 1865 the Cheyenne survivors surrendered unconditionally and gave up their Sand Creek lands.

SOURCE A

A description by Robert Bent, a half-Cheyenne, who had been forced to guide Chivington's expedition quoted in Ezra Brown, editor, *The Old West: The Indians*, Time Life Books, 1973, p. 187.

I saw five squaws [women] under a bank. When troops came up to them they ran out and showed their persons to let the soldiers know they were squaws and begged for mercy but the soldiers shot them all. Some thirty or forty squaws, collected in a hole for protection, sent out a little girl about six years old with a white flag on a stick. She was shot and killed. I saw one squaw cut open with an unborn child lying by her side. I saw the body of White Antelope with the privates cut off, and I heard a soldier say he was going to make a tobacco pouch out of them.

Examine Source A. Why did Chivington's men commit such atrocities?

Fighting in the southwest

In the southwest, the Chiricahua Apaches, led by **Cochise**, relentlessly attacked white settlers and soldiers. (Cochise claimed he killed ten white men for every Indian slain: 'We kill ten', he mused 'and a hundred come in their place.') Union commander **Kit Carson** put down the Mecsalero Apaches in 1863, crushed the Navajos in Arizona in January 1864, and defeated the Kiowas at the battle of Adobe Walls in November 1864. However, small bands of Apaches continued to attack farms and travellers.

Congressional action

In March 1865, Congress created a joint committee to investigate 'the condition of the Indian tribes and their treatment by the civil and military authorities of the United States'. Congress also authorised a treaty commission to approach the Sioux tribes of the upper Missouri. These two measures marked the first steps towards a different kind of Indian policy: a policy of 'conquest by kindness' rather than extermination. Many easterners, while having no wish to halt western expansion, felt some sympathy for Native Americans. Some of the leading humanitarians of the day (for example, abolitionists like William Lloyd Garrison) became active in Indian reform movements. Essentially, they advocated large chunks of land being set aside as **reservations** and supported efforts to educate and civilise Native Americans.

The situation 1865–9

Throughout 1865 intermittent clashes continued. Bands of Sioux, Cheyenne and Arapaho, often no more than ten to twenty strong, wiped out dozens of isolated

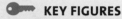

KEY FIGURES

Cochise (c.1805–74)

A war leader of the Chiricahua Apaches, led a rebellion against the USA which began in 1861 and continued through most of the 1860s. He finally made peace in 1872.

Kit Carson (1809–68)

Well informed about Indian ways, he was a guide in Frémont's western expeditions in the 1840s and served with distinction in the Mexican War and Civil War.

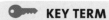

KEY TERM

Reservations Areas of land 'reserved' for the use of Native Americans.

Figure 8.1 The opening up of the West.

white families and ambushed small army patrols on the northern and central Plains.

Army tactics

With the Civil War's end, thousands of regular troops, many of them African Americans, took the offensive against Native Americans. Thousands more manned frontier forts defending travel routes and settlements. While the forts helped to establish control of areas, large-scale military operations often had little success. Soldiers, operating in an inhospitable country, far from their base, required massive logistical support. Most troop columns, moving at the speed of their wagons, stood little chance of finding bands to fight. Military commanders found that small, fast-moving patrols, using mules for supplies and friendly

Native Americans as scouts, were far more effective in locating and defeating hostile tribesmen.

Red Cloud's War

From 1865 to 1867, Lakota Sioux chief Red Cloud led resistance to the army's attempt to build the Powder River Road (part of the Bozeman Trail – see the map on page 232), which would have cut across the Lakota's hunting grounds in Montana. Red Cloud's men harassed the soldiers so effectively that the road could not be built and most troops were bottled up in their forts. The Indians' greatest success came in December 1866 when 82 soldiers under Captain Fetterman were killed near Fort Phil Kearny.

Peace efforts

Army chiefs, wanting vengeance for the 'Fetterman massacre', urged vigorous military countermeasures. But President Andrew Johnson's government supported a peaceful solution. So did a majority of Congressmen, for humanitarian and for financial reasons. (It cost $2 million a year to maintain a single regiment on the Plains.)

In 1867, Congress set up a Peace Commission to tour the Plains and find a means of ending the fighting. Its *Report on the Condition of the Indian Tribes* blamed the Plains' wars mainly on the white people and called for just and humane treatment of Native Americans. Congress now endorsed a plan to concentrate all the Plains Indians in two large reservations:

- In October 1867, a conference at Medicine Lodge, Kansas ended with an agreement that the Kiowa, Comanche, Arapaho and Cheyenne would accept lands in western Oklahoma.
- A meeting at Fort Laramie in the spring of 1868 resulted in the Sioux tribes being given a reservation in the Black Hills of Dakota.

In both cases, the US government offered money and supplies to ease the Native American transition to reservation life. Most chiefs yielded to US pressure because they realised that reservations offered the only alternative to extinction.

More fighting 1868–9

Some tribesmen still refused to yield, resisting their chiefs in an effort to preserve their traditional way of life. Hard fighting on the southern Plains continued through 1868–9 as troops under the command of Civil War hero General Philip Sheridan beat the renegades into submission. 'The more [Plains Indians] we can kill this year', said Sheridan, 'the less will have to be killed next year.' He ordered an autumn and winter campaign to force the Native Americans on to the reservations. In November 1868 Colonel **George Armstrong Custer** attacked a Cheyenne village along the Washita River, killing over 100 warriors and 40 women.

 KEY FIGURE

George Armstrong Custer (1839–76)

Fought with distinction in the Civil War. He went on to command the Seventh Cavalry during campaigns against the Plains Indians. Politically and militarily ambitious, he was killed at the battle of the Little Bighorn.

President Grant's Peace Policy

The continuing bloodshed divided eastern humanitarians and western settlers. Easterners continued to have some sympathy with Native Americans. Most westerners, by contrast, echoed the traditional view that the only good Indian was a dead one. They claimed that there would be no peace until the tribes had been vanquished in battle and the survivors placed in reservations under military control.

Grant's actions

In his 1869 inaugural speech, President Grant promised to 'favour any course … which tends to … [the] civilizing and ultimate citizenship' of the 'original occupants of this land':

- Grant favoured the reservation policy, hoping that Native Americans would, in time, become American citizens.
- In 1869 Congress established a new civilian Board of Indian Commissioners, ending the long-standing division of authority between the Department of the Interior and the War Department. The Board's main purpose was to supervise conditions on the reservations, moulding reservation life along the lines that the reformers (not Native Americans) thought best.
- In an effort to stamp out laxity and corruption, Grant replaced present Indian agents, first with Quakers and then with nominees of other Protestant denominations.
- One of Grant's close friends and advisers, Colonel Ely Parker, a full-blooded Seneca Indian, was appointed to head the Bureau of Indian Affairs.

Grant's 'Peace Policy' delighted eastern reformers. The measures he supported were not new; they had long been advocated. What was new (it was hoped) was a serious attempt to make them work.

Failure of the Peace Policy

Proclaiming high-sounding objectives in Washington, DC was one thing, but making them work out on the frontier was another. Unfortunately, the new system soon showed itself to be as inefficient as previous systems. Incompetent and corrupt officials slipped through the screen of missionary appointments in large numbers. Moreover, an 'Indian Ring' in the Department of the Interior systematically stole the funds and supplies intended for the reservations. Consequently, many Indians did not receive the welfare to which they felt entitled. In 1871, Parker, suspected of corruption, was forced to resign as Commissioner of Indian Affairs.

Given the lack of adequate funding, Indian agents found it difficult to keep tribesmen on the reservations where the wildlife was too sparse to support them. Even more serious was the fact that as the 1870s wore on army authorities found it equally hard to keep white settlers out of Native American territory.

Ironically, the eight years of Grant's Peace Policy were years of savage warfare. Within Native American tribes there was intense factionalism, some chiefs supporting peace, others favouring war. While renegade tribesmen were often rounded up by troops and herded into reservations, it was not easy to keep them there. In 1874, for example, renegade Kiowas, Comanches and Cheyennes attacked freight wagons and trading posts. US soldiers, in a fierce winter campaign (known as the Red River War), destroyed Indian supplies and slaughtered scores of Cheyenne fugitives near the Sappa River in Kansas. With the exile of the ringleaders to reservations, Native American independence on the southern Plains ended.

The Great Sioux War 1876

In the north, the Fort Laramie Treaty kept the Sioux relatively quiet for several years. In 1870 Red Cloud led his Lakota on to a reservation and never again took up arms. This seemed a major victory for the Peace Policy. But some Sioux, northern Cheyenne and Arapaho opposed the reservation system. These non-treaty Indians, who looked to the leadership of Sitting Bull, a Hunkpapa Sioux chieftain, opposed continued white encroachment on their territory in Dakota and Montana. By 1875–6, they won support from disenchanted warriors who had settled on the Sioux reservation in the Black Hills of Dakota.

Sioux unrest

Reservation Sioux Indians were unsettled by:

* the poor supplies they received from the USA
* the advance of the North Pacific Railroad, which threatened Sioux hunting grounds
* Colonel Custer's exploring expedition into the Black Hills in 1874. Accompanying prospectors found gold and thousands of miners were soon streaming into Sioux lands. Despite promises to the contrary, the army did little to keep them out.

The Black Hills' situation led to a large spring migration of reservation Sioux to the camps of the non-treaty tribes, concentrated in the region of the Bighorn River in south Montana. By mid-1876 many Sioux were on the warpath. Troops were sent to deal with the trouble.

The battle of the Little Bighorn

In June, Custer found the Sioux and Cheyenne encampment on the Little Bighorn River. Some 8000 Native Americans had gathered. Unaware of enemy numbers, and fearing that the enemy might slip away, Custer determined to attack. Dividing his small force of Seventh Cavalry, he sent Major Reno to attack the Sioux/Cheyenne village from the south while he headed north with over 200 men, intending to outflank the enemy. Sioux warriors forced Reno to retreat. Then 2500 Native Americans, led by Crazy Horse and Sitting Bull, attacked Custer's force, killing him and his entire command. Reno, surrounded by tribesmen, managed to hold out for two days until more US troops arrived, causing the Sioux to withdraw.

The Native Americans' last stand

The Little Bighorn battle is often referred to as 'Custer's Last Stand'. In reality, it was the Sioux's last stand. President Grant and the military authorities determined to avenge the Bighorn massacre. The army thus continued its remorseless pressure. Shortages of food and ammunition soon forced most of the Sioux bands to surrender and return to reservation life. Crazy Horse was captured and murdered before he was brought to trial. Sitting Bull led the remnants of his tribe to Canada. In 1881 he finally surrendered. After 1876 there were only a few sporadic outbreaks of violence on the northern Plains.

The Nez Perce

In 1877 the Nez Perce took to the warpath rather than surrender their lands in the northwest. Their leader, Chief Joseph, with some 700 tribesmen, conducted a remarkable retreat of over 2400 km through Idaho, Wyoming and Montana, defeating US forces in numerous small skirmishes on the way. He was finally caught by troops just 50 km short of the Canadian border. He and his people were uprooted from their traditional lands and sent first to Kansas and then to Oklahoma.

The Apache wars

Fighting continued for a little longer in New Mexico and Arizona. Cochise finally agreed to peace terms in 1872. While many Apaches agreed to settle on a reservation, two leaders, Victorio and Geronimo, continued to resist. The wildness of the terrain, and the fact that it straddled the Mexican–US border, enabled the small bands of Apaches to hold out for several years.

- Victorio was finally defeated and killed by Mexican forces in 1880.
- Geronimo's capture by US troops in 1886 ended Apache resistance.

Reasons for US success

Plains Indian resistance to white settlement was ultimately futile. The disunited and relatively few Native Americans never stood much chance of retaining their tribal lands against the flood of white settlers. Those settlers were supported by a professional army and by far superior technology, which included the railway, the electric telegraph and the Winchester repeating rifle. Although the Plains Indians fought a skilful (and savage) guerrilla-type war, army officers like Generals Sherman and Sheridan, toughened by their Civil War experiences, were prepared to use equally savage methods. Winter campaigns proved particularly effective.

Army leaders also encouraged the wholesale killing of the buffalo herds, aware that this would make life difficult for the Plains Indians. However, the buffalo's destruction was not deliberately planned by the army; rather, it was mainly the result of professional hunters (like **Buffalo Bill Cody**) killing the beast as food for railway construction workers or simply as sport. Railways ran excursion trains for hunters who were allowed to gun down buffalos from train carriages. In the years 1872–4 some 3 million buffalo a year were killed. In 1865 there were two great buffalo herds on the Plains, comprising an estimated 13 million animals. By 1883 the southern herd had been exterminated and a scientific expedition could find only 200 survivors of the northern herd. The destruction of the buffalo meant the destruction of the Plains Indians' way of life.

Civilising Native Americans

By 1880 most Native Americans were settled on reservations. On paper the reservations appeared large. Even after the cession of the Black Hills, the Great Sioux reservation which sprawled over southwest Dakota encompassed some 100,000 km². But most of the land was unsuitable for agriculture.

Americanisation

Eastern politicians, churchmen and some of the leading humanitarians of the day continued to speak out against Native American mistreatment. In 1877, newly elected President Rutherford Hayes accepted white responsibility and admitted: 'Many if not most, of our Indian wars have had their origin in broken promises and acts of injustice on our part.' Under Hayes, renewed efforts were made to reform the Indian Bureau and prevent corruption. However, even those white Americans who were sympathetic to Native Americans had little inclination to respect or preserve their way of life. Most liberal reformers, who belonged to organisations such as the Indian Rights Association, believed that the best way forward was assimilation – 'Americanisation' – and the eradication of tribal culture. Native Americans must be weaned from their nomadic ways, encouraged to support themselves by farming, learn English and become Christian. In the 1880s Congress provided funds for Native American education. Boarding schools were established where Native American children could be isolated from parental influences and taught white American skills and attitudes. Native American religious practices were outlawed, rations being withheld from those tribes which did not conform.

The Dawes Act

The climax of the integrationist policy came with the Dawes General Allotment Act (1887). This broke up reservation land into small units held by individuals or families. Each head of family could receive 160 acres (65 hectares) of farmland (or 320 acres of grazing land), each single male adult 80 acres. Native Americans who accepted the allotments and 'adopted the habits of civilized life' were to be granted US citizenship after 25 years.

 KEY FIGURE

William Frederick Cody (1846–1917)

Better known by his nickname of Buffalo Bill. An army scout and Pony Express rider, he gained his nickname from his success in supplying the men working on the Union Pacific Railroad with buffalo, killing 4280 in eight months in 1867–8. In 1883 he began touring the USA and Europe with his Wild West Show.

Reformers at the time hailed the Dawes Act as a great achievement, hoping that it would end the old tribal relationships and the need to provide Native Americans with rations. But the effects of the measure were deplorable. The assumption that Native Americans could be transformed into farmers was naive. Within a very short time, most had sold or lost their land to whites and fallen into poverty. Ironically, the 'soft' humanitarian policies of easterners thus proved as destructive to Plains Indians' traditional way of life as the 'hard' policies advocated by westerners.

The battle of Wounded Knee

The last tragic episode came in 1890. Despairing Sioux in South Dakota rallied to the teachings of Wovoka, who promised that if they took up a ceremonial dance their lands and power would be restored. The Ghost Dance craze spread rapidly and with such fervour that it soon alarmed white authorities. An effort to arrest Sitting Bull, one of the chiefs encouraging the Ghost Dance, led to his death. Bands of Lakota Sioux fled their reservations with the army in pursuit. In December 1890, nervous Seventh Cavalry fired into a group of Sioux at Wounded Knee. Some 200 Sioux, many of them women and children, died. So did 31 soldiers. The 'battle' was an accident: neither side had really wanted to fight. The whole affair, an accident born of mutual distrust, misunderstanding and fear, epitomised relations between Plains Indians and Americans in the late nineteenth century.

Conclusion

In less than two decades, the Plains Indians' political, cultural, social and economic systems had been destroyed. The result was the moral and physical decline of a once proud people. Disease, alcoholism, dependency and poverty were the fate of most Plains Indians, whose numbers halved between 1865 and 1900. The USA had pursued a mixed policy – benevolence, coercion cloaked in legality, and violence – to change the Plains Indian lifestyle in the name of civilisation and progress. But several things might be said in defence of US action:

- The USA's record with regard to Native Americans was not very different from that of European powers, who (at the same time) were carving out empires in Africa and Asia at the expense of native peoples.
- There were so many different views about how to deal with Native Americans that it was difficult to agree a consistent policy. Settlers, for example, talked of their continuing fears. Congress talked of peace, military leaders talked of suppression, and reformers talked of conversion and Americanisation.
- Even with the benefit of hindsight, it is difficult to come up with a better solution than a reservation policy, given American settlers' determination to occupy the West. Native Americans might have been given more land and been allowed to maintain their way of life. But that life was dependent on the buffalo, an animal soon on the point of extinction.

- There is now a tendency to glorify the Plains Indians, to see them as a noble minority, fighting bravely for their alternative cultures. However, they also fought brutally, slaughtering white settlers, sometimes torturing their captives to death. No prisoners were taken at the Little Bighorn.

Not all Native Americans suffered as severely as the Plains Indians:

- The pacific Pueblos in the southwest retained their lands and their autonomy.
- The Five Civilised Tribes in the Oklahoma territory made a rapid recovery from the devastation and demoralisation resulting from their support of the Confederacy in the Civil War. By 1880 they had attained a reasonable prosperity that set them apart from all other western Native Americans.
- There was no warfare in Alaska, the USA's last frontier (purchased from Russia for $7.2 million in 1867). The 70,000 natives – Eskimo, Aleut and Native American – continued to live peacefully. No treaty extinguished native title to land, no reservations were established and no agency sought to impose a civilisation programme.

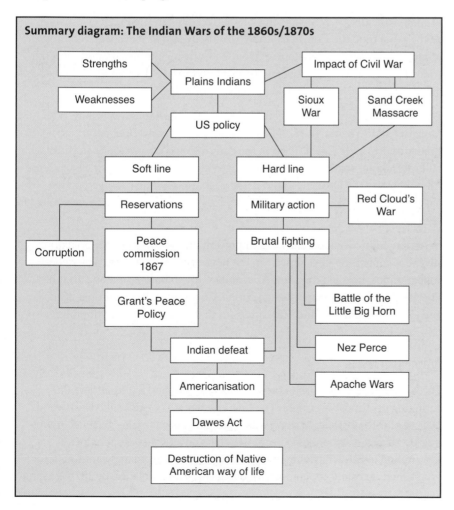

Summary diagram: The Indian Wars of the 1860s/1870s

The mining frontier

▶ *Why was mining so important to western development?*

Miners, seeking gold or silver, often paved the way for other western settlers. Unlike previous frontiers, the miners' frontier was one that advanced from west to east. The first prospectors in any given area were usually experienced 'forty-niners' from California (see page 50). The miners' frontier was never so much a frontier as a scattering of settlements, usually in remote highland and barren desert regions. Whenever news of a 'strike' reached mining towns, prospectors flocked to the site. The excitement of the California gold rush of 1848–9 was re-enacted time and again in the following three decades. Frustration and hard labour were the lot of most miners. Only a tiny fraction succeeded in striking it rich.

The 'strikes'

In 1858–9 the discovery of gold in Colorado resulted in the Pike Peak rush. At the same time the Comstock Lode was discovered in Nevada. It required prodigious amounts of labour to exploit the Comstock mines properly. But the scale of the effort was matched by the yield. In the two decades after the Lode's discovery, its total output of gold and silver yielded $350 million.

The encroachments of miners continued through the 1860s, especially in Montana and Arizona. In 1870, Leadville, Colorado had a brief boom, as did Creede and Cripple Creek. Then in the early 1870s gold was found in the Black Hills of Dakota, sparking a great rush on to territory owned by the Sioux. Both tribesmen and the US army found it impossible to exclude prospectors (see page 235). In 1877 discovery of the Lucky Cuss silver mine in Arizona resulted in yet another rush.

In Arizona and Montana, the most important mineral was neither gold nor silver but copper (needed for wire in the new electrical industry). The richest copper mines included the giant Anaconda mine in Butte, Montana and the Phelps–Dodge mine near Bisbee, Arizona. Coal mines (in Oklahoma, Kansas and Colorado) and zinc and lead mines (in Colorado, Idaho and Montana) also prospered.

Mining towns

The sudden disorderly rush of prospectors to a new find led to settlements springing up almost overnight. The first inhabitants of places like Deadwood, Dakota and Tombstone, Arizona were young, transient males. But such towns quickly attracted saloon-keepers, prostitutes and assorted desperadoes, determined to extract a living from the miners. Not surprisingly, mining towns established notorious reputations for debauchery and violence. By 1873, Virginia

City, which grew up as a result of the Comstock Lode, had 20,000 people. Men outnumbered women by three to one and the town had 131 saloons and numerous gambling houses and brothels. Deadwood, which sprang up in 1875, was much the same. In its brief heyday, it was one of the most lawless spots on earth. Gunfights were commonplace. However, it does seem that most men adhered to a rough code of conduct. The majority of those involved in shoot-outs chose to be involved. Women, children, elderly citizens and those unwilling to fight were rarely the targets of attack.

Generally, crime, disorder and vice flourished for only a short time. As well as the prospectors, each new rush brought permanent settlers – farmers, cattlemen, storekeepers, lawyers, ministers – who usually made a better living by supplying the needs of the gold-seekers than by looking for the elusive metal. If a settlement survived and prospered, the law-abiding and responsible majority soon took matters into their own hands, given that Washington, DC proved unable to provide orderly government. Informal codes of law were established and rough and ready justice was meted out by vigilantes. Although these groups have often had a bad press, they seem to have meted out justice at least as fairly as the official system. A few summary punishments usually drove the 'bad men' out of town.

Many towns did not survive. Miners' expectations faded in the light of reality – high prices, low yields, hardship and deception – and many of the towns that sprang up in the 1860s and 1870s disappeared almost as quickly as they had risen.

SOURCE B

A photograph of Deadwood in the 1860s.

> How useful is Source B for understanding what life was like in a western mining town? **?**

Corporate mining

Throughout the mountain country, mining methods developed according to a set pattern. In the initial stages of mining, individual prospectors could hope to make themselves rich simply by sifting off dirt and gravel from surface deposits of gold by **panning**. But once the surface metals had gone, efficient mining required shafts sunk into the ground and crushing mills built to extract the precious metal, embedded deep in hard rock and locked in quartz. Deep-level quartz-mining required extensive outlays of capital and considerable engineering skill. Western mining thus quickly became big business as most of the mining wealth fell into the hands of a few investment bankers and mining company owners. The mines around Deadwood, for example, were soon controlled by one large company, Homestake Mining. By 1880 the wild rush of individual prospectors had given way to organised enterprises. Most miners settled down to work for the mining bosses or took up farming.

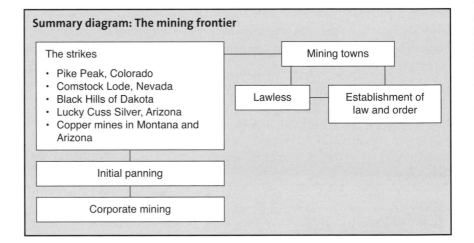

Summary diagram: The mining frontier

The strikes
- Pike Peak, Colorado
- Comstock Lode, Nevada
- Black Hills of Dakota
- Lucky Cuss Silver, Arizona
- Copper mines in Montana and Arizona

Mining towns

Lawless — Establishment of law and order

Initial panning

Corporate mining

4 The impact of the railways

▶ *Why were railways so important for western development?*

The settlement of Oregon and California in the late 1840s pointed to the need for a transport network that would link the Pacific coast with the Atlantic. That network did not really arrive until after the Civil War. It then came with a vengeance.

Mail services

In 1857, the government awarded a federal mail contract to a syndicate headed by John Butterfield. In return for an annual subsidy of $600,000, Butterfield's Overland Express Company undertook to provide a mail service, in each direction, between St Louis and San Francisco – a 4500-km route – and to guarantee delivery within 25 days. The first eastbound stagecoach arrived on schedule in 1858 and by 1860 Butterfield's company was carrying a greater volume of mail than was going to California by sea.

In 1860, the firm of Russell, Majors & Waddell, which ran a western overland freight company, set up the Pony Express to provide a faster mail service to the Pacific coast. Relays of pony-riders, operating between St Joseph, Missouri, the western terminus of the railways, and Sacramento, California, covered the distance across the central Plains in ten days. But the completion of a transcontinental telegraph line in 1861 made the Pony and Butterfield Express services obsolete.

The Pacific Railroad Act

By the 1850s there was considerable support for a transcontinental railway. The enormous expense in building such a railway meant that federal aid was essential. Prior to 1861, sectional jealousies prevented Congress taking action. Southern Congressmen demanded a southern route, while northerners pressed for a northern or central route. The secession of the Confederate states enabled northerners to agree on a central route. The July 1862 Pacific Railroad Act chartered the Union Pacific Company to build westward across the continent from Omaha; it also authorised the Central Pacific Company to build eastward from Sacramento. Both companies were given enormous land grants – a 120-metre right of way and twelve square kilometres of public land on each side of the track for each mile of track laid. The land was allotted in alternate sections, forming a pattern like a chessboard: the squares of one colour represented railway property, the squares of the other colour government property. Adjacent government lands were not open to homesteaders on the grounds that free land in the immediate vicinity of a line might prevent the railways from selling their properties at good prices. The companies were also granted huge government loans, varying in amount (from $16,000 to $48,000 per mile) with the difficulty of the terrain.

Building the line

The building of the first transcontinental line began in earnest after 1865, with government land grants and financial support ensuring that money flowed in from both American and European investors.

The builders of the line inevitably faced major problems. Everything required had to be transported over long distances, together with supplies for the thousands of labourers. The Union Pacific construction gangs were chiefly Irish immigrants and discharged Union soldiers, while the Central Pacific relied heavily on 12,000 imported (and cheap) Chinese labourers. The Central Pacific faced the challenge of building a track across – or through – the Sierra Nevada mountains. The Union Pacific, working with military precision, had an easier job building across the Plains. In May 1869 the two lines met (after initially missing!) at Promontory Point in Utah. The Union Pacific company had built 1738 km of track and the Central Pacific had built 1102 km.

The economic side of the transcontinental line was sordid. Unscrupulous shareholders of both railway companies devised an ingenious scheme to enrich themselves. Instead of inviting competitive tenders, they created dummy construction companies to do the actual building: the Crédit Mobilier for the Union Pacific and the Contract and Finance Company for the Central Pacific. The Crédit Mobilier charged the Union Pacific $94 million for construction that cost at most $44 million. The Credit and Finance Corporation did almost as well, taking the Central Pacific for $79 million, of which an estimated $36 million was profit. While the building companies made huge profits, the two railway companies were burdened with debt.

Moreover, the terms under which government aid was granted turned the transcontinental project into a race between the two railways, simply in order to get government money. This put a premium on speed of construction rather than quality. The result was that the lines of both companies soon had to be extensively resited and rebuilt. Nevertheless, the successful completion of the transcontinental line was a remarkable feat of engineering and planning.

Railway expansion

By the 1890s there were four other transcontinental lines:

- The Northern Pacific, completed in 1883, stretched from Duluth, Minnesota to Portland, Oregon.
- The Southern Pacific, linking New Orleans with San Francisco, was also completed in 1883.
- The Atchison, Topeka and Santa Fe, linking Kansas City with Los Angeles and San Diego, was completed in 1884.
- The Great Northern, extending westwards from St Paul, Minnesota reached the Pacific coast at Seattle, in 1893.

The building of the transcontinental lines accounted for only a fraction of western rail construction. Each of the transcontinental railways built numerous branch-lines. By 1900 there was some 139,200 km of track west of the Mississippi, nearly half the national total.

Although there were no more federal loans to railways after 1873, all the transcontinental lines, apart from the Great Northern, received lavish federal land grants, as did most of the infill lines. In all, the federal government gave the western railways 70 million hectares of public land, an area larger than France. These land grants were hugely important, providing a basis of credit which enabled construction to start. However, the federal government's involvement was matched by that of the states, which advanced over $200 million and made land grants totalling 19 million hectares, and by municipalities and counties whose desire for railway connections led them to provide some $300 million. But most of the capital for railway building came from private sources, especially European investors and New York banking houses.

Few railway fortunes were built by methods of pristine purity. Most railway companies bribed federal and state politicians on a huge scale. But compared to some contemporary businessmen, most railway magnates were giants of probity. They at least took some interest in the welfare of their companies, if not always in that of the public.

A wise investment?

Corruption was part of the price the USA had to pay for opening up the West. On the whole, the federal government received a substantial return on its support for railways:

SOURCE C

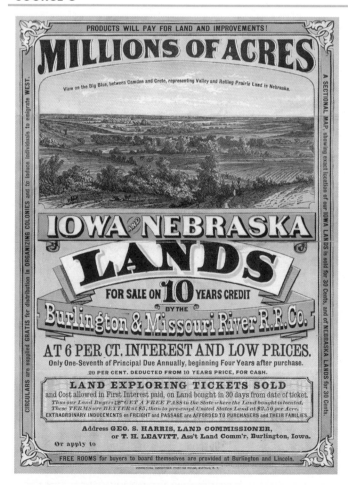

An 1872 railway advertisement for land.

How does Source C attempt to attract settlers to the West? What does it not say about life in the West?

- The alternate sections of land it retained along the railway tracks fetched twice the normal price of $1.25 an acre.
- Government traffic on the land-grant lines enjoyed a 50 per cent discount.
- By 1900, the loan of $60 million to the Union and Central Pacific had been repaid in full, together with interest at six per cent, totalling more than $104 million.
- Most importantly, the railways served the national purpose of binding the country together. They revolutionised the West, ensuring that a flood of people (and goods) moved in and an abundance of raw materials moved out.
- The railways were gigantic markets for iron, steel, lumber and other capital goods.
- The New West of cattlemen and farmers was largely the product of the railways.

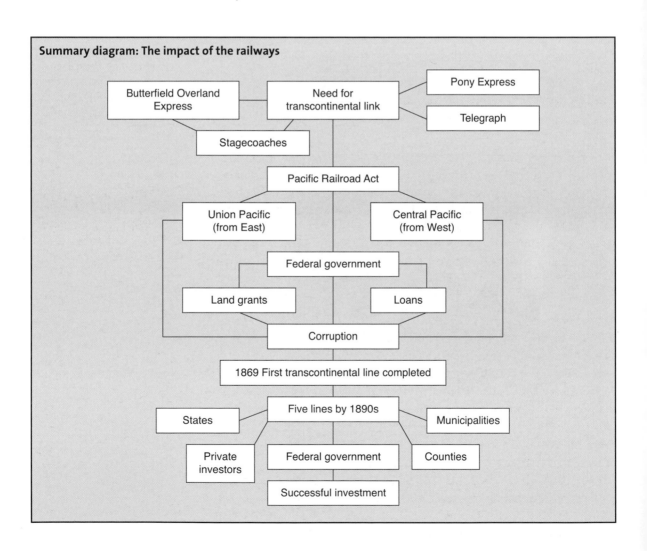

Summary diagram: The impact of the railways

Farmers, cowboys and shepherds

▶ *How were farmers able to make a living in the West?*

Most settlers who went westwards earned their living from the land. A few were ranchers, cowboys and shepherds. But most depended on crops for their livelihood. How successful were western farmers in the three decades after the Civil War?

The Homestead Act

Under the Homestead Act (1862) farmers could claim western land for free simply by staking out a claim and living on it for five years. Those Congressmen who passed the act assumed that the free lands would attract poor easterners and that the Plains would soon be dotted with 160-acre (65-hectare) family farms.

Problems with the Homestead Act

Congressional assumptions did not work out as planned. Most landless Americans were too poor to become independent farmers, even when they could obtain free land. A great deal of capital was needed to move west, purchase the necessary tools, seed, stock and machinery, build a house, farm buildings and fences, and to survive for a year before the first crops could be harvested. Industrial workers, for whom the free land was supposed to provide a 'safety valve', lacked the skills and inclination to become farmers. Most **homesteaders** were already farmers, usually from districts not far removed from frontier regions. Yet even for these experienced farmers, there were serious problems with the Homestead Act. The framers of the measure failed to realise that 160 acres was too small a unit on which to make a living on the Plains.

There were other problems with the Homestead Act, not least the fact that it invited fraud. Many of the men who claimed free land had no intention of farming the land themselves: they were dummy registrants acting for speculators, cattlemen, mining or lumber companies who were simply trying to acquire huge tracts of land. Consequently, much of the land claimed under the act passed quickly to large concerns.

Further acts

Subsequent land laws, for example the 1873 Timber Culture Act, which permitted individuals to claim an additional 160 acres if they agreed to plant a quarter of it with trees within ten years, and the 1877 Desert Land Act, which allowed a settler to buy 640 acres at $1.25 an acre providing the holding was irrigated within two years, did not really help the small homesteader. Fewer

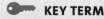 **KEY TERM**

Homesteaders Farmers who received land by the 1862 Homestead Act.

than a quarter of the 245,000 who took up land under the Timber Culture Act obtained final title to the property, as raising large numbers of seedling trees on the Plains proved difficult. Indeed, most measures of this kind were adopted largely in response to pressure from ranchers and timber interests intent on plundering the public domain. Thanks to wholesale fraud in the administration of the acts, both interests achieved their aims.

State and railway lands

Between 1862 and 1900, the government awarded to 600,000 claimants under the Homestead Act a total of 32 million hectares – a mere fraction of the 211 million hectares surrendered to the railways and the states or sold to land speculators.

The Homestead Act and subsequent federal measures thus contributed far less to the settlement of the West than the colonising activities of states and railways. Western states and territories made strenuous efforts to promote settlement, stationing agents in the east and in Europe to advertise opportunities. These efforts were overshadowed by those of the land-grant railway companies. Having millions of acres for sale and seeing in settlement a means of generating rail traffic, railways spent lavishly in attempts to attract settlers. Their promotional literature depicted the West as a land of milk and honey. In addition, they held out a variety of inducements: long-term loans, reduced steamship rates, free 'land-exploring tickets' and temporary accommodation for new arrivals.

Railway advertising proved effective. Large numbers of immigrants were lured to the Plains from Europe. Many clustered together to form compact homogeneous settlements, so that by 1890 hundreds of small German, Swedish and British colonies were dotted across the West. But most settlers were from American states further east, mainly those in the Mississippi Valley.

Life on the Plains

Despite the colonisation literature's glowing descriptions, newcomers soon discovered that the treeless and arid Plains presented huge challenges. Life was invariably a grim struggle, involving long hours of backbreaking work in isolated surroundings. The first settlers took up their land along the rivers and creeks, where they found timber for home-building, fuel and fencing. Later arrivals had to build houses of sods of earth (Source D). The nearest neighbours were often miles away, a problem for women who were about to give birth. While the soil was rich, pioneer families fought a constant battle with the elements: tornadoes, hailstorms, droughts, prairie fires, blizzards and pests. Swarms of locusts would sometimes cover the ground 15 cm deep, consuming everything in their path. Although land was relatively cheap, horses, livestock, wagons, wells, fencing, seeds and fertilisers were not. Freight charges and interest rates on loans were often cripplingly high. The tough conditions wore down many farmers and their

SOURCE D

An 1886 photograph of a family and its sod house.

Would the photograph in Source D have attracted or discouraged new settlers intending to go west?

families. The high transiency rate on the frontier reflected the frequent failure to adapt to the new environment.

Plains' agriculture

Most of the problems of Plain's agriculture were overcome sufficiently to make farming possible and (sometimes) profitable.

Important innovations

- In 1873 Joseph Glidden produced the first effective barbed wire, making it possible to fence land cheaply.
- Deep-drilled wells and steel windmills provided much-needed water.
- **Dry farming** methods enabled farmers to grow particular types of corn and wheat even when there was scant rainfall.
- American factories turned out an ever-increasing quantity of farm machinery – reapers, threshing machines, binders, combine harvesters – making possible wheat and maize farming on a colossal scale.

The Morrill Land Grant Act

The Morrill Land Grant Act (1862) provided land grants to the states for the founding of colleges to teach 'agriculture and the mechanic arts.' Most land-grant colleges struggled at first, lacking both students and a body of useful scientific knowledge to teach. However, they eventually prospered, fostering a system of agricultural education that brought useful knowledge to the farmers.

 **KEY TERM**

Dry farming A method of tillage involving deep ploughing and frequent harrowing which serves to hold water in the soil.

Bonanza farms

In good years, western agriculture could be made to pay. Large farms, in particular, prospered, often becoming larger as they did so. In Minnesota and the Dakotas, gigantic **bonanza** farms with machinery for mass production became one of the marvels of the age. These farms, sometimes over 4000 hectares in size and employing scores of men, were usually controlled by wealthy corporations which employed managers to run the farms at a profit. But even the biggest farms could not cope with prolonged drought and most failed in the dry years of the late 1880s. Those farmers who diversified their crops and cultivated their land intensively fared better in the long run.

The impact of western farming

Despite the various hazards, the eastern Plains from Minnesota and North Dakota down to Texas emerged as the new breadbasket for both the USA and Europe. In 1865, the USA had exported 1.2 billion litres of wheat. By 1900 it exported 7 billion litres, most of which was produced in states west of the Mississippi. Wheat exports evened the USA's balance of payments and spurred economic growth. The Plains also accounted for heavy percentages of the USA's other cereal crops, together with huge quantities of beef, pork and mutton. The population of the middle and northern Plains steadily increased. Between 1860 and 1900 the number of people in Kansas, Nebraska, the Dakotas, Iowa and Minnesota rose from less than a million to more than 7 million.

Boom and bust farming

Given the fact that much of the cereal crop was exported, western farmers' success depended increasingly on international market forces. Farmers were also dependent on other Americans.

- Bankers and loan companies provided the capital to expand farm operations and purchase machinery in good years.
- Middlemen stored – and sometimes sold – the farmers' produce.
- Railways carried the goods to market.

Western farmers were thus unable to determine the price of things they bought and sold, and most suffered in the 1870s as cereal prices tumbled as a result of a glut on the American and world markets. Corn, which sold for 78¢ a **bushel** in 1867, fell to 31¢ a bushel by 1873. Farmers who had borrowed heavily to finance their homestead and to purchase machinery went bankrupt. Many small farmers, believing that the 'system' of corrupt middlemen and greedy bankers and railway companies was against them, joined the Granger movement, which campaigned for regulation of the 'villains'. The situation was not so simple. The years after 1873 saw the entire US economy caught in a depression in which railway operators and middlemen also had to struggle to survive. While farm prices fell, so too did prices of manufactured goods and railway rates, often faster than farm prices.

The situation for farmers improved in the late 1870s as cereal prices rose. But over the next two decades economic boom and bust was the norm on the Plains. In the bust years of the late 1880s and early 1890s many hard-hit Plains' farmers were almost in open revolt against big business and state and federal governments. Most supported the Populist – or People's – Party. The Populists called for government control of transport and communications, a graduated income tax, regulation of monopolies and utilities, and more silver in the currency, ensuring there was more money in circulation. Populist presidential candidate James B. Weaver won a million votes in 1892.

The cattle bonanza

In the 1860s, some entrepreneurs realised there was no need to breed or stock their own cattle. On the grasslands of Texas an estimated 5 million longhorn cattle roamed free and unowned. These cattle could be had just for the effort of rounding them up. They were worth only $3 or $4 a head in Texas. But if they reached northern meat markets they fetched ten times as much. The key was getting the cattle to a convenient point on a railway from which they could be sent to St Louis and Chicago.

In 1866 some enterprising Texans headed a large herd northwards on the first post-war 'long drive', a huge mile trek across the open range to Sedalia, Missouri, the western terminus of the Missouri Pacific Railroad. The venture was not a total success. There were heavy losses *en route*. Moreover, Arkansas and Missouri farmers opposed the march of (possibly disease-carrying) cattle across their states.

Joseph McCoy was more successful. Helped by the liberalisation of the Kansas cattle quarantine laws in 1867, McCoy developed a more suitable **railhead** at Abilene in Kansas. In 1867, 35,000 head of cattle trudged along the Chisholm Trail to Abilene. In 1868 this number doubled and by 1871, 700,000 cattle reached Abilene. Overnight the place grew from a small hamlet into the first flourishing Kansas cattle town.

As the railways and farming frontiers extended further westwards, new trails came into being, new railheads eclipsed Abilene, and new cattle towns – Ellsworth, Wichita and Dodge City – developed. Between 1866 and 1888 some 6–10 million cattle were driven to the cattle towns, from where they were shipped to Chicago and other stockyards of the mid-west. Other herds were driven on a second long drive to be fattened or to stock the ranches of Colorado, Wyoming, Montana and the Dakotas.

Cowboys: myth and reality

During the 20 years after the Civil War 40,000 cowboys roamed the Plains. Most were in their teens or early twenties. They came from diverse backgrounds. Some were ex-Confederate soldiers seeking adventure. Perhaps a third were Mexican, black, Asian or Native American. Virtually all were expert horsemen,

KEY TERM

Railhead A railway terminus; in this context a collecting station to which cattle were herded for slaughter or to be sent to northern markets.

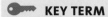 **KEY TERM**

Dime novel A cheap (10¢) and usually not very well-written adventure novel which appealed to the masses.

an essential skill given that cowboys virtually lived on horseback for the two months that most cattle drives took.

Cowboy life was rarely as glamorous as the **dime novel** of the time or cinema and television since has depicted it. For a wage of only $25–30 a month, the average cowboy worked an eighteen-hour day, mostly in the saddle, trying to coax forward a sprawling mass of cattle, coping with a continuous cloud of dust, and facing a variety of other potential hazards – floods, poisonous snakes and scorpions, blizzards, stampedes, rustlers and occasionally Native Americans. At journey's end, cowboys not surprisingly whooped it up in the cattle towns.

Cattle-ranching

The cattle drives were relatively short lived. As railway lines spread across the west, cattlemen realised that they could best function by establishing cattle ranches on the Plains. By 1880 ranching had spread northwards from Texas as far as Canada. Huge tracts of grazing land were quickly appropriated by ranchers who rarely bothered (initially) to acquire legal title to what was still almost wholly the public domain. They then maintained their position by force, fraud and perjury. Water rights were usually more important than land rights: whoever controlled the water effectively controlled the land. Disputes over land and water rights and rustling of livestock were endemic, often leading to violence between ranchers. Vigilante systems quickly sprang up, providing a measure of order. Leading ranchers also banded together to form livestock associations which developed a code of rules defining land and water rights and the recording of cattle brands. The associations operated reasonably effectively in most cases but they were by no means universally popular. Some behaved arbitrarily and sometimes unjustly, often favouring big ranchers at the expense of small.

The greatest boom in the range-cattle trade came in the early 1880s when eastern and European investors poured money into the 'Beef Bonanza'. By 1883 British companies owned or controlled nearly 8 million hectares of western grazing land. By the mid-1880s the open range-cattle business thus resembled the kind of large-scale corporate enterprise characteristic of US industry in the late nineteenth century. The Swan Land & Cattle Company of Wyoming, for example, owned a huge area of land on which roamed 100,000 head of cattle. Cowboys, in effect, became farmhands, riding only that part of the range which was owned (or controlled) by their employer.

The end of the open range

Two exceptionally severe winters between 1885 and 1887, straddling a summer drought, resulted in the death of millions of western castle (possibly 90 per cent of the total). Thousands of cattlemen (including the Swan Land & Cattle Company) were ruined.

Most of those who survived retreated into the security of smaller, fenced-in ranches (using barbed wire to enclose land actually owned), equipped with shelter for their animals against the elements. Such methods ensured that cattle could be more scientifically bred. By 1890 the days of the open range and the cowboy were effectively over. But the rise of the range-cattle industry, aided by the extension of the railways and the development of the refrigerator carriage (introduced in 1875), had changed the nation's eating habits: Americans became a primarily beef-eating rather than a pork-eating people.

The sheep bonanza

In some territories, particularly in the foothills of the Rockies, there was a sheep rather than a cattle bonanza. Cattlemen and sheep ranchers sometimes (literally) fought for control of water holes and grazing rights. Sheep were reputed to pollute precious drinking water and to ruin pasture by close-cropping. The prolonged warfare, which reached its height in the 1880s, resulted in the deaths of dozens of cattlemen and sheep-herders and the slaughter of hundreds of thousands of sheep, especially along the Colorado–Wyoming border. But the sheep-herders survived. By 1900 there were some 25 million sheep in the West.

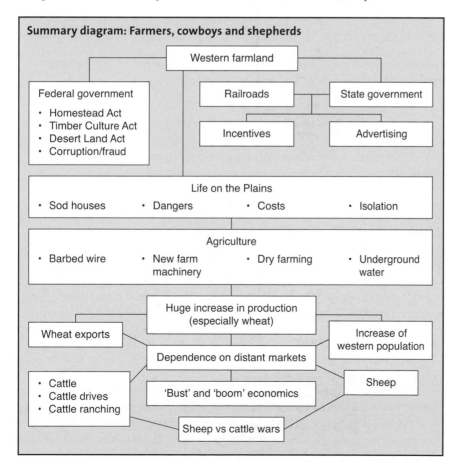

Summary diagram: Farmers, cowboys and shepherds

6 # The romance of the West

▶ *Was the winning of the West a heroic and romantic achievement?*

Many Americans liked to believe that the West was won by individuals successfully overcoming natural and economic obstacles and that this success had little to do with government initiatives. Many also regarded the winning of the West as a heroic and romantic achievement. Is there any truth in these views?

Federal government inaction

In many ways the US government had limited control over the process of western expansion:

- Most US politicians favoured *laissez-faire* government: they supported individual enterprise.
- Many domestic matters in the USA were state, not federal government concerns.
- Even law and order in the western territories was often left to vigilantes.

Federal government action

The federal government, the single most powerful force in the nation, by no means washed its hands of western developments:

- The fact that the government had clear rules defining the process by which western areas were incorporated into the USA was crucially important (see page 3).
- The federal government used the army to support white settlers against Native Americans. Throughout the period, it tried to maintain control of Indian policy.
- Acts like the Pacific Railroad Act (1862) and the Homestead Act (1862) had a major effect on western expansion.
- By the late nineteenth century many Congressmen were seriously concerned with the threat to the USA's natural resources – water, soil, animals, minerals and trees – and supported controlling and managing the western environment. The first National Park in the USA – indeed in the world – was created in 1872 when Congress passed an act designating 800,000 hectares of Wyoming Territory, an area of geysers, waterfalls and mountains, as Yellowstone National Park.

Western political developments

The demand for orderly government in the West led to the creation of territories: the Dakota, Colorado and Nevada territories were created in 1861, the Idaho and Arizona territories in 1863 and the Montana territory in 1864. Silver-rich Nevada was fast-tracked into the Union in 1864, in time to cast its electoral votes for

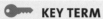 **KEY TERM**

Laissez-faire A French term meaning letting events find their own course. It refers to the view that governments should not intervene in economic and social matters.

Figure 8.2
The New
West.

Lincoln. Colorado was admitted in 1876. Thereafter, Democrats were reluctant to create new states out of territories that were heavily Republican. Only after the sweeping Republican victory of 1888 did Congress admit the Dakotas, Montana and Washington in 1889 and Idaho and Wyoming in 1890. Utah entered in 1896 (after the Mormon Church agreed to abandon the practice of polygamy). By 1900, only three areas within the continental USA, all sparsely populated, remained under territorial government: Oklahoma, Arizona and New Mexico. (All three territories had become states by 1912.)

The romance of the West

The frontier experience of the people settled in the Wild West caught the imagination of contemporary easterners. As farmers, miners, cowboys and prostitutes pursued their various real activities, a parallel legendary West took deep roots in US consciousness. This mythic West was shaped primarily by western dime novels which Erastus Beadle began publishing in 1859. These novels and the many imitators, featuring such legendary (albeit real-life) characters as Buffalo Bill and Calamity Jane, sold in huge numbers. The novels, which paid little regard to accuracy, familiarised readers with a world of stagecoaches and outlaws, cowboys and Indians. They emphasised the qualities Americans admired most: manliness, individualism, self-reliance. According to historian William C. Davis (2000), the legend of the west was 'a legend of struggle, of individual and collective men and women fighting hostile elements to create a place for themselves, the very essence of the American ethic of self-reliance, hard work, egalitarianism … . It stood for what men could do. It stood for never giving up. It stood for the limitless potential awaiting those who kept pressing on.'

Romantic pictorial representations of the West were also influential in shaping popular conception. The two most highly regarded western artists, Charles Russell and Frederic Remington, drew on first-hand experience. Their romantic images of Indians, cowboys, soldiers and frontiersmen captured the public's imagination. So did Buffalo Bill Cody's Wild West Show, which toured the USA and Europe in the 1880s and 1890s, attracting huge audiences. Half circus, half pageant, Cody's show glamorised the West. It included ace-shot Annie Oakley and re-enactments of Indian attacks on stagecoaches and US cavalry.

The West continued to fascinate future generations when adapted to cinema and television in the early twentieth century. Both media also tended to romanticise western life, with white Anglo-American heroes invariably defeating Indians and a mix of other villains. Some of the villains – murderers, bank and railway robbers like Jesse James and Billy the Kid – became heroes. So did the gunmen who (sometimes) had the law on their side – Wyatt Earp and 'Wild Bill' Hickok.

The impact of the frontier

In 1893 historian Frederick Jackson Turner, in a lecture, 'The Significance of the Frontier in American History', advanced his thesis that the conquest of the western frontier had shaped the national character in fundamental ways: it made Americans practical and inventive and led to 'dominant individualism, buoyancy and exuberance'. Turner's view – that the frontier was the source of America's democratic politics, open society, unfettered economy and **rugged individualism** – had enormous influence and appeared to give some academic credence to the romantic and heroic view of the West.

Greed and exploitation

In truth, Turner's frontier thesis was at best a gross exaggeration. White settlers had far more influence on the frontier than the frontier had on white settlers. That influence was often negative. There was little that was obviously romantic or heroic about the fact that:

- Native American culture was destroyed
- western settlers left behind an ever-lengthening trail of devastation, wantonly slaughtering wildlife, squandering mineral resources, felling forests and

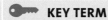
KEY TERM

Rugged individualism
The ability of an individual to succeed by his or her own endeavours, without relying on the government or other people for help.

displaying a similarly careless attitude towards the soil, with little heed to its future fertility

- most prospectors, cowboys or farmers laboured hard for little reward
- stockholders of large corporations made off with the lion's share of the West's mineral wealth
- (often corrupt) big business interests exploited most of the West's resources for their own profit, to the detriment of small entrepreneurs and without regard for the general interest
- the West was often a place of injustice, discord and conflict.

An achievement?

Nevertheless, the winning of the West, if not necessarily heroic or romantic (except in the public's imagination), can certainly be seen as a formidable and formative episode in the USA's history. Western mining bolstered the financial position of the USA. Western crops fed the growing populations of the USA and Europe. Between 1869 and 1899 the USA's population nearly trebled, farm production more than doubled and the value of manufacturers grew six-fold. Western expansion was major factor in the USA becoming the world's greatest economic power by 1900.

While western expansion undoubtedly exacted a fearful price on Native Americans, the perceived crimes of conquest should not overshadow all that happened. Perhaps there was something romantic and heroic about the struggle of people, usually of modest means – immigrants from all over Europe, Hispanics, Chinese, and American farming families (black and white) from further east – to better themselves. Not all succeeded. But many did.

Rugged individualism was part of the story. But so was cooperation – a practical necessity, a form of insurance in a tough environment where almost everyone was vulnerable to instant misfortune or economic disaster. Joint effort was essential to deal with problems of law enforcement, protection against Native American attack, prairie fires and a host of other problems. Individual and joint effort eventually ensured that remote farm settlements blossomed into thriving communities.

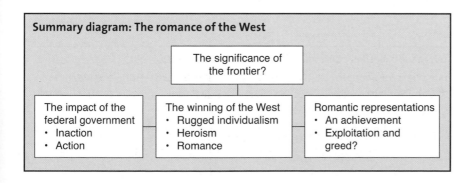

Summary diagram: The romance of the West

The significance of the frontier?

The impact of the federal government	The winning of the West	Romantic representations
• Inaction • Action	• Rugged individualism • Heroism • Romance	• An achievement • Exploitation and greed?

Chapter summary

In the second half of the nineteenth century, hundreds of thousands of settlers moved into the Wild West. They did so for a number of reasons. These included new finds of gold, silver and other minerals, completion of transcontinental railways, the rise of the range-cattle industry, and – most importantly – the ability of farmers to make the land fruitful. In little more than a generation the West was tamed and the power of the Plains Indians broken. With the division of the West into states, the political organisation of the continent was complete. But in the process of taming the region, the natural resources of the West were exploited ruthlessly and thoughtlessly. So were its human resources – the Native Americans.

 ## Refresher questions

Use these questions to remind yourself of the key material covered in this chapter.

1 How 'wild' was the West in 1865?

2 What impact did the Civil War have on western development?

3 How and why were the Plains Indians defeated?

4 Why did President Grant's Peace Policy fail?

5 How successful were attempts to 'Americanise' the Plains Indians?

6 What can be said in defence of US Native American policy?

7 Why was mining so important to western development?

8 Why did mining so quickly become 'big business'?

9 Why were railways important for western development?

10 Why did the federal government give the railways generous land grants and was it wise to do so?

11 How were farmers able to make a living in the West?

12 How important was government action in opening up the West?

13 How romantic was the winning of the West?

 ## Question practice

ESSAY QUESTIONS

1 How important were railways in westward expansion in the period c.1830–c.1900?

2 Which of these had the greater consequences for Native Americans in the years 1861–90: a) the Indian Wars or b) the Dawes Act? Explain your answer with reference to both a) and b).

3 Assess the reasons for the Plains Indians losing their lands.

4 'Farmers were the most important settlers in the west.' How far do you agree with this statement?

OCR A level History

Essay guidance

The assessment of OCR Units Y216 and Y246: The USA in the 19th Century: Westward expansion and the Civil War 1803–c.1890 depends on whether you are studying it for AS or A level:

- for the AS exam, you will answer one essay question from a choice of two, and one interpretation question, for which there is no choice
- for the A level exam, you will answer one essay question from a choice of two, and one shorter essay question also from a choice of two.

The guidance below is for answering both AS and A level essay questions. Guidance for the shorter essay question is at the end of this section. Guidance on answering interpretation questions is on page 264.

For both OCR AS and A level History, the types of essay questions set and the skills required to achieve a high grade for Unit Group 2 are the same. The skills are made very clear by both mark schemes, which emphasise that the answer must:

- focus on the demands of the question
- be supported by accurate and relevant factual knowledge
- be analytical and logical
- reach a supported judgement about the issue in the question.

There are a number of skills that you will need to develop to reach the higher levels in the marking bands:

- understand the wording of the question
- plan an answer to the question set
- write a focused opening paragraph
- avoid irrelevance and description
- write analytically

- write a conclusion which reaches a supported judgement based on the argument in the main body of the essay.

These skills will be developed in the section below, but are further developed in the 'Period Study' chapters of the *OCR A level History* series (British Period Studies and Enquiries).

Understanding the wording of the question

To stay focused on the question set, it is important to read the question carefully and focus on the key words and phrases. Unless you directly address the demands of the question you will not score highly. Remember that in questions where there is a named factor you must write a good analytical paragraph about the given factor, even if you argue that it was not the most important.

Types of AS and A level questions you might find in the exams	The factors and issues you would need to consider in answering them
1 Assess the reasons why the Union won the American Civil War.	Weigh up the relative importance of a range of factors as to why the Union won the Civil War.
2 To what extent was Confederate weakness the most important cause of the victory of the Union in the American Civil War?	Weigh up the relative importance of a range of factors, including comparing the importance of Confederate weakness with other factors.
3 'The leadership of Lincoln was the most important reason for the victory of the Union in the American Civil War.' How far do you agree?	Weigh up the relative importance of a range of factors, including comparing the importance of Lincoln's leadership with other issues to reach a balanced judgement.

Types of AS and A level questions you might find in the exams	The factors and issues you would need to consider in answering them
4 How successful was Lincoln as leader of the Union?	This question requires you to make a judgement about Lincoln's leadership. Instead of thinking about factors, you would need to think about issues such as: • Lincoln's success as a politician and his relationship with ministers. • Lincoln's success as a statesman. • The issuing of the Emancipation Proclamation. • Lincoln's role as a war leader and the organisation of the war. • Lincoln's handling of particular issues and crises. • Lincoln's administrative abilities.

Planning an answer

Many plans simply list dates and events: this should be avoided as it encourages a descriptive, or narrative, rather than an analytical answer. The plan should be an outline of your argument. This means you need to think carefully about the issues you intend to discuss and their relative importance before you start writing your answer. It should therefore be a list of the factors or issues you are going to discuss and a comment on their relative importance.

For question 1 in the table, your plan might look something like this:

• Military campaigns – link to resources and the impact of battles such as Gettysburg.
• Leadership – military – not important at start as South better.
• Leadership – political – importance of Lincoln compared with Davis.

• Morale – kept war going as South fighting for way of life.
• Resources – vital as the North had men and war resources, such as iron.
• International support – failure of South to get British/French support.

The opening paragraph

Many students spend time 'setting the scene'; the opening paragraph becomes little more than an introduction to the topic – this should be avoided. Instead, make it clear what your argument is going to be. Offer your view about the issue in the question – what was the most important reason for the victory of the Union – and then introduce the other issues you intend to discuss. In the plan it is suggested that resources were the most important factor. This should be made clear in the opening paragraph, with a brief comment as to why – perhaps that the resources allowed the Union to sustain losses and pursue a lengthy war that the South could not sustain. This will give the examiner a clear overview of your essay, rather than it being a 'mystery tour' where the argument becomes clear only at the end. You should also refer to any important issues that the question raises. Here is an example:

There are a number of reasons why the Union won the Civil War, including leadership, military strength and resources[1]. However, the most important reason was resources, both in terms of population and materials[2]. These were particularly important once the war was not over quickly as in this area the Union was far stronger than the Confederacy[3].

1 The student is aware that there were a number of important reasons.
2 The student offers a clear view as to what they consider to be the most important reason – a thesis is offered.
3 There is a brief justification to support the thesis.

Avoid irrelevance and description

Hopefully the plan will stop you from simply writing all you know about why the Union won and force you to weigh up the role of a range of factors. Similarly, it should also help to prevent you from simply writing about the military events of the Civil War. You will not lose marks if you do that, but neither will you gain any credit, and you will waste valuable time.

Write analytically

This is perhaps the hardest, but most important skill you need to develop. An analytical approach can be helped by ensuring that the opening sentence of each paragraph introduces an idea, which directly answers the question and is not just a piece of factual information. In a very strong answer it should be possible to simply read the opening sentences of all the paragraphs and know what argument is being put forward.

If we look at the second question on the importance of Confederate weakness (see page 259), the following are possible sentences with which to start paragraphs:

- Confederate weakness became an important factor once the war was not over quickly, but at the start of the war it was not an important factor … .
- Union strength, particularly economic, ensured that in a long war they were more likely to be successful … .
- The political leadership of Lincoln was important because he was able to keep factions working together and work with his critics … .
- Grant and Sherman provided the Union with the military leadership that they had lacked in the early years and were able to use their superior resources … .

You would then go on to discuss both sides of the argument raised by the opening sentence, using relevant knowledge about the issue to support each side of the argument. The final sentence of the paragraph would reach a judgement on the role played by the factor you are discussing in the victory of the Union. This approach would ensure that the final sentence of each paragraph links back to the actual question you are answering. If you can do this for each paragraph you will have a series of mini

essays which discuss a factor and reach a conclusion or judgement about the importance of that factor or issue. For example:

Military leadership was an important factor in securing Union victory, but this was only in the latter stages of the war when Grant and Sherman provided the Union with the leadership they had lacked at the start[1]. *It was only with the Grant's appointment as overall commander in March 1864 that the Union was given military direction as he had the concept of the total war strategy needed to win the conflict and the skill to carry out the strategy. Similarly, Sherman with his marches through Georgia and the Carolinas reached areas that the Confederacy were unable to reach and therefore weakened it logistically, politically and psychologically*[2].

1 The sentence puts forward a clear view that military leadership was only important for the Union victory in the later stages of the war.
2 The claim that it was important in the later stages is developed and some evidence is provided to support the argument

The conclusion

The conclusion provides the opportunity to bring together all the interim judgements to reach an overall judgement about the question. Using the interim judgements will ensure that your conclusion is based on the argument in the main body of the essay and does not offer a different view. For the essay answering question 1 (see page 259), you can decide what was the most important factor in the victory of the Union, but for questions 2 and 3 you will need to comment on the importance of the named factor – Confederate weakness or Lincoln's leadership – as well as explain why you think a different factor is more important, if that has been your line of argument. Or, if you think the named factor is the most important, you would need to explain why that was more important than the other factors or issues you have discussed.

Consider the following conclusion to question 2: to what extent was Confederate weakness the most important cause of the victory of the Union in the American Civil War?

Although the Confederates certainly had numerous weaknesses, such as low levels of economic production, the poor leadership of Davis and the failure to win British support, it was not the most important factor in their defeat[1]. After all, in the early years of the war the Confederacy had been more than a match for Union armies on the battlefield. It was therefore Union morale that was crucial; as long as that held, and Lincoln's leadership was important in that respect, the superior resources, both in terms of manpower and war materials, along with the determination of Grant as a military commander would ensure that the Union would win a long war[2].

1 This is a strong conclusion because it considers the importance of the named factor – Confederate weakness – but weighs that up against a range of other factors to reach an overall judgement.
2 It is also able to show links between the other factors to reach a balanced judgement, which brings in a range of issues, showing the interplay between them.

How to write a good essay for the A level short answer questions

This question will require you to weigh up the importance of two factors or issues in relation to an event of development. For example:

Which had the greater consequences for Native Americans in the years 1861–1890?

(i) The 'Indian Wars'

(ii) The Dawes Act

Explain your answer with reference to both (i) and (ii).

As with the long essays, the skills required are made very clear by the mark scheme, which emphasises that the answer must:

- analyse the two issues
- evaluate the two issues
- support your analysis and evaluation with detailed and accurate knowledge

- reach a supported judgement as to which factor was more important in relation to the issue in the question.

The skills required are very similar to those for the longer essays. However, there is no need for an introduction, nor are you required to compare the two factors or issues in the main body of the essay, although either approach can still score full marks. For example, you could begin with:

The Dawes Act had a significant impact on the Native American population as it resulted in the significant loss of their land with the allotment policy and the selling off of excess land[1]. Reservations that had been created after the Indian Wars were broken up. Not only was some of this land sacred, but it also went a long way to undermining the economic and social structures of Native American life and the tribal bonds that held Native Americans together and, according to many Americans, prevented them from being 'Americanised'[2]. Its impact was also far reaching as all Native American were affected by the policy[3].

1 The answer explains one of the problems created by the Dawes Act.
2 The implications of this development are considered.
3 The wider implications are hinted at and this could be developed and contrasted with the Indian wars, which did not affect all Native Americans.

The answer could go on and argue how the Dawes Act affected American policy both in the short and long term, leading to attempts to 'Americanise' the Native Americans.

Most importantly, the conclusion must reach a supported judgement as to the relative importance of the factors in relation to the issue in the question. For example:

Both of the issues had a significant impact on Native Americans. Although the Dawes Act affected all Native Americans, whereas the wars only impacted on some, it was the Indian Wars that had the greater impact[1]. Not only were a significant number of Native Americans killed, but the subsequent creation of reservations began the destruction of Native American life which was continued by the Dawes Act. It was the treaties after the Indian Wars which started the Americanisation policy and attack on their culture, which the Dawes Act continued. The conditions on the reservations were often appalling and many died, therefore it could even be suggested that the Dawes Act saw some improvement and thus had a less negative impact**[2]**.

1 The response explains the relative importance of the two factors and offers a clear view.
2 The response supports the view offered in the opening sentence and therefore reaches a supported judgement.

Interpretations guidance

How to write a good essay

The guidance below is for answering the AS interpretation question for OCR Unit Y246: The USA in the 19th Century: Westward expansion and the Civil War 1803–c.1890. Guidance on answering essay questions is on page 259.

The OCR specification outlines the two key topics from which the interpretation question will be drawn. For this book these are:

- Westward expansion; causes and impacts.
- The growth of sectional tension 1850–61.

The specification also lists the main debates to consider.

It is also worth remembering that this is an AS unit and not an A level historiography paper. The aim of this element of the unit is to develop an awareness that the past can be interpreted in different ways.

The question will require you to assess the strengths and limitations of a historian's interpretation of an issue related to one of the specified key topics.

You should be able to place the interpretation within the context of the wider historical debate on the key topic. However, you will *not* be required to know the names of individual historians associated with the debate or to have studied the specific books of any historians. It may even be counterproductive to be aware of particular historians' views, as this may lead you to simply describe their view, rather than analyse the given interpretation.

There are a number of skills you need to develop if you are to reach the higher levels in the mark bands:

- To be able to understand the wording of the question.
- To be able to explain the interpretation and how it fits into the debate about the issue or topic.
- To be able to consider both the strengths and weaknesses of the interpretation by using your own knowledge of the topic.

Here is an example of a question you will face in the exam:

Read the interpretation and then answer the question that follows:

'It was an emotional force as much as an economic one that persuaded American citizens to move into the lands west of the Mississippi River.'

Adapted from: *Modern America: The USA, 1865 to the Present*, Joanne de Pennington

Evaluate the strengths and limitations of this interpretation, making reference to other interpretations that you have studied.

Approaching the question

There are several steps to take to answer this question.

1 Explain the interpretation and put it into context

In the first paragraph you should explain the interpretation and the view it is putting forward. This paragraph places the interpretation in the context of the historical debate and explains any key words or phrases relating to the given interpretation. A suggested opening might be as follows:

The interpretation puts forward the view that there was more than one factor which caused America to expand westwards. The author suggests that emotional force was just as important as economic factors in encouraging Americans to move west. In raising the issue of 'emotional force' Pennington is referring to the idea of 'manifest destiny', the concept by which many Americans believed that it was their God-given right to settle the continent[1]. The idea of 'destiny' encouraged the idea of expansion and linked the developing idea of nationalism with geography. For many Americans the large, unspoilt landscapes of the west symbolised freedom. The interpretation suggests that this was just as important as economic factors, which many historians emphasise[3].

1 The opening two sentences are clearly focused on the given interpretation, it clearly explains that there was more than one factor in American westward expansion, but there is no detailed own knowledge added at this point.

2 The third sentence explains what is meant by 'emotional force' and this is developed in the following sentence.

3 The last sentence begins to place the concept of manifest destiny in the wider historical debate and suggests that this historian's emphasis on it might challenge the more frequent view that it was economic factors.

In order to place Pennington's view in the context of the debate about the importance of various factors, you could go on to suggest that there are a wide range of economic factors that could be considered, including the fur trade, mining, agriculture and the development of various methods of transport.

2 Consider the strengths of the interpretation

In the second paragraph consider the strengths of the interpretation by bringing in your own knowledge to support the given view. A suggested response might start as follows when considering the strengths of the view:

There is some merit to Pennington's view as it acknowledges that there was more than one factor. Many Americans did believe in the idea of manifest destiny, which was first used in 1845[1]. The Republic was fairly new and there was much energy among its citizens, who saw in the west the chance to make their fortunes and acquire land, while escaping from the industry and growing cities in the east[2]. These motives bring together the two factors mentioned by Pennington of emotion and the economy[3].

1 The answer clearly focuses on the strength of the given interpretation.

2 The response provides some support for the view in the interpretation from the candidate's own knowledge, this is not particularly detailed or precise, but this could be developed in the remainder of the paragraph.

3 The final sentence links together the two motives.

In the remainder of the paragraph you could show how these two factors were linked and how this was played on by posters, which showed California offering great economic opportunities, or in popular songs, such as 'America the Beautiful.'

3 Consider the weaknesses of the interpretation

In the third paragraph consider the weaknesses of the given interpretation by bringing in knowledge that can challenge the given interpretation and explains what is missing from the interpretation.

A suggested response might start as follows when considering the weaknesses of the view:

However, there are a number of weaknesses in Pennington's interpretation[1]. Most importantly, it fails to explain what the economic factors were. Moreover, the economic factors changed as the period progressed; at first trapping encouraged some movement west and this followed by mining and the 'gold rush' of 1849[2]. However, developments in agriculture and transport were more important economic factors in the later period, with the first transcontinental railway opening in 1869[3]. The interpretation also fails to consider government legislation, such as the Homestead Act of 1862.

1 The opening makes it very clear that this paragraph will deal with the weaknesses of the interpretation.

2 It explains clearly the first weakness and provides evidence to support the claim, the evidence is not detailed and could be developed, but the answer focuses on explaining the weakness, rather than providing lost of detail.

3 Although more detail could have been provided about the changing nature of economic factors, the answer goes on to explain a second weakness, the ignoring of government legislation, and this could be developed in the remainder of the paragraph.

Answers might go on to argue that government legislation was vital as it encouraged the economic exploitation of the West. The answer might discuss other government measures that further encouraged westward movement, including protection from

Native Americans, the financing of transport and the imposition of acceptable behaviour in the new settlements. The paragraph might therefore suggest that the interpretation provides a partial answer which needs further development.

There is no requirement for you to reach a judgement as to which view you find more convincing or valid.

Assessing the interpretation

In assessing the interpretation you should consider the following:

- Identify and explain the issue being discussed in the interpretation: the factors that encouraged people to move west of the Mississippi river.
- Explain the view being put forward in the interpretation: the interpretation is arguing that the idea of manifest destiny, a God-given right, was just as important in explaining westward expansion as economic issues, such as mining or agriculture.
- Explain how the interpretation fits into the wider debate about the issue: the relative importance of manifest destiny and economic factors in westward expansion, but also a wider range of issues such as religious persecution, actions of the federal government, the development of transport links.

In other interpretations you might need to do the following:

- Consider whether there is any particular emphasis within the interpretation that needs explaining or commenting on, for example, if the interpretation says something is 'the only reason' or 'the single most important reason'.
- Comment on any concepts that the interpretation raises, such as 'total war', 'authoritarian system', 'liberalisation'.
- Consider the focus of the interpretation, for example, if an interpretation focuses on an urban viewpoint, what was the rural viewpoint? Is the viewpoint given in the interpretation the same all areas of society?

In summary, this is what is important for answering interpretation questions:

- Explaining the interpretation.
- Placing the interpretation in the context of the wider historical debate about the issue it considers.
- Explaining the strengths *and* weaknesses of the view in the extract.

AQA A level History

Essay guidance

At both AS and A level for AQA Component 2: Depth Study: America: A Nation Divided, c1845–1877, you will need to answer an essay question in the exam. Each essay question is marked out of 25:

- for the AS exam, Section B: answer **one** essay question from a choice of two
- for the A level exam, Section B: answer **two** essay questions from a choice of three.

There are several question stems which all have the same basic requirement: to analyse and reach a conclusion, based on the evidence you provide.

The AS questions often give a quotation and then ask whether you agree or disagree with this view. Almost inevitably, your answer will be a mixture of both. It is the same task as for A level – just phrased differently in the question. Detailed essays are more likely to do well than vague or generalised essays, especially in the Depth Studies of Paper 2.

The AQA mark scheme is essentially the same for AS and the full A level (see the AQA website, www.aqa.org.uk). Both emphasise the need to analyse and evaluate the key features related to the periods studied. The key feature of the highest level is sustained analysis: analysis that unites the whole of the essay.

Writing an essay: general skills

- *Focus and structure.* Be sure what the question is asking and plan what the paragraphs should be about.
- *Focused introduction to the essay.* Be sure that the introductory sentence relates directly to the focus of the question and that each paragraph highlights the structure of the answer.
- *Use detail.* Make sure that you show detailed knowledge, but only as part of an explanation being made in relation to the question.

No knowledge should be standalone; it should be used in context.

- *Explanatory analysis and evaluation.* Consider what words and phrases to use in an answer to strengthen the explanation.
- *Argument and counter-argument.* Think of how arguments can be balanced so as to give contrasting views.
- *Resolution.* Think how best to 'resolve' contradictory arguments.
- *Relative significance and evaluation.* Think how best to reach a judgement when trying to assess the relative importance of various factors, and their possible interrelationship.

Planning an essay

Practice question 1

To what extent would you agree that the election of a Republican president in 1860 was the main reason for the outbreak of the Civil War?

This question requires you to analyse why Civil War broke out in 1861. You must discuss the following:

- The significance of Lincoln's victory in the 1860 presidential election and the events between November 1860 and April 1861 (your primary focus).
- The longer-term factors that brought about the situation in 1860–1 (your secondary focus).

A clear structure makes for a much more effective essay and is crucial for achieving the highest marks. You need three or four paragraphs to structure this question effectively. In each paragraph you will deal with one factor. One of these *must* be the factor in the question.

A very basic plan for this question might look like this:

- Paragraph 1: the effects of Lincoln's election, especially the secession of the Lower South.

- Paragraph 2: failure to effect a compromise, resulting in the outbreak of war.
- Paragraph 3: the long-term factors dividing North and South pre-1860; factors which made secession and Civil War a real possibility once Lincoln was elected.

It is a good idea to cover the factor named in the question first, so that you don't run out of time and forget to do it. Then cover the others in what you think is their order of importance, or in the order that appears logical in terms of the sequence of paragraphs.

The introduction

Maintaining focus is vital. One way to do this from the beginning of your essay is to use the words in the question to help write your argument. The first sentence of question 1, for example, could look like this:

While Lincoln's election success in November 1860 undoubtedly triggered the crisis that culminated in the outbreak of Civil War in April 1861, there were deep-seated factors which brought about the conflict.

This opening sentence provides a clear focus on the demands of the question, though it could, of course, be written in a more exciting style.

Focus throughout the essay

Structuring your essay well will help with keeping the focus of your essay on the question. To maintain a focus on the wording in question 1, you could begin your first main paragraph with 'weakness'.

Within weeks of Lincoln's election success, southern states had begun the process of seceding from the Union.

- This sentence begins with a clear point that refers to the primary focus of the question (Lincoln's coming to power) while linking it to a factor (the secession of the southern states).
- You could then have a paragraph for each of your other factors.

- It will be important to make sure that each paragraph focuses on analysis and includes relevant details that are used as part of the argument.
- You may wish to number your factors. This helps to make your structure clear and helps you to maintain focus.

Deploying detail

As well as focus and structure, your essay will be judged on the extent to which it includes accurate detail. There are several different kinds of evidence you could use that might be described as detailed. This includes correct dates, names of relevant people, statistics and events. For example, for question 1 you could use terms such as sectionalism and secession. You can also make your essays more detailed by using the correct technical vocabulary.

Analysis and explanation

'Analysis' covers a variety of high-level skills including explanation and evaluation; in essence, it means breaking down something complex into smaller parts. A clear structure which breaks down a complex question into a series of paragraphs is the first step towards writing an analytical essay.

The purpose of explanation is to provide evidence for why something happened, or why something is true or false. An explanatory statement requires two parts: a *claim* and a *justification*.

For example, for question 1, you might want to argue that one important reason for the coming of war was the issue of slavery. Once you have made your point, and supported it with relevant detail, you can then explain how this answers the question. For example, you could conclude your paragraph like this:

The issue of slavery, which had long divided North from South[1], ultimately brought about Civil War because[2] southerners were not prepared to recognise a Republican president who was pledged to stop slavery expanding[3].

1 The first part of this sentence is the claim while the second part justifies the claim.

2 'Because' is a very important word to use when writing an explanation, as it shows the relationship between the claim and the justification.
3 The justification.

Evaluation

Evaluation means considering the importance of two or more different factors, weighing them against each other, and reaching a judgement. This is a good skill to use at the end of an essay because the conclusion should reach a judgement which answers the question. Your conclusion to question 1 might read as follows:

Clearly, Lincoln's election was a crucial event in bringing about Civil War. However, the fact that it did so was the result of a long-term division between northerners and southerners over the issue of slavery. For many southerners the election of Lincoln was the last straw: an affront to their honour but also a threat to their peculiar institution. Therefore, slavery, as much as Lincoln's election, was 'somehow' the cause of Civil War.

Words like 'however' and 'therefore' are helpful to contrast the importance of the different factors.

Complex essay writing: argument and counter-argument

Essays that develop a good argument are more likely to reach the highest levels. This is because argumentative essays are much more likely to develop sustained analysis. As you know, your essays are judged on the extent to which they analyse.

After setting up an argument in your introduction, you should develop it throughout the essay. One way of doing this is to adopt an argument–counter-argument structure. A counter-argument is one that disagrees with the main argument of the essay. This is a good way of evaluating the importance of the different factors that you discuss. Essays of this type will develop an argument in one paragraph and then set out an opposing argument in another paragraph. Sometimes this will include

juxtaposing the differing views of historians on a topic.

Good essays will analyse the key issues. They will probably have a clear piece of analysis at the end of each paragraph. While this analysis might be good, it will generally relate only to the issue discussed in that paragraph.

Excellent essays will be analytical throughout. As well as the analysis of each factor discussed above, there will be an overall analysis. This will run throughout the essay and can be achieved through developing a clear, relevant and coherent argument.

A good way of achieving sustained analysis is to consider which factor is most important. Here is an example of an introduction that sets out an argument for question 1:

While Lincoln's election success in November 1860 undoubtedly triggered the crisis that culminated in the outbreak of Civil War in April 1861, there were deep-seated factors which brought about the conflict[1]. The key factor was the issue of slavery. For more than two decades prior to 1860, the peculiar institution had divided North from South[2]. By 1860, northerners had come to support the Republican Party, which was pledged to stop slavery expansion. Southerners were equally determined to defend their peculiar institution. Fearful that Republican rule might threaten slavery[3], Lincoln's election impelled southern states to secede from the Union.

1 The introduction begins with a claim.
2 The introduction continues with another reason.
3 Concludes with outline of argument of the most important reason.

- This introduction focuses on the question and sets out the key factors that the essay will develop.
- It introduces an argument about which factor was most significant.
- However, it also sets out an argument that can then be developed throughout each paragraph, and is rounded off with an overall judgement in the conclusion.

Complex essay writing: resolution and relative significance

Having written an essay that explains argument and counter-argument, you should then resolve the tension between the argument and the counter-argument in your conclusion. It is important that the writing is precise and summarises the arguments made in the main body of the essay. You need to reach a supported overall judgement. One very appropriate way to do this is by evaluating the relative significance of different factors, in the light of valid criteria. Relative significance means how important one factor is compared to another.

The best essays will always make a judgement about which was most important based on valid criteria. These can be very simple, and will depend on the topic and the exact question. The following criteria are often useful:

- Duration: which factor was important for the longest amount of time?
- Scope: which factor affected the most people?
- Effectiveness: which factor achieved most?
- Impact: which factor led to the most fundamental change?

As an example, you could compare the factors in terms of their duration and their impact.

A conclusion that follows this advice should be capable of reaching a high level (if written, in full, with appropriate details) because it reaches an overall judgement that is supported through evaluating the relative significance of different factors in the light of valid criteria.

Having written an introduction and the main body of an essay for question 1, a concluding paragraph that aims to meet the exacting criteria for reaching a complex judgement could look like this:

No one doubts that Lincoln's election success in November 1860 sparked the fuse of Civil War. It led to southern secession and ultimately the firing of the first shots of the war at Fort Sumter in April 1861. However, the election of a northern president would hardly have led to war had it not been for the issue of slavery which had long divided North and South. By 1860 white southerners felt that their peculiar institution, to which most were committed, was under threat. Thus, the election of a Republican president, pledged to stop slavery's expansion, was the last straw: an affront to southern honour and a challenge to their way of life. For this reason a majority of southerners were prepared to secede from the Union and risk Civil War.

Sources guidance

Whether you are taking the AS exam or the full A level exam for AQA Component 2: Depth Study: America: A Nation Divided, c1845–1877, Section A presents you with sources and a question which involves evaluation of their utility or value.

AS exam	A level exam
Section A: answer question 1 based on two primary sources. (25 marks)	Section A: answer question 1, based on three primary sources. (30 marks)
Question focus: with reference to these sources and your understanding of the historical context, which of these two sources is more valuable in explaining … ?	Question focus: with reference to these sources and your understanding of the historical context, assess the value of these three sources to an historian studying …

Sources and sample questions

Study the sources. They are all concerned with the defeat of the Confederacy in 1865.

SOURCE I

Part of President Lincoln's Second Inaugural Address, 4 March 1865.

Fellow-countrymen: at this second appearing to take the oath of the presidential office there is less occasion for an extended address than there was at the first. Then a statement somewhat in detail of a course to be pursued seemed fitting and proper. Now, at the expiration of four years, during which public declarations have been constantly called forth on every point and phase of the great contest which still absorbs the attention and engrosses the energies of the nation, little that is new could be presented. The progress of our arms, upon which all else chiefly depends, is as well known to the public as to myself, and it is, I trust, reasonably satisfactory and encouraging to all. With high hope for the future, no prediction in regard to it is ventured.

SOURCE 2

President Jefferson Davis's last message to the people of the Confederacy, 4 April 1865.

The General in Chief of our Army has found it necessary to make such movements of the troops as to uncover the capital and thus involve the withdrawal of the Government from the city of Richmond. It would be unwise, even if it were possible, to conceal the great moral as well as material injury to our cause that must result from the occupation of Richmond by the enemy. It is equally unwise and unworthy of us, as patriots engaged in a most sacred cause, to allow our energies to falter, our spirits to grow faint, or our efforts to become relaxed under reverses, however calamitous … If by stress of numbers we should ever be compelled to a temporary withdrawal from her limits, or those of any other border state, again and again will we return, until the baffled and exhausted enemy shall abandon in despair his endless and impossible task of making slaves of a people resolved to be free. Let us not, the, despond, my countrymen; but relying on the never-failing mercies and protecting care of our God, let us meet the foe with fresh defiance, with unconquered and unconquerable hearts.

SOURCE 3

Robert E. Lee's General Order No. 9 to the Army of Northern Virginia, 10 April 1865.

After four years of arduous service marked by unsurpassed courage and fortitude the Army of Northern Virginia has been compelled to yield to overwhelming numbers and resources.

I need not tell the survivors of so many hard fought battles, who have remained steadfast to the last, that I have consented to this result from no distrust of them. But feeling that valor and devotion could accomplish nothing that could compensate for the

loss that would have accompanied the continuance of the contest, I determined to avoid the useless sacrifice of those whose past services have endeared them to their country …

With an unceasing admiration of your consistency and devotion to your country and a grateful remembrance of your kind and generous consideration of myself, I bid you all an affectionate farewell.

AS style question

With reference to Sources 1 and 2, and your understanding of the historical context, which of these two sources is more valuable in terms of explaining the war situation in the spring of 1865?

The mark schemes

AS mark scheme

See the AQA website (www.aqa.org.uk) for the full mark schemes. This summary of the AS mark scheme shows how it rewards analysis and evaluation of the source material within the historical context.

Level 1	Describing the source content or offering generic phrases.
Level 2	Some relevant but limited comments on the value of one source *or* some limited comment on both.
Level 3	Some relevant comments on the value of the sources and some explicit reference to the issue identified in the question.
Level 4	Relevant well-supported comments on the value and a supported conclusion, but with limited judgement.
Level 5	Very good understanding of the value in relation to the issue identified. Sources evaluated thoroughly and with a well-substantiated conclusion related to which is more valuable.

A level style question

With reference to Sources 1, 2 and 3, and your understanding of the historical context, assess the value of these sources to a historian studying the reasons for Confederate defeat in 1865.

A level mark scheme

This summary of the A level mark scheme shows how it is similar to the AS, but covers three sources. The wording of the question means that there is no explicit requirement to decide which of the three sources is the most valuable. Concentrate instead on a very thorough analysis of the content and evaluation of the provenance of each source, using contextual knowledge.

Level 1	Some limited comment on value of at least one source.
Level 2	Some limited comments on the value of the sources *or* on content or provenance *or* comments on all three sources but no reference to the value of the sources.
Level 3	Some understanding of all three sources in relation to both content and provenance, with some historical context; but analysis limited.
Level 4	Good understanding of all three sources in relation to content, provenance and historical context to give a balanced argument on their value for the purpose specified in the question.
Level 5	As Level 4, but with a substantiated judgement.

Working towards an answer

It is important that knowledge is used to show an understanding of the relationship between the sources and the issue raised in the question. Answers should be concerned with the following:

- provenance
- arguments used (and you can agree/disagree)
- tone and emphasis of the sources.

The sources

The two or three sources used each time will be contemporary – probably of varying types (for example, diaries, newspaper accounts, government reports). The sources will all be on the same broad topic area. Each source will have value. Your task is to evaluate how much – in terms of its content and its provenance.

You will need to assess the *value of the content* by using your own knowledge. Is the information accurate? Is it giving only part of the evidence and ignoring other aspects? Is the tone of the writing significant?

You will need to evaluate the *provenance* of the source by considering who wrote it, and when, where and why. What was its purpose? Was it produced to express an opinion; to record facts: to influence the opinion of others? Even if it was intended to be accurate, the writer may have been biased – either deliberately or unconsciously. The writer, for example, might have only known part of the situation and reached a judgement solely based on that.

Here is a guide to analysing the provenance, content and tone for Sources 1, 2 and 3.

Analysing the sources

To answer the question effectively, you need to read the sources carefully and pull out the relevant points as well as add your own knowledge. You must remember to keep the focus on the question at all times.

Source 1 (page 271)
Provenance:

- The source is from a speech by President Abraham Lincoln in March 1865 made at his second presidential inauguration.
- Presidents generally use the occasion of their inaugural address to say something about the present situation and to give some indication of their main aims in the four years ahead of them.

Content and argument:

- Lincoln declares that he can say little that is new.
- While he does suggest that the war is going very well militarily, he is still not prepared to predict the outcome.
- He states that the war's outcome is dependent on the Union army.

Tone and emphasis:

- Lincoln might not be prepared to predict the outcome, but his tone is positive. He is not particularly boastful. Nevertheless, he declares that the Union army was doing well.

Own knowledge:

- Your knowledge to agree/disagree with the source, for example: details about the military situation in March 1865: just how well was the war going for the Union? To what extent was the war's outcome dependent on the Union army?

Source 2 (page 271)
Provenance:

- This is President Jefferson Davis's final message to the people of the Confederacy. The military situation meant that he had to flee from his capital Richmond.
- Davis is attempting to maintain southern morale in dire circumstances in April 1865.

Content and argument:

- Davis argues that the Confederacy can still maintain the war, despite the loss of Richmond – a terrible blow.

- Davis asserts that the Confederacy can still win the war if the people maintain their opposition to the Union.

Tone and emphasis:

- The tone remains positive. The struggle will go on. Southerners, with God on their side, will continue to fight the good fight.

Own knowledge:

- Your knowledge to agree/disagree with the source, for example: evidence about the dreadful situation the Confederacy faced in April 1865. Was guerrilla warfare a serious possibility? Robert E. Lee was against the idea (see Source 3).

Source 3 (page 272)

Provenance:

- The source is an order from Robert E. Lee to the Army of Northern Virginia, following his surrender at Appomattox.
- Given Lee's role in the Confederacy, it is an important source.

Content and argument:

- The source praises the Army of Northern Virginia.
- It declares that the Confederacy lost the war because of the Union army's superior numbers and resources.
- Lee says that enough is enough. There is no point continuing the fight.

Tone and emphasis:

- Lee is typically steadfast. He praises his men for their courage. But that courage has not been enough. The Army of Northern Virginia must accept that it has been defeated.

Own knowledge:

- Your knowledge to agree/disagree with the source, for example: detailed knowledge about the debate about Confederate defeat: was it due to the Union's numbers and resources or was it the result of lack of will or even poor leadership on Lee's part?

Answering AS questions

You have 45 minutes to answer the question. It is important that you spend at least one-quarter of the time reading and planning your answer. Generally when writing an answer, you need to check that you are remaining focused on the issue identified in the question and are relating this to the sources and your knowledge.

- You might decide to write a paragraph on each 'strand' (that is provenance, content and tone), comparing the two sources, and then write a short concluding paragraph with an explained judgement on which source is more valuable.
- For writing about content, you may find it helpful to adopt a comparative approach, for example when the evidence in one source is contradicted or questioned by the evidence in another source.

At AS level you are asked to provide a judgement on which is more valuable. Make sure that this is based on clear arguments with strong evidence, and not on general assertions.

Planning and writing your answer

- Think how you can best plan an answer.
- Plan in terms of the headings above, perhaps combining 'provenance' with 'tone and emphasis', and compare the two sources.

As an example, here is a comparison of Sources 1 and 2 in terms of provenance, and tone and emphasis:

The two sources are important speeches by the respective heads of the Union and the Confederacy. Lincoln, albeit not boastful or overconfident, is clearly pleased with the way that the war is going in March 1865 – with good cause. Victory for the Union was in sight. That was even more obvious a month later after the capture of Richmond. Faced with the loss of his capital, Davis remains resolute. His intent (on 4 April 1865) was to try to sustain the morale of the people of the Confederacy.

Then compare the *content and argument* of each source, by using your knowledge. For example:

Lincoln, in Source 1, has relatively little to say about the war – which he suggests was nearing its end. In general, although not in this particular extract, his second inaugural address was more concerned with the issues of reconstruction and reconciliation.

Davis, in Source 2, is not yet prepared to accept defeat. He declares that southerners will continue the struggle, despite the calamitous loss of Richmond. His exhortations fell on deaf ears. By April 1865 most southerners had had enough of war. General Robert E. Lee, when surrendering at Appomattox a few days later, accepted that the Confederacy had been defeated. Rather than prolonging the South's misery, he told his men to return to their homes. Davis's hopes of fighting a guerrilla war came to nothing. The war spluttered to an end and he was captured in May.

Which is *more valuable*? This can be judged in terms of which is likely to be more valuable in terms of where the source came from; or in terms of the accuracy of its content. However, remember the focus of the question: in this case, explaining the war situation in 1865.

> With these sources, you could argue that Source 1 is the more valuable because it provides a thoughtful analysis of the situation in March 1865. From Lincoln's perspective, thanks to the Union army ('upon which all else chiefly depends') the war was going well. Source 2, by contrast, is an unrealistic (albeit understandable) declaration from Davis that the Confederacy will somehow continue the war.

Then check the following:

- Have you covered the 'provenance' and 'content' strands?
- Have you included sufficient knowledge to show understanding of the historical context?

Answering A level questions

The same general points for answering AS questions (see 'Answering AS questions') apply to A level questions, although of course here there are three sources and you need to assess the value of each of the three, rather than choose which is most valuable. Make sure that you remain focused on the question and that when you use your knowledge it is used to substantiate (add to) an argument relating to the content or provenance of the source.

If you are answering the A level question with Sources 1, 2 and 3 above:

- Keep the different 'strands' explained above in your mind when working out how best to plan an answer.
- Follow the guidance about 'provenance' and 'content' (see the AS guidance).
- Here you are *not* asked to explain which is the most valuable of the three sources. You can deal with each of the three sources in turn if you wish.
- However, you can build in comparisons if it is helpful, but it is not essential. It will depend to some extent on the three sources.
- You need to include sufficient knowledge to show understanding of the historical context. This might encourage cross-referencing of the content of the three sources, mixed with your own knowledge.
- Each paragraph needs to show clarity of argument in terms of the issue identified by the question.

Glossary of terms

Abolitionism   The desire to end slavery.

Agrarian   Relating to land and farming.

Agrarian civilisation   An advanced and sophisticated society based on farming.

American Dream   The idea that the American way of life offers the prospect of economic and social success to every individual.

Annex   To take possession of an area.

Arsenal   A place where military supplies are stored or made.

Article of faith   A central belief.

Batteries   Units of artillery.

Battleground state   A state whose voters might well determine the outcome of the presidential election.

Belligerent status   Recognised legally as waging war.

Blockade running   Attempts by ships to avoid the Union navy's blockade of Confederate ports.

Bonanza   Any source of wealth or good luck.

Border states   The states between the North and the deep South (for example, Kentucky, Maryland, Tennessee, Delaware and Missouri). These states supported slavery but were not committed to secession.

Bureau of Indian Affairs   Created within the War Department in 1824 and charged with handling all matters relating to Native Americans. In 1849 the Bureau was shifted from the War Department to the Department of the Interior.

Bushel   A unit of dry volume: 1 US bushel = about 35 litres.

Call to arms   A presidential order calling up troops and putting the USA on a war-footing.

Capitalistic   Concerned essentially with making money.

Carpetbaggers   Northern whites who settled in the South. (A carpetbag was the suitcase of the time.)

Casualties   The number of soldiers dead, wounded, taken prisoner and missing.

Civil liberties   The rights of individuals.

Colonisation   The movement of people to a different country or area, which they then take over.

Commerce raiders   Confederate warships that attacked Union merchant ships.

Confederate commissioners   Men representing the Confederate government.

Confederate socialism   The Richmond government's attempts to control the Confederate economy.

Constitution   A set of rules by which an organisation or a country is governed.

Contraband of war   Goods which can be confiscated from the enemy.

Crimean War   In 1854, Britain and France went to war against Russia to protect Turkey. Most of the war was fought in the area of Russia known as the Crimea.

Cult of domesticity   The notion that women's place was in the home.

Democratic   A form of government in which ultimate power is vested in the people and their elected representatives.

Dime novel   A cheap (10¢) and usually not very well-written adventure novel which appealed to the masses.

Draft evaders   Those who avoided conscription.

Draft exemptions   Workers in key industries, such as the railways, did not have to serve in the armed forces.

Dry farming   A method of tillage involving deep ploughing and frequent harrowing which serves to hold water in the soil.

Egalitarian   A society in which people are equal.

Electoral college   The body that elects the president. Each state has the same number of electoral college representatives as it has members of Congress.

Electoral college representatives are selected by the party with the most votes in each state.

Emancipation   The act of setting free from slavery or bondage.

Evangelical   Having a passionate belief in Christianity and a desire to share that belief with others.

Federal   A government in which several states, while largely independent in home affairs, combine for national purposes.

Federal government   The national government.

Filibuster   A military adventure, aimed at overthrowing a government. (It can also refer to someone who obstructs legislation by making lengthy speeches in Congress.)

Fire-eating/fire-eaters   Southerners who wanted to leave the Union.

Five Civilised Tribes   The Creeks, Cherokees, Choctaws, Chickasaws and Seminoles. Some of these tribes had accepted Christianity and attempted to adapt to white ways.

Founding Fathers   The American politicians who drew up the American Constitution.

Free homesteads   The Republicans hoped to provide 160 acres (65 hectares) of land to farmers who settled in the West.

Freeport Doctrine   A view that voters in a territory could exclude slavery by refusing to enact laws that gave legal protection to owning slaves, thus effectively invalidating the Dred Scott ruling.

Frontiersman   Someone who lived near the edge of 'civilisation' and knew something about the West.

Fugitive Slave Act of 1793   This provided for slaves who had escaped and fled into a different state to be returned to their owners. It was ignored by most northern states by the 1840s.

Gold reserves   Gold bullion held by a country. This gold usually underpins the country's currency.

Gone With the Wind   A novel, written by Margaret Mitchell (a southerner), published in 1936. It sold over 10 million copies and was soon made into a successful film. Both book and film suggested that the pre-war South was a civilised society.

Gross national product   The total value of all goods and services produced within a country.

Guerrilla war   Warfare by which small units harass conventional armies.

Homesteaders   Farmers who received land by the 1862 Homestead Act.

Impeach   To charge a public official with an offence committed while serving in office.

Impressing   Forcing into government service.

Impressment of supplies   Confiscation of goods.

Inaugural address   A new president's first speech, made after he has been sworn in as president.

Industrialising capitalism   A society in which industry and big business are developing.

Inflationary pressure   An undue increase in the quantity of money in circulation. The result is that the value of money goes down.

Ironclad warship   Ship made of iron or protected by iron plates.

Jim Crow laws   Segregation laws, passed in most southern states in the 1890s. (It remains something of a mystery why they were called Jim Crow laws.)

King Cotton   Cotton was so important to the US economy that many Americans claimed that 'cotton was king'.

Laird rams   The distinguishing feature of these vessels was an iron ram that projected from the bow, enabling them to sink an enemy by smashing its hull.

Laissez-faire   A French term meaning letting events find their own course. It refers to the view that governments should not intervene in economic and social matters.

Liberal Republican Party   A new party that came into existence in 1872, largely because of dissatisfaction with Grant. While some major Republican figures joined the party, it had little support from Republican rank and file. The party quickly disappeared after 1872.

Lower South   The deep southern states: Alabama, Louisiana, Georgia, Texas, Florida, South Carolina and Mississippi.

Lynched   Put to death without the usual forms of law.

Manifest destiny   The USA's supposed right to take over North America.

Manumission   Freeing of slaves.

Martial law   The suspension of ordinary administration and policing and, in its place, the exercise of military power.

Mass production   Making large quantities of goods by a standard mechanised process.

Merchant marine   Ships involved in trade, not war.

Mid-term elections   The whole of the House of Representatives and a third of the Senate are re-elected every two years. This means that there are major elections half way through a president's term of office.

Militia draft   Conscription of men in the state militias.

Minié ball   A lead ball that expanded into the rifling of the rifle-musket's barrel.

Mission   A religious settlement, set up by the Spanish to try to convert Native Americans to Christianity.

Mobilisation   Preparing for war, especially by raising troops.

Mormons   Members of a religious sect founded in the 1820s by Joseph Smith. In 1846–7 Brigham Young established a Mormon 'state' in Utah, centred on Salt Lake City.

Muzzle-loading   Loaded down the barrel.

Native Americans   The people, often known as Indians, who first inhabited North America.

Nativist   Someone who is suspicious of immigrants and usually aggressively nationalistic.

Ordnance Bureau   The government agency responsible for acquiring war materials.

Panic of 1819   A major economic crisis 1819–23. While the entire country was affected, westerners were hit especially hard. It was mainly caused by a decline in demand for US products in Britain and Europe.

Panning   Shovelling gravel from a stream or hillside into a wash-pan or sluice box and swilling it round with water to (hopefully) isolate the grains of gold.

Papal plot   A fear, mainly held by Protestants, that the Roman Catholic Church was conspiring to increase its influence.

Paternalistic   Concerned with looking after, protecting and caring for a family.

Patronage   The giving of jobs or privileges to supporters.

Patronage pressure   Using the offer of government jobs and offices effectively to bribe Congressmen.

Peculiar institution   Southerners referred to slavery as their 'peculiar institution'.

Pioneer settlers   Those who were among the first people to explore and occupy a region.

Plantation agriculture   Sugar, rice, tobacco and cotton were grown on southern plantations.

Planters   Men who owned plantations with twenty or more slaves.

Platform   The publicly declared principles and intentions of a political party.

Polygamy   A state of marriage to more than one partner.

Posse   A group of men called out by a sheriff or marshal to aid in enforcing the law.

Postmaster   The person in charge of a local post office.

Potato famine   In 1845–6 the Irish potato crop was hit by a devastating fungus, resulting in a serious famine. Millions of Irish people died or emigrated to Britain or the USA.

Prospectors   People who searched for precious metals, especially gold.

Proviso   A term or condition.

Quakers   Members of Religious Society of Friends, founded in England by George Fox in the 1640s. Quakers were (and remain) committed to pacifism.

Railhead A railway terminus; in this context a collecting station to which cattle were herded for slaughter or to be sent to northern markets.

Rebels Confederates were called rebels or 'rebs' by Union forces.

Redeem To restore to white rule.

Referendum A vote on a specific issue.

Republican A form of government without a monarch (or someone who supports such a government).

Reservations Areas of land 'reserved' for the use of Native Americans.

Revolutionary and Napoleonic Wars The wars, waged by France, lasting from 1792 to 1815. France's main opponents were Britain, Austria, Russia and Prussia.

Rugged individualism The ability of an individual to succeed by his or her own endeavours, without relying on the government or other people for help.

Saltpetre Potassium nitrate – an essential ingredient of gunpowder.

Scalawags Southern whites who supported the Republican Party.

Secede To leave or quit.

Second party system The period from the mid-1830s to the mid-1850s when the Democrats and Whigs were the two main parties.

Secretary of State The US government official responsible for foreign policy.

Segregation The system whereby blacks and whites are separated from each other (for example, in schools and housing) on grounds of race.

Seminole Indians Native American people of Creek ancestry who migrated from Georgia to Florida in the late eighteenth century. They were regarded by the USA as one of the Five Civilised Tribes.

Slave patrol Armed men who rode round slave areas, especially at night, to ensure that there was no disorder.

Slave Power conspiracy A northern notion that southerners were plotting to expand slavery. Those who believed in the conspiracy were never very specific about who exactly was conspiring.

Sovereignty Supreme power.

State militia All able-bodied men of military age (in most states) could be called up to fight in an emergency. By the 1850s most militias were shambolic; many men did not bother turning up for drill practice.

Strike breakers Workers employed to do the work of those on strike.

Supply lines Links with sources of food, equipment, ammunition and so on.

Tariff Customs duty on imported goods.

Temperance Opposition to the drinking of alcohol.

Territorial status Areas in the USA that had not yet become states and which were still under federal government control.

Underground railroad A network of anti-slavery houses that helped runaway slaves to escape to the North and to Canada.

Vigilantes Self-appointed and unofficial police.

War Democrats Those Democrats who were determined to see the war fought to a successful conclusion.

War of attrition A conflict in which each side tries to wear down the other.

West Point The main US military academy.

Writ of habeas corpus The right of a prisoner to know why he or she has been arrested.

Further reading

General texts

J.M. McPherson, *Battle Cry of Freedom* **(Penguin, 1988)**
The best single-volume survey of the causes and course of the Civil War

J.M. McPherson, *Ordeal by Fire: The Civil War and Reconstruction* **(McGraw-Hill, 1992)**
Another excellent work by McPherson. (Everything he writes is excellent!)

D.M. Potter, with D. Fehrenbacher, *The Impending Crisis 1846–61* **(Harper & Row, 1976)**
Still an essential text on the causes of the war

R.M. Sewell, *A House Divided: Sectionalism and Civil War, 1848–1865* **(Johns Hopkins University Press, 1988)**
A short and succinct account of both the causes and course of the war

Books on slavery and abolitionism

J.W. Blassingame, *The Slave Community: Plantation Life in the Antebellum South* **(Oxford University Press, 1979)**
This book stresses the theme of a persisting and identifiable slave culture

S.M. Elkins, *Slavery: A Problem in American Institutional and Intellectual Life* **(University of Chicago Press, 1959)**
A bit long in the tooth but still raises some important issues

D.F. Ericson, *The Debate over Slavery: Antislavery and Proslavery Liberalism in Antebellum America* **(New York University Press, 2000)**
This deals with the contemporary debate about slavery and the Slave Power

R.W. Fogel and S.L. Engerman, *Time on the Cross: The Economics of American Negro Slavery* **(University Press of America, 1974)**
Beware of statistics!

E.D. Genovese, *Roll, Jordan, Roll: The World the Slaves Made* **(Random House, 1974)**
An important book, albeit its framework is Marxist

P.J. Parish, *Slavery: History and Historians* **(Icon Editions, 1989)**
This provides a splendid overview of the main debates about slavery

K.M. Stampp, *The Peculiar Institution: Slavery in the Ante-bellum South* **(Eyre & Spottiswoode, 1956)**
This remains an essential text

J.B. Stewart, *Holy Warriors: The Abolitionists and American Slavery* **(Hill & Wang 1976)**
A solid introduction to the abolitionist movement

Books on US politics 1846–61

W.E. Gienapp, *The Origins of the Republican Party* **(Oxford University Press 1987)**
The most detailed account of the rise of the Republican Party

M. Holt, *The Fate of Their Country: Politicians, Slavery Extension, and the Coming of Civil War* **(Hill & Wang, 2005)**
This book distils the wisdom of several of Holt's vast books about the politics of the 1840s and 1850s into an incisive, short overview

E.B. Smith, *The Presidency of James Buchanan* **(University Press of Kansas, 1975)**
A good introduction to Buchanan's troubled presidency

K.M. Stampp, *America in 1857* **(Oxford University Press, 1990)**
A readable snapshot of a momentous year (in Stampp's view)

Biographies

D.H. Donald, *Lincoln* **(Jonathan Cape, 1995)**
A very good single-volume biography of Lincoln

W.S. McFeely, *Grant* **(W.W. Norton, 1981)**
Perhaps the best biography of Grant

M.E. Neely, Jr, *The Last Best Hope of Earth: Abraham Lincoln and the Promise of America* **(Harvard University Press, 1993)**
A penetrating analysis which examines the important questions about Lincoln

P.S. Paludan, *The Presidency of Abraham Lincoln* **(University of Kansas Press, 1994)**
A succinct analysis of all aspects of Lincoln's work as president

E.M. Thomas, *Robert E. Lee* **(W.W. Norton, 1981)**
Perhaps the best biography of Lee

Books on military aspects of the Civil War

R.E. Beringer, H. Hattaway, A. Jones and W.N. Still, *Why the South Lost the Civil War* **(University of Georgia Press, 1986)**
An interesting (if not convincing) interpretation of why the Confederacy lost

R.N. Current, editor, *The Encyclopedia of the Confederacy,* **4 volumes (Simon & Schuster, 1993)**
A collection of essays on every conceivable topic and person by the best historians

D. Donald, editor, *Why the North Won the Civil War* **(Collier, 1960)**
A superb collection of essays providing different explanations for the war's outcome

D.G. Faust, *The Republic of Suffering: Death and the American Civil War* (Alfred A. Knopf, 2008)
This book deals with the soldiers' experience of combat and death

S. Foote, *The Civil War* (Pimlico, 1958–74)
This three-volume work, while too long for most students, is a tremendous read

G.W. Gallagher, *The Confederate War* (Harvard University Press, 1997)
This book has eminently sensible things to say about Confederate morale

G.W. Gallagher, S.D. Engle, R.K. Krick and J.T. Glatthaar, *The American Civil War: This Mighty Scourge of War* (Osprey Publishing, 2003)
A lucid and concise narrative of the main campaigns, as well as penetrating analyses of strategies and leadership

J.M. McPherson, *For Cause and Comrades: Why Men Fought in the Civil War* (Oxford University Press, 1997)
An important book examining why northerners and southerners fought and died for their respective causes

G.C. Ward (with R. Burns and K. Burns), *The Civil War: An Illustrated History* (Alfred A. Knopf, 1990)
This book accompanied Burns' splendid television documentary. It is magnificently illustrated

Books on the Union and Confederate home fronts

P.S. Paludan, *A People's Contest: The Union and Civil War 1861–1865* (Harper & Row, 1988)
A good survey of the impact of the war on northern society

G.C. Rable, *Civil Wars: Women and the Crisis of Southern Nationalism* (University of Illinois Press, 1989)
This considers southern women's role in the conflict

Britain and the Civil War

A. Foreman, *A World On Fire* (Allen Lane, 2010)
A good read, as well as a good account of British involvement in the Civil War

Primary material

H.S. Commager, editor, *The Blue and the Gray* (Wings Books, 1950)
A tremendous collection of primary source material

R.U. Johnson and C.C. Buel, editors, *Battles and Leaders of the Civil War*, 4 volumes (Castle, 1887)
The fact that the four volumes are still in print is very revealing

Books on Reconstruction and the African American experience of war

I. Berlin *et al.*, *Slaves No More* (Cambridge University Press, 1992)
A concise summary of a two-volume work on emancipation

E.F. Foner, *Reconstruction: America's Unfinished Revolution 1863–1877* (Harper & Row, 1988)
Remains the best book on Reconstruction

E.F. Foner, *Forever Free: The Story of Emancipation and Reconstruction* (Knopf Doubleday, 2013)
A short and very satisfactory survey

M. Penman, *Struggle for Mastery: Disfranchisement in the South, 1888–1908* (University of North Carolina Press, 2001)
An important book dealing with an important issue

R.L. Ransom and R. Sutch, *One Kind of Freedom: The Economic Consequences of Emancipation* (Cambridge University Press, 2001)
A lucid examination of the economic consequences of emancipation

C. Vann Woodward, *The Strange Career of Jim Crow* (Oxford University Press, 1974)
This small book, once very influential, is somewhat dated but still worth a read

Internet resources

Interviews with former slaves can be found at www.gutenberg.org/ebooks/11255
A massive Civil War portal with thousands of links: **www.civil-war.net**

A decent site for primary sources: **www.civilwar.org/education/students**

The Library of Congress has many online sources. A good starting point for research would be: **www.loc.gov/topics/content.php?subcat=8**

It's also worth searching the archives of the *New York Times* for contemporary accounts of the Civil War.
See: **www.nytimes.com**

Index